ALIGN IT

ALIGN IT

Business Impact Through IT

Richard Wyatt-Haines

BICENTENNIAL
1807
WILEY
2007
BICENTENNIAL

John Wiley & Sons, Ltd

Other Wiley Editorial Offices

John Wiley & Sons Inc., 111 River Street, Hoboken, NJ 07030, USA

Jossey-Bass, 989 Market Street, San Francisco, CA 94103-1741, USA

Wiley-VCH Verlag GmbH, Boschstr. 12, D-69469 Weinheim, Germany

John Wiley & Sons Australia Ltd, 42 McDougall Street, Milton, Queensland 4064, Australia

John Wiley & Sons (Asia) Pte Ltd, 2 Clementi Loop #02-01, Jin Xing Distripark, Singapore 129809

John Wiley & Sons Canada Ltd, 6045 Freemont Blvd, Mississauga, Ontario, L5R 4J3, Canada

Wiley also publishes its books in a variety of electronic formats. Some content that appears in print may not be
available in electronic books.

Library of Congress Cataloging-in-Publication Data

Wyatt-Haines, Richard.
    Align IT : business impact through IT / Richard Wyatt-Haines.
        p. cm.
    Includes bibliographical references and index.
    ISBN 978-0-470-03039-4 (pbk. : alk. paper)
1.   Management information systems. 2.   Strategic planning. I.   Title.
    HD30.213.W86 2007
    658.4′038011—dc22

British Library Cataloguing in Publication Data

A catalogue record for this book is available from the British Library

ISBN-13: 978-0-470-03039-4

Typeset in 10/14pt Futura by Laserwords Private Limited, Chennai, India
Printed and bound in Great Britain by Bell & Bain, Glasgow
This book is printed on acid-free paper responsibly manufactured from sustainable forestry
in which at least two trees are planted for each one used for paper production.

Copyright

Figure 10, chapter 10, p.291:
McCall Jr., M. W. and Hollenbeck, G. P. (2002) *Developing Global Executives*. Harvard Business School Publishing. Reproduced from Harvard Business School Publishing.

Figure 11, chapter 10, p.292:
McCall Jr., M. W. and Hollenbeck, G. P. (2002) *Developing Global Executives*. Harvard Business School Publishing. Reproduced from Harvard Business School Publishing.

Figure 12, chapter 10, p.298:
Herb, E., Leslie, K. and Price, C. (2001) Teamwork at the Top. McKinsey Quarterly, No. 2. Reproduced from McKinsey Quarterly.

Figure 4, chapter 11, p.315:
Kotler, P. (1994) Marketing Management: Analysis, planning, implementation and control. Prentice Hall International. Reproduced with permission from Prentice Hall.

Figure 4, chapter 12, p.358:
Morton, M. S. (1991) *The Corporation in the 1990s: Information Technology and Organizational Transformation*. Oxford University Press, New York. Reproduced from Oxford University Press.

Table 1, chaper 12, p.366:
Higgs, M. J., Rowland, D. (2000) Building Change Leadership Capability. *Journal of Change Management*, 2(1). Reproduced from Journal of Change Management.

Figure 9, chapter 12, p.368:
Turner, D. and Crawford, M. (1998) *Change Power: Capabilities that Drive Corporate Renewal*. Business & Professional Publishing Limited. Reproduced with permission from Business & Professional Publishing Limited.

Figure 18, chapter 12, p.387
Scholes, K., Johnson, G. and Whittington, R. (2006) *Exploring Corporate Strategy: Text and Cases*. FT Prentice Hall. Reproduced with permission from Prentice Hall.

Figure 2, chapter 13, p.412:
Thornbury, J. (1999) KPMG: Revitalizing culture through values. *Business Strategy Review*, Winter. Reproduced with permission from Blackwell Publishing.

To Suzanne, Emma, Amy and Samuel. Thank you.

To aspiring CIOs everywhere. Good luck.

Contents

Who is this book for?

Principally, this book is for all levels of IT management including CIOs, IT Directors, Heads of IT and Team Managers, regardless of whether you work in the public or private sectors, medium sized or global companies.

Equally, though, it is written for you if you wish to be a senior IT manager within an organization, or if you simply wish to understand what it is to be an effective CIO.

Similarly, this book is also written for a much wider audience including CEOs, functional directors, business unit heads, and team leaders. Or if you aspire to any of these positions, then this book is for you.

This book is also for you if you simply want to gain an understanding of how you can ensure that IT is pointing in the right direction, doing the right things and is delivering the right results.

Therefore, this book will also bring enormous benefits if you are a consultant seeking to support a business to achieve more through the use of information, or technology.

Introduction

This book will provide you with both the understanding and the tools to more tightly align your IT function with the goals and strategies of your organization, and in consequence, enable your IT function to deliver real value to the business and hence enable your business to enjoy greater success, and faster.

Any business strategy only has any value when it is implemented. In that regard, IT is a key element in implementation and success. Over time and with the development of the necessary capabilities, it can also become an integral part of the development of strategy by the organization.

This book will focus on enabling IT managers to implement strategy rather than develop it. In this regard, it has to be recognized at the outset that IT can indeed truly deliver value to the business, but it demands that IT managers and their teams understand a number of aspects in the strategy arena:

- Firstly, the need to understand what strategy is today in the competitive and fluid environment in which businesses operate. This is not necessarily about analysis and planning, but how strategy operates both as a way of thinking and as a way of acting so that organizations can deliver value to their customers and enjoy competitive success.

- With that foundation, and a direction on which to focus, it is possible for the IT function to develop its own strategy which must be tightly aligned to and effectively support the business strategy. This degree of alignment is critical to both the success of the business, the effective utilization of its resources and, in turn, the perceived value of the IT function. How can this be done?

- Once clear about the direction to be taken, it is possible to be much more specific about what and how an IT function delivers to the business and in turn, the service that it wraps around the core products and role. How is this made clear and reinforced?

– In turn what capabilities are required across the function IT so that it has the ability to deliver consistently and reliably?

– For this to be achieved, there is the need to develop the necessary skills and capabilities in your IT staff and managers and set these in a culture that will support and facilitate success. This will demand consideration of issues such as management and leadership skills, change capabilities, the operation of the team, technical skills, etc.

– This all demands that the IT team build the ability to think and act in a strategically aligned way. This is not about strategy as plans, systems and processes; it is about communication, fluidity of thought, awareness and a passion to see IT as the key strategic resource in your business, one delivering value and success continuously.

This book is structured in a simple manner; comprising four main sections and three or four chapters in each section that will take you through the story of understanding what strategy is, and what it means to the IT function. We end up by considering how you can deliver your strategy with impact.

Section 1 – The business & its strategy
Chapter 1 – Strategy today

– So what is strategy?

– Some strange strategic terms and what they mean

– Strategy as a way of behaving

Strategy today has developed from being an analytical process into something that is far more fluid and dynamic. This chapter explores that shift and provides you with a context and language for the rest of the book.

Chapter 2 – Competing businesses

– Competitive advantage and added value

– The strategy hierarchy

– Coherent strategic planning

At the level of individual businesses, we need to understand how they compete, what resources they use to do so, the elements that they need to piece together to give their plans coherence, and their delivery impact. This chapter will enable you to understand the component elements of a business's competitive position so that you can gain a deeper understanding of what your own business is trying to achieve and how it is trying to do it. As a result, you will be able to see the strategy that your IT function must align itself behind and prepare itself to support.

Chapter 3 – The setting for strategy

– The individual user

– The challenge of teams

– Different types of organization

– Living with lifecycles

This chapter will take you outside of the IT function and force you to look at the needs of the different types of users that you will serve. This will build and develop your understanding of the context in which the IT function has to operate and the specific needs that you need to satisfy.

Section 2 – Aligning IT with the strategy
Chapter 4 – The potential value of IT

– Does IT matter?

– IT strategy versus business strategy

At the heart of this book is the need to get IT directors and managers to understand deeply what your business is trying to achieve and your role in making that happen. To do this you have to understand the potential of IT to really have strategic impact, and the differences between an IT strategy and that of the business.

Chapter 5 – Aligning IT

– Planning – who cares?

– Planning – some approaches

– Strategy mapping

– IT strategy maps

– Aligning IT

This chapter is about enabling you to translate the business strategies and needs into clearly articulated IT strategies and plans that are cascaded throughout the IT function. On the way we explore some key principles around business planning, and understand various tools and approaches that you could adopt.

Chapter 6 – Focusing on outcomes

– Performance measures – some principles

– Performance measures – some approaches

– Creating performance measures

Sound business disciplines demand that the rigour of measurement is attached to a strategy. This chapter reinforces this principle and guides you through the development of strategically aligned performance measures.

Section 3 – Following, Enabling and Leading
What does this mean in practice?

Chapter 7 – Following

– Some general principles

– The specifics

– Other aspects

We understand the business and the strategy, and we have a pretty good idea of what that will mean in terms of what we have to deliver. But how will the IT function operate; what does it need to be good at in order to be efficient, reliable and cost effective? Indeed, what does it meant to be a Follower?

Chapter 8 – Enabling

– A context

– What does it mean?

– Making it happen

The concept of Enabling is central to this book, and many of the principles are reinforced elsewhere. But what does it mean in terms of structure, management systems and technology or the application of knowledge? What capabilities will you need and how can you establish the agility and flexibility that will enable you to cope in disruptive environments?

Chapter 9 – Leading

– Leveraging emerging technologies

– Leading the debate

The potential for IT to lead is enormous and yet it is rarely grasped. Why is that? In part it is because the role is poorly understood, and equally, it is because the challenge of becoming a strong Follower and Enabler is so demanding that IT functions rarely succeed in breaking through to this ultimate layer. So, what does Leading mean and what do you have to be doing to realize the potential benefits for your company?

Section 4 – Delivering with impact

Chapter 10 – Leadership & management in IT

- The context

- Your objectives

- Your role

- The skills and behaviours you need

- developing the IT manager

The leader and manager is critical in providing the impetus and energy that initiates the change necessary to deliver your strategy. The leader in IT has to reach right across the organization in order to create the context in which the IT function can perform, and the business can enjoy success. What is the role of the IT leader and what must that leader deliver?

Chapter 11 – Building and sustaining your brand

- Where? Where are you going, what are you trying to achieve and what are your objectives?

- The brand

- Who? Who is involved in successfully building your brand?

- The relationship management role

- How? Making it happen on the ground?.

Our starting point is one where the perception and reputation of IT is often negative. Thus IT managers must be able to manage their brand across the business and often across outsourced providers. Unfortunately they have very little guidance of what to do and how to do it. This chapter provides you with the necessary approaches to managing the IT brand.

Chapter 12 – Change plus

– The context for change

– Taking the pulse

– Building the route map

– Telling the change story

– Managing stakeholders

– The CEO's role

– Maintaining momentum

Any strategy will demand change. In this chapter we identify the key components in designing and implementing a change plan with particular focus on the people and organizational capability issues rather than the technology and procedural elements.

Chapter 13 – Culture

– What is it?

– How to analyse your culture

– How do you change your culture?

Culture is a strange and woolly concept for the IT community; not only will this chapter provide clear guidance on the issues of cultural change, but it will also make culture tangible and accessible. In doing so, it will provide you with an approach and understanding to which you can relate and in turn apply in the workplace.

Chapter 14 – In closing

A concluding chapter to draw together all the strands and identify the key issues on which you need to focus.

The style of this book

Every chapter is considered in three ways, each to reflect the range of the readers' individual learning styles. You may only choose to refer to one of each type throughout the book, or you may use all three; that is up to you and the way you respond to the world. The three styles are what I have called Touching, Looking and Doing:

– Touching – provides the detail to link the underlying thinking with the world in which the CEOs, IT managers and directors operate, using models and diagrams to provide the meat of the topic

– Looking – providing stories, case studies and examples that bring the topic alive

– Doing – focuses on highlighting what you need to do.

This will not be an academic book, even though it will build on strong and proven academic approaches. It will be grounded in practice. Neither will this book be technical, either in an IT or strategic sense.

The benefit will be that you will be able to use selected parts of the book to address specific issues, or the whole book to provide a context and approach to the development and improved performance of your IT function.

Fundamentally though, the book will enable you to align your IT function with the goals and strategies of your organization, and in consequence enable IT to deliver real value to the business, resulting in business growth and higher levels of performance, plus a more stimulating role and less stress for you.

Section 1

The business & its strategy

1 Strategy today

- What is strategy?

- Some strange strategic terms and what they mean

- Strategy as a way of behaving

Strategy today has developed from being an analytical process into something that is far more fluid and dynamic. This chapter explores that shift, and provides you with a context and language for the rest of the book.

Touching

What is strategy?

To enable you to really benefit from this book, you need to have an understanding of the core components of strategy; but that doesn't mean that you need to become skilled in all tools and language that academics, consultants and some business people seem fascinated by. So if you want to delve into the detail of the jargon then this book isn't you. However, if you want to understand the key issues that drive organizational performance, the success of high performing organizations, and if you need an understanding of the context in which your IT function has to operate, then this is the book for you.

Firstly, strategy is not the tools that carry names such as PEST Analysis, SWOT Analysis, Resource Analysis, Competitor Analysis, Five Forces Analysis, Scenario Analysis, etc. These are tools that help business people to understand the environment in which they are operating. And there are all sorts of debate over whether these tools remain appropriate in today's very unpredictable business environment. We won't have that debate here.

More importantly, strategy today has a broader and deeper meaning that allows organizations to operate in an environment where the competitive pressures are greater and more varied than ever before; where customer expectations are increasing both in terms of the speed of change and the degree of change; and where the expectations for an uplift in performance increase almost exponentially. And these pressures come from investors, marketplace commentators (e.g. the press and analysts), customers and staff.

Strategy today has developed from being an analytical process into something that is far more fluid, and if working well, central to organizational success. Indeed, strategy is now more akin to a way of acting and thinking within an organization. When doing its job, strategy is evident everywhere in a business by the way the people, systems and processes are operating in alignment with the organizational goals. In this way strategy permits (indeed facilitates) a decision-making ability, a speed of responsiveness, and a desire to deliver that enables the business to operate in a more entrepreneurial manner, pursuing and taking advantage of opportunities as they occur and are spotted.

Is it timebound?

Strategy is traditionally considered to be a medium or long-term issue because strategic plans were those set for 5 or 10 year periods of time. This is no longer the case. Strategy is no longer time bound in that narrow sense. Yet it does force us to look into the future and determine what sort of business we will be at some point in time, though that time span may be as short as 12 months or as long as 10 years. However, in practice the timescales have become shorter over the last 15 years, and the key role of strategy is one by which today's activities are linked to the development of tomorrow's capabilities and the delivery of tomorrow's results and performance.

This change of emphasis reflects the fluidity of the marketplace and the fact that many organizations change their strategies more often than many would consider healthy. Indeed, you may today be working in an organization that has recently changed CEO, been visited by consultants, or carried out yet another strategy review, and if so, you will know what I mean. But this is reality and there is no point pretending or hoping that this pattern will change; you might as well live with it and make the most of it.

Perhaps this is the first lesson from this book. This fluidity demands a great deal of flexibility in the organization to enable it to cope. Have you built the necessary flexibility in your team? And I don't just mean in terms of systems, I also mean in terms of culture, people skills and leadership capabilities.

Strategy is also about growth. It is about building a bigger organization in one or a number of domains; turnover, profit, capability, customer base, brand value, market awareness, market perception, customer loyalty, processes and systems, sustainability, resources, market share, and many, many more.

Who cares?

For anyone in IT, this is an important issue to remember, because the board cares, your CEO cares, and your finance director cares. And on top of that, your investors and your customers care. Everyone of them is looking to see your organization achieve more, and they see IT as an integral player in the delivery of that success. So that you can achieve and support their strategic goals, there should be no doubt in your mind that you need to understand where the business is pointing, what it is trying to achieve and what your role is in that success. To do this you need to understand how the business mind works, especially when thinking strategically.

How does it work?

Wonderful stuff, you may say, but what does it mean on the ground; what are the key components?

In this section I am going to cover only a few of the main components, but don't feel that this is too simplistic a view. Each aspect is critical in its own right and provide the core understanding that will enable you to have a meaningful dialogue with the business regarding its

TOUCHING

strategy. Indeed as a result of reading this, many of you will find that your thinking will have leapfrogged that of other members of your board; if so, enjoy the moment.

A simple view of strategy

When a business decides upon its strategy, where does it start and what would it be trying to achieve?

In respect of what it is trying to achieve, the following diagram provides a useful understanding of the key questions we are trying to answer.

The Why
Why are we doing this?

The Who
Who should we target as customers?

The What
What products and services should we be

The How
How can we do this in an efficient and

Figure 1: A simple view of strategy (Markides, 1999)

In other words, if somebody were to explain their strategy to you, then you should be able to quickly understand why they exist, who they serve, what they offer them and how they do it.

Regrettably, many business strategies fail to answer these core questions, or wrap them up in such convoluted language that as a result only a very few people really understand the strategy, let alone deliver the sort of results the directors had hoped for when they set the strategy in the first place.

Focus and simplicity

Therefore, there are big issues here regarding focus and simplicity. If you always remember that a good strategy is one that delivers rather than one that looks good on paper, you will start to measure the quality of strategies on their ability to focus and align the activities of large numbers of people so that organizations can achieve more as a unified force. Complex

TOUCHING

strategies, whilst well meaning, often serve to confuse and dissipate the energy and effec tiveness of staff and organizational resources.

Indeed, unnecessarily complicated strategies also manage to confuse customers. In this re-spect there is an old retail adage which says that "confused customers don't buy". I am sure that you will recognize this in your own shopping behaviour. Think of the stores and shops from which you buy regularly and repeatedly and those that you have visited infrequently or only once. There is a strong chance that those that you visit regularly have made very clear to you what it is they do, what they sell, and which customers they want to serve. Indeed, you may have noticed a how strange it is that there are a lot of customers just like you in that shop. Alongside, I bet you find yourself spending more in those shops and also feeling comfortable about recommending them to your friends and neighbours because you can predict how they will perform. Thus, clarity of purpose shines through to the customer. It must also shine thorough in a strategy and not confuse.

Returning to my four questions (why, who, what and how), this is not to say that you should see simplicity as representing a lack a depth of thought and understanding. Indeed, very often, a great deal of analysis, debate, argument and discussion is required to distil a clear strategy from the complex environment in which most businesses operate. As Winston Churchill once said, "I am afraid that you will have to put up with a long speech, as I have not had the time to prepare the short one."

The difficulty you may have as a CEO is that you may be working in one of those businesses where the strategy is unnecessarily complicated. As you will see later in the book, this maybe just because the directors haven't properly understood or agreed it, or perhaps the business is just making things too complicated. Whatever, you will have to extract the wheat from the chaff so that your staff can make sense of the strategy and can develop and deliver an IT strategy that is suitably aligned. This means that you will need to become adept at extracting the core themes and issues that exist within the business strategy and explaining them to your staff so that they can understand them and transact against them.

To enable you to be able to do this, it is worthwhile taking a quick look at some of the issues underpinning the four questions I highlighted above.

The Why

Every business must understand why it is in existence. For a large multinational corporate, it may be the delivery of shareholder value through the returns it delivers to its investors. For the public sector provider it will be the delivery of certain services or products to a particular part of the community (not for financial gain, but for the well-being of that community). And for the entrepreneur running a small business it may simply be the pride and the desire to work on their own, or to balance their home and business lives.

Whatever, the answer to the 'why' question has massive implications on the strategic choices that are subsequently taken. In other words, the solutions that you identify as a result of the other three questions have to jointly deliver the returns that you have identified in this section.

For example, if you are the entrepreneur, working in a home office, you can select and choose a narrow range and a small number of customers with whom you do business. You can offer them a personalized service, build close relationships with them and custom-build every product and service that you deliver. It may not be very efficient, and it may not even be very profitable, but the personal rewards may be great.

On the other hand, you may be the chief executive of Tesco serving large swathes of the United Kingdom and Europe, and having to provide a return of something like 20% to investors on their investment each year. To achieve this, you have to reach a lot more customers and deliver your products and services very efficiently indeed.

Or, you may be the chief executive of a town council. Here you have little choice over your customers and your reason for existing has little to do with individual well-being or financial rewards for investors. But you must still be very efficient, and increasingly effective.

The Who

Once you understand why you are in business, you can start to think about your target market. Clearly the returns you want from the previous question (The Why) will impact on your choice of customer.

In this regard, strategists have all sorts of tools to enable them to 'slice and dice' the world into little bits and pieces (segments) that they can serve, sell to, and hopefully satisfy. For the purpose of this book, it is sufficient to know that we don't have to serve everyone in the world. But that we do need to make sure we know who we are serving and that we understand their needs aspirations intimately so that we can focus our energies on satisfying those desires.

"Oh, I forgot about the customer"

One point of caution here; many businesses don't understand who they are serving and neither do they understand the needs of those markets. As a result, they offer a service or product that has limited benefit to that bit of the marketplace that it reaches. It has been proven by many failed and underperforming organizations that sustainability and long-term success does not flow from such muddled thinking.

This implies a need for the organization to be able to gain proximity to, sense and understand the markets in which it operates and the customers it serves. Companies that do this effectively are called 'market oriented', and this is one of four high level descriptions that is used to classify companies;

Product focused

To these organizations the product itself, innovation, improvement and product features are everything. Here you will be surrounded by engineers, techies, and generally people who are excited by what the product or service can do, how it operates and its technical features. However, these people may not have considered whether or not the customer really wants all the features they have introduced, or whether they are willing to pay for them at a price that makes a profit.

Process focused

In these companies, the process of making the product is the most exciting thing on earth. The operations team dominates and spends its life improving production processes, using techniques such as total quality management, business process reengineering and Kaisen, and gets really excited when a 'root cause analysis' shows up a previously undetected fault. These types of businesses can produce their high quality products on time, at a lower cost, and in greater quantities than others. However, it is this last feature, which often causes these organizations problems. So good are they at producing in volume that the system produces more than the market wants and then oversupply occurs and a fall in prices results. One only needs to look at car manufacturing to get a flavour of this problem. If like me, you have driven past enormous car parks of new cars waiting months to be distributed to showrooms, you can tangibly see the problem of oversupply. Further, one look at a profit and loss account of the Ford Motor Company will show you what oversupply in the industry has done to their profit margins.

Sales driven

These are organizations whose focus and energy is driven into sales processes and getting the customer to buy, whether or not the product and service really meets their needs. In its extreme form, this can be seen as hard selling. You will recognize this place of work, because the sales function will be the dominant team, and this is where power resides.

TOUCHING

Market oriented

And so we come back to market orientation. Here products and services are designed, made and sold as a result of a deep understanding of the marketplace, the company's customers and their evolving needs and desires. In the extreme form, companies such as these have the customer at the centre, with everything from organizational structure to team meetings focused around their requirements. Marketers and strategist have proclaimed this as the ideal company and what we should all be striving for. However, problems reside here too; product proliferation, mass customization, reactivity, all of which can lead to poor profit performance are common. Often smaller enterprises find it much easier to achieve this state, because of their greater proximity to the customer.

In reality, very few organizations evidence a single trait; most have a mix of two or three of these cultures. The challenge is determining which type is appropriate to a company and its market in order to maximize performance. Without doubt, the marketing orientation should be evident in all companies, but Wal-Mart would not succeed if it did not also benefit from a process orientation. That enables it to operate the logistics capability that keeps it competitive through stocked shelves and low distribution costs, and hence prices.

So what?

You need to be conscious of the approach or approaches that dominate in your company, as each type places different demands on the IT function.

Product focused organizations need systems that support the innovation process, the sharing of information and knowledge about technological breakthroughs. They need a system architecture which supports approaches such as multidisciplinary teams and project management.

In the process driven organization, it is the efficiency of manufacturing systems that is critical. So, the IT team needs to provide reporting and analysis on issues such as process speed and reliability, and capacity planning. They need to provide systems to run the main manufacturing processes, cope with preventative maintenance systems and deliver visibility of performance.

In the sales oriented organization, on the other hand, performance management systems are central to the way of working. IT must provide performance reports, sales information, profit figures, etc., and at all levels of the organization, very quickly, in various levels of detail, and with tools that facilitate interrogation. Also, they must be able to collate and analyse data regarding competitor performance.

The marketing oriented organization needs support and information regarding the marketplace and its customers and how they are behaving. These systems need to gather and share large quantities of information from a wide range of sources and in widely differing formats, making it accessible and usable by managers and staff, so that decisions can be readily taken. Scenario planning, product launches, performance, and organizational learning will also need to be enabled by the IT team

Therefore, even at this very high level, we start to see influences on IT arising out of the orientation of the company and you and your team need to be able to recognize the demands that arise as a result.

The What

Having determined why we are here, and who we serve, we are now in a position to identify the products and services that we will offer to our chosen customers. As noted above, many businesses are product driven and this tends towards a habit to first design a product and service and then try to find a market to sell into. This can work in the short-term, but over the long-term the thinking has to be reversed; we need to understand the customer first and then build and deliver products and services that meet their needs. Given this proviso, what do we see organizations doing?

Doing it again, better and differently

In endeavouring to determine 'The What', companies tend to adopt a mix of three approaches.

Doing it again

"This is what we've always done, so we will continue to do it." This may be a bit harsh, but I am sure you will recognize that the history of the organization (what it was set up for initially, and what it is skilled at doing) will dominate when choosing the 'What'. However, this can be constraining and if the market moves on because of technological advances or replacement products and services, or evolving customer needs, there is a risk that you may be left making something that nobody wants any more. You need only to speak to the manufacturers of video recorders and video tapes to see this happening in front of our eyes today. Of course, many of these companies will progress and start to manufacture DVD machines and the discs themselves, but their existing reliance on their current product range and skills set may slow their entry into new markets with the result that they miss the best opportunities. Of course, they may not see the change coming at all, in which case they are likely to go out of business. Also, the shift may be so substantial that they simply do not have the skills nor resources or capabilities to respond. For example, there has to be a good chance that we could receive all films in the near future by way of a download through broadband. If this was the case, then what is the role of DVD, let alone videos in the world such as this?

Doing it better

Some companies simply copy existing products and services delivered by other organizations and seek to do it better. They focus on incremental improvements, enhances to distribution processes, wrapping new services around the core product, and linking with other partners to provide greater value.

Doing it differently

Other companies set out to find new products and services to bring to market in order to satisfy the evolving needs and changing behaviours of their customers. This demands the ability to innovate, be creative, and above all understand what it is that customers want and what they are likely to value in the years to come. Often, it can mean trying to guess what it is that customers will want, even when those customers haven't recognized the need themselves. For example, I am sure that you didn't know that you needed a Blackberry when you first started receiving and sending e-mails. However, someone at RIM clearly spotted the behavioural shift towards a need for immediacy of information, availability and response and created a global product on the back of this shift.

Once again, these high level strategic issues have an impact on the IT director. If your company is one that seeks simply to do things better, then the system and information demands will be in the area of efficiency, control and process development. On the other hand, if your organization seeks to do things differently you will be asked to support an organization that will be hungry for knowledge and will need to use information in a variety of ways. They will have a need to manipulate it, whilst trying to determine and identify new opportunities for income generation. Therefore, your IT team needs to be established in a way that can respond to these differing demands.

Product or service?

Additionally, you will need to recognize that your company will either be providing a product or service, and most likely, a mix of the two. In most mature economies these days, about 70% of the gross domestic product arises from services, and this represents a complete reversal from some 30 years ago.

Such is the shift that it is unusual now to see a product that does not have some kind of service attaching to it, and even more common is the stand-alone service. Even if your company is primarily a manufacturer or producer of a product, it is likely that you will be providing support services such as call centres, internet support, knowledge sharing with partners, combined distribution chain management, point of sale support materials, etc. All these elements demand IT systems support and information management.

If you are a service company, then the need for information is arguably even greater, especially with the move into providing an enhanced experience in addition to the delivery of the core service. We all know that the Walt Disney Company runs theme parks, and as a consequence we appreciate that we are being taken through a service process, both in the park generally and on each ride. But for Disney this is only the core product. What makes them different from other theme parks is their ability to provide an experience throughout the day and your stay. The rides themselves may not be particularly spectacular, but the overall experience is. This trend is only echoed through venues such as Nike town.

It will be clear to you whether your company is focused on products or services, but you may not have considered the implications of this for your IT strategy. As I noted earlier, these big strategic issues impact on the way in which you focus and run your team and the sorts of tasks that they undertake. Product based companies need you to support the manufacturing and distribution processes, whereas service companies need your help in managing the most complex part of the service, namely, the people. In other words your staff, and your company's customers. In a service, the mix of people in the delivery process adds all sorts of complexities and unexpected behaviours which conspire to undermine your best intentions. A member of staff who has been poorly treated by their manager, or a customer who had a bad experience in the shop next door, and suddenly that planned experience the customer was meant to enjoy is gone forever. IT has a massive role in minimizing the risks of failure in a service, as well as supporting the experience and management of information and knowledge that derives from processing each customer.

The How

The challenge now is to make sure we serve our customers in a way that provides us with the returns that we want. It is no good a multinational company offering products and services in a way which results in them making a loss or just breaking even. If they do, they won't be able to provide the required returns to their investors. However, for the small entrepreneur, breaking even may be acceptable.

So, what are the strategic issues that we need to consider and be aware of when determining how we are going to deliver our products and services in an efficient and effective manner? Clearly, the choices made here will be strongly influenced by the decisions already taken in the preceding three questions. Once you know what you want to achieve, who you want to serve and what you want to offer them, all you need to do is to find a way of pulling it altogether, so that you can do it consistently and sustainably.

Doing it better, doing it differently – again

Once again, the choice between doing things better and doing things differently will feature. If your company believes success will be won through doing things better, they will pursue process efficiency, management controls, and approaches such as lean manufacturing and continuous improvement. System simplicity, speed and dependability will be key areas of focus as well as the need to drive down the cost of production. Alongside will be a desire to benefit from economies of scale which can be achieved through organic growth, entry into new markets and acquisition.

Each of these poses challenges for IT, but there it is clear from this list that there is a thrust and focus which your IT strategy must support. Additionally, if growth is going to be achieved through entering new countries, you will need an ability to cope with cross-border issues such as languages, systems, culture and the differing timescales. Acquisitions will demand an ability to integrate systems or roll out your existing systems in the acquired companies.

Alternatively, doing things differently may be the solution adopted by your organization. In the technology driven age, IT will be at the centre of the development of options and possibilities, and in turn delivery. Can you imagine Amazon without an IT function and IT strategy that could support and develop its business model. If you can, you are probably visualizing a traditional bookshop. At Amazon, IT was not just a support function, but the key player in the developmental process.

And in these 'doing it differently' companies, IT is not just involved in the creative processes, but also in the delivery of the products and services in conjunction with the marketing and operations teams.

Reuters, knowledge and resources

Apart from these core considerations, new strategic developments have occurred over recent years, which make even greater demands on the IT function. In this respect, competing through the provision of knowledge or by using knowledge to find new opportunities has been accelerated by the availability and capability of information systems. You only need to consider roles of Bloomberg's and Reuters in providing information to the investment banking community and stock markets of the world to see the influence of knowledge on the commercial world. On a smaller scale, every university sees itself as a knowledge base supporting a global learning community. Accountants compete by providing tax updates and information and avoidance schemes, and no self-respecting lawyer would open for business if they couldn't readily access and utilize the latest case law and legislation.

Finally, IT has a role in maximizing the utilization of the company's resources. Perhaps this is a rehearsal of the long-running debate regarding productivity about which much has been written already. Or perhaps it is about our role in maximizing the use of all the company's resources, including physical (buildings, plant and machinery), people (their well-being, pay and reward and motivation), and intangible assets (intellectual property, copyright, knowledge, and the brand). In any of these areas, IT has to reach across the functional boundaries, and sometimes organizational boundaries to create, use and maintain systems that support, make available and maximize the performance of each resource.

So what?

From the issues outlined in this chapter you will have seen that the choices companies have to make are many and varied. There is not a single answer, and all companies are subject to the whims of the market, the changing tastes of your customers and the actions of your competition. Indeed, it would seem that the range, variety and scale of those challenges increases all the time and the general nature of the business environment becomes increasingly unpredictable. To protect yourself you need to be able to respond flexibly and fluidly to these challenges.

In such an environment, traditional analytical tools have a smaller part to play, whereas there is a greater demand for senior management, and perhaps the whole organization, to be able to think strategically, flexibly and with a more entrepreneurial mindset. This demands that information can be gathered and used more quickly to make decisions that are delivered with great pace and precision.

Thus, it is clear from this discussion that IT has a central role in the strategic choices your organization makes and its subsequent performance. Therefore, it is incumbent on you to understand strategy in its generic format, its evolution, and its core components so that you and your function can respond to the needs of the market place and your company.

We can now see that this demands that you and your team clearly understand what it is your organization is trying to achieve, who it is serving, what it is offering them, and how it operates.

– This means that you clearly understand what those plans are, and also the implications for the IT function.

TOUCHING

– It means that you appreciate the implication of the organization choosing between doing things better of doing things differently, or doing both.

– It means that you understand the implications of pursuing economies of scale, of choosing to provide services rather than products, or choosing to be a sales driven organization, rather than a marketing oriented one

– It means that you understand how companies compete using knowledge.

With the benefit of that level of understanding you can appreciate the challenges and opportunities that are presented to you and your team and you can start to identify the role that IT has in the future performance of your organization in response to your business' strategy.

More attractive still is the picture of IT taking a leading role in the development and delivery of your company's aspirations. And perhaps in reality this is the essence of this book:

– It is about IT leading not following

– It is about IT, enabling not blocking

– It is about IT presenting opportunities and possibilities, not constraining.

So, this is the focus of the rest of this book. Now that you have an understanding of some of the core principles of strategy, we need to delve much more deeply into what this means specifically in your company and how you make sure that your IT function can align its activities, projects, thinking, behaviours, and performance behind your company's strategy, and in turn deliver outstanding results.

So that, IT moves from *following*, through *enabling*, to *leading*.

Looking

In the Looking section of each chapter I will provide examples, short case studies and analogies that help you to see how the topics discussed in the chapter come alive in the world around us. In other words, this section is about helping you to visualize and engage with the issues that will challenge you as you establish an IT function that is aligned with and delivering your business's strategy.

What has IT got to do with anything anyway?

"The trouble with IT departments is that they have so little understanding of the world in which our business operates and the challenges we face. Therefore, their role in the delivery of strategy is vastly diminished which leaves me feeling that as long as they put machines on desks, then I have to be satisfied."

These were the words of Andy Chapman, Chief Executive of Pioneer (www.pioneer-friendly.co.uk), an award winning insurer established in 1888 which is entirely dedicated to providing market leading income protection products and putting its customers' interests first. Andy's director level experience across a wide range of companies in the financial services sector provides him with vast experience of why there is such conflict between the business units and IT.

Andy went on, "The trouble is, IT in many companies pretend that they know what's going on. Their lack of understanding causes other managers mirth at the outset. But then, it quickly translates to frustration and frustration is followed by conflict. From there the relationship just breaks down, IT falls down the pecking order and simply becomes a support function which we could easily outsource."

"So" I asked, "what are the big issues and what could IT be doing?"

"That's easy." he said. "There are four big issues that stretch my business at the moment and I know that they also apply to my colleagues around the world. These things are:

– Having an intimate knowledge of our customers, and being able to use information about them,

– An increasing need for organizational flexibility,

– Having the ability to coordinate a wide variety of partners, and

– Exercising ever tighter cost controls on the business.

In each of these areas, I believe IT has a key role to play, but often they really don't understand the issues or the principles, and neither can they see the opportunities available to them to really add value to my business."

"Could you expand?" I asked.

"Yes, let's look at each in turn."

An intimate knowledge of customers

"If we start with a need to have a much greater understanding of our customers, I think the real issue is about being able to recognize how their behaviour is changing and then being able to respond and provide services in a focused way that meet those needs.

Wal-Mart are doing this well at the moment in the way they are using their website. Like everyone else, they recognized that their customers were increasingly using the web to buy things, and therefore they were exposed to the risk that they would lose out on income. This could be income lost either by way of people not coming into the store or because their customers started using other providers, who could supply over the Internet. What they also noticed through their research into customer behaviour was the customers were increasingly confused by the multiplicity of products and services available to them, and in many cases, the technology involved in those products. You just think of buying a digital camera, and there are so many options that it is easy for the customer to say `Oh, I just won't bother.'

Separately, Wal-Mart had noticed from their customers' in-store behaviour that if they were provided with information guides about products and services, customers were not only more likely to buy, but also were likely to up trade to a higher model.

So they pulled this information together when deciding upon their website strategy. They decided to:

– Target existing customers, rather than new ones,

– With the aim of drawing increasing numbers into their store, rather than less, and

– Getting them to spend more as a result of being more informed.

Their website does two main things. Firstly, it provides information regarding products and services so that their customers are better informed. Yes, their customers can buy on-line, but it also encourages them to come into the store to purchase or collect. And when they are in the store, they spend on other goods and services.

Separately, there are other triggers that draw those same customers into the store, so that they can spend more money when they get there. For example, you can upload your digital photos from your digital camera and within a few hours you can go to your local store to pick up the pictures. And whilst there, why not pick up a bottle of wine and some snacks so that you can enjoy your pictures with your family and friends."

"To me" said Andy "this is a great example of a business understanding how customers behave and using that knowledge to achieve more. And there are other examples around us all the time. Look at the last election, both in the US and United Kingdom. All the political parties in both these countries have recognized that voters increasingly want a dialogue with their service providers. And they expect to be an important part of the sales process, whether it is buying banking services, designing the interior of their house or voting in an election.

What we saw was political parties and their leaders engaging in that dialogue. From John Kerry, running his fundraising and election campaign through his blog, to Tony Blair making sure that he was seen talking to patients in hospitals, to voters in town halls, and to teachers and parents and children in schools. Very rarely did he carry out any one-to-one interviews with reporters, and when he did make speeches they were in town halls, with him wherever possible standing in the centre carrying out a dialogue with the voters around him. This conversational approach was echoed through the dialogue that was encouraged through the website, by text messaging and advertising. Both Bush and Kerry increasingly used voter segmentation tools to target their messages and methods of delivery to respond to the expectations and needs of their chosen groupings.

On the other hand, Kodak didn't see the shift in customer behaviour; or if they did they were unable to respond quickly enough. Their customers moved rapidly from film to digital cameras and Kodak struggled to keep up with them. They are doing it now, but along the way, that failure to see the seismic shift early enough prevented them from responding quickly enough. As a result, they lost out."

Flexibility

"The Kodak story really also serves to highlight the second issue I raised regarding the need for increased organizational flexibility," continued Andy, now getting into his stride. "In other words it is not only necessary for business to have the knowledge of their customers, they also need to be able to respond quickly to catch the opportunities that arise as a result. Kodak couldn't and over time they missed out.

Sony have been another company that has not been able to respond. In this respect, you only need to look at the iPod story to see how Sony have missed a massive opportunity. Surely, Sony were much better placed to launch the iPod than Apple?

For years, Sony had developed a capability and reputation for miniaturization, by shrinking the size of everything from camcorders to televisions, and so surely they had to be the ideal candidate to launch in a mini-sized music player.

Not only that, but Sony had the content too. Robbie Williams is under contract to Sony and so are many of the world's leading artists, and they own 50% of the rights to all the Beatles songs. And on top of that, they own a film studio. On the surface it would appear that they had everything in their grasp to create a video iPod. But they didn't; or perhaps, they *couldn't*. They couldn't because of their structures and hierarchies, and their inability to coordinate software development and focus their research, and their ability to recognize changes in customers' habits. Sir Howard Stringer, the new CEO, is trying to change these constraints on their performance, and in some ways I bet this feels harder than launching the PS3.

Similarly, you only need to look at the history of acquisitions around the world to see organizations that have failed to deliver value from their purchases, because they have been unable to respond to the changes wrought on the whole organization by a major purchase."

Coordination

Andy continued:

"Increasingly" he said, "we can only deliver in partnership with others. The resources in our own company are insufficient alone, and we need to link with other companies around the world. Not only to achieve cost savings, but more importantly, to improve the offer we make, develop our capabilities and also to be much more innovative in the services that we provide.

Take Li & Fung Ltd in Hong Kong. They provide clothes, handbags, footwear, toys, and fashion accessories to the Western world. They don't have a manufacturing capability of their own, but what they do is combine the resources of thousands of manufacturers across the world. In other words, they combine the world's manufacturing capabilities and resources to respond to the needs of the developed nations shoppers. They rely on their ability to create a massive network, and hence massive capacity. And they don't just use that network to act as an outsourced provider, they are now moving beyond the manufacture to design, and then using that network to innovate in the area of new materials and manufacturing processes.

Cisco do much the same. They link with partners globally, to provide their products and services (with Cisco at the centre) using standard tools to loosely couple and connect all the players. And by using standard tools and stipulating the methods by which partners can join this network, Cisco make massive operational cost savings, as well as being able to offer such a competitive range of services.

To me the problem is not about technology. In all these examples, it is about being able to link and connect suppliers and providers, managers and businesses, and IT systems and infrastructure. And to do this we need IT functions that can cope with this sort of complexity."

Cost management

"The last big strategic issue facing us today relates to the need to manage our costs.

My problem is that operating in a global world means that my costs go up. I have to provide different packaging and labelling; I have to use a wide variety of distribution channels and sales forces, and need to respond to different regulatory environments. All this increased complexity, potentially increases the cost of doing business. So I have to find ways of managing my business better so that I can either reduce cost or improve my margin. Also, I have to cope with the complexity of managing costs in the service sector, rather than the relative simplicity of cost control in manufacturing.

So what are we doing?

Increasingly, I am seeing a move away from individual product and service profitability to customer profitability, and we try to manage our business on this basis. It means that we have to be even better at segmentation, so that we understand which groups of customers generate profits, and which don't. For example, you may recently have noticed the Cable & Wireless, the UK telecoms Company has decided to shed 30,000 of its smaller customers to focus its energy and resources on its top 3,000 customers. This is seen by some as being very risky, but what I know is that it reflects the fact that Cable & Wireless don't believe they make any profit from those smaller customers.

And it's not just the profitability of customers on a transaction by transaction basis that I am interested in. No, we have to focus on the lifetime value of our customers. In my sector the acquisition costs of winning a customer for an insurance policy is very high, and I need to keep that customer and make them profitable over the long-term if I'm going get the sort of return that satisfies my shareholders.

Increasingly, I also see more and more of my peers managing their businesses from the balance sheet rather than the profit and loss. It's no good for a distributor to improve turnover at the expense of increased stock holding and longer credit terms. Such an approach is only likely to weaken his cash position, and most probably would also hit their margins. On the other hand, if he reduces his stockholding too much or manages it poorly it means he won't have the goods on the shelves and the customers cannot buy. So, he has to be much more sophisticated in the management and utilization of his limited resources.

To me, IT has a key role in helping me manage effectively in this world of cost containment and profit maximization. They can provide me with the tools to control lifetime customer (not product) profitability, and they can deliver the logistics systems that make sure the right stock is on the right shelf at the right time."

So what?

"I believe therefore, you will now understand my frustration with IT functions", said Andy. "The big strategic issues with which we struggle across the industry demand that we gather more information, and use it more quickly and effectively to make decisions and deliver greater results for the shareholders.

This means:
– I need IT to help me gather that information

– I need them to help me play with the information and understand what it means

– I need them to provide the tools by which we can manipulate it

– I need them to provide the cross-organizational view

– I need them to provide the systems by which we deliver and compete not only today but in the future, and

– I need them to tell me how we're doing."

"Thank you," I said "that poses quite a challenge."

LOOKING

Doing

In this final section of each chapter I will focus your thoughts on what you need to get on and do. So this part of each chapter is for those of you who learn best by practical application.

Throughout this chapter, you will have seen that strategy is a living and breathing activity that sustains, focuses and energizes an organization. It is also fluid and dynamic, and that there are many options and possibilities for organizations to pursue, and many issues to consider. To be effective, you need a strong understanding of the breadth of issues and how they impact on your own organization. Therefore, the actions proposed below focus on broadening your experience and providing you with a wider range of perspectives.

Going shopping

I do not believe that you can gain this type of understanding from reading alone. You need to go out into the marketplace and to see what people are up to, how they are competing and how customers are behaving. Accordingly, I would like you to go into a bit of shopping. By this, I don't mean some form of random stroll along your local mall, but something a little more structured and educationally rewarding.

How do our emotions get excited when shopping?

In the earliest stages of sensing and feeling the market, you can learn a lot from just looking at companies in a wide assortment of sectors and identifying how they are seeking to excite and stimulate their customers. Every business approaches this in different ways, not only because company histories vary, as do their staff, location and ownership, but most importantly it is the enormous breadth of customer types, and their behaviours and emotions that presents so much opportunity.

The exercise you are about to embark on will give you the opportunity to explore and investigate in a way that you will rarely undertake in your busy life. So please open your mind, seek out the sensory pleasures and identify how you are stimulated by the businesses you are going to visit.

This is not an easy exercise, unless you are intent on enjoying yourself – if you are, you will have a great time.

Where are you going?

Firstly, you are being asked to consider the differing ways in which the retail shopping sector presents its offering to the market.

So, I would like you to go out into your high street and visit one of the major supermarkets and a convenience store and compare them using the guidance shown below.

What will you be looking for?

This exercise is about your senses and emotions.

☑ I need you to visit the stores and as you move around the store please record the multitude of ways (and yes, there are a great many of them) in which all your senses are stimulated at each store.

☑ As you note how each sense is stimulated, note the emotion that is aroused as a result. Now, you will recognize that this will entail both positive and negative emotions – make a note of both. In other words, how do you feel?

☑ Then, why not sit down in the café and watch the world go by! But don't just watch idly, watch other customers and see how they respond to the stimuli that you have just experienced yourself.

☑ Look at their emotions and how they change and interact with other people. Consider whether they are doing this of their own volition, or whether this is being encouraged by the retailer

☑ Take your time, enjoy yourself and try to spot things that you would normally take for granted.

☑ Having visited a supermarket, do the same thing in a convenience store and identify how it differs.

☑ Then move on, and choose another part of the retail environment. Perhaps record stores or clothing retailers or drug stores. Compare once again how different players are seeking to stimulate the senses and trigger different emotions.

DOING

The world of leisure

In this exercise, I would like you to move on from the high street and indulge yourself in the world of hotels, coffee shops, night clubs, fast food joints, possibly beauty parlours and hairdressers.

What will you be looking for?

The services offered by companies in these sectors differ most markedly in terms of the speed of offering. As a result, their whole service design should be tailored towards reinforcing either fast delivery or slowing you down (amongst other things). Record what you see?

☑ In each site that you visit, how do they slow you down or speed you up?

- Either through the service process through which you are guided

- The approach and training of their staff

- The physical layout, colours and feel of the site

- Through the picture created by their brand image?

☑ What are your main impressions of the companies and how they seek to deliver their service?

- Do they succeed in their aims?

- How could they improve?

☑ What type of customers buy from each and why?

- How do they communicate with and reach those different types of customers – both in-store and externally?

☑ What are the main price points – are there any messages for you here?

☑ What is your overall reaction to the offer being made to you?

☑ Take your time, enjoy yourself and try to spot things that you would normally take for granted.

☑ What are your key observations and insights?

☑ What are the key messages and lessons for your own business?

And please remember, this is not a race and there is no need to rush.

Some other reading

One other thing that you can do to broaden your strategic awareness is to read some key columns in the leading business press.

For example, you could read the Lex column on the back page of the *Financial Times* where you will regularly find commentary on the ways in which organizations are adapting their strategies to the world in which they operate.

Your business

Your next task is to think about strategy as it relates to your own business.

In this activity, I would like you to explore how the main themes discussed in the Touching section of this chapter relate to your own business.

The Why

☑ What are you trying to achieve and for whom?

☑ Who are your masters and what do they expect?

The Who

☑ Identify and describe your target customers. Try to put them into groups, and not just by geographic location, but by how they behave, or what they expect or by the benefits they get from what you do as a business.

☑ Is your company sales driven, process or product focused, or market orientated?

• How do the differences evidence themselves to you?

- If there is a mix of approaches, which one dominates?

- In which bits of the organization does power reside?

The What

☑ Are you about being better than others or being different?

- How do you achieve this?

☑ Do you offer a product or a service?

- List the products and services that you offer.

- What are the obvious groupings of these?

☑ Try to group these products and services slightly differently.

- Group them by way of the benefits that your customers receive from using them. Perhaps you have one group of products that stimulate the emotions of your customers, and another which make their lives easier, and another which makes it the more profitable.

- When you group them like this, does it alter your view of what your company does?

The How

☑ How do you deliver the products and services in your business so that you are both efficient and effective?

☑ Are you trying to be better or do things differently?

☑ Are your operations focused on manufacturing the product, delivering a service or competing through knowledge?

- How do they do that?

☑ Are you seeking economies of scale, and if so through what means?

- What are the organizational implications of this?

☑ What are the main resources you use to compete?

  • How do you make sure you use them productively?

With the benefit of the opportunity to reflect on these issues, I need you to step back and ask yourself what this means for you and your IT function:

☑ What will the business expect from you?

☑ What do you need to be good at?

☑ What sort of knowledge will you be handling?

☑ What resources do you need to have at hand?

☑ What sort of systems do you need to provide?

As a result of these activities...

So what?

As a result of these activities you will have immersed yourself in, and gained a much deeper understanding of how different organizations decide to compete, what they are trying to achieve, who they are trying to serve, what they offer them and how they try to deliver effectively and efficiently. And more importantly, you will have started to develop a strong feel of strategy, what it is and how it works. You will also have gained a strong understanding of the implications for your own business and your IT function.

Therefore, you are now ready to look at how your organization competes in much greater detail and in turn, identify more specifically, what it is you need to be doing so that you can play your full part in your company's success.

DOING

2 Competing businesses

- Competitive advantage and added value

- The strategy hierarchy

- Coherent strategic planning

At the level of individual businesses, we need to understand how they compete, what resources they use to do so, the elements that they need to piece together to give their plans coherence, and their delivery impact. This chapter will enable you to understand the component elements of a business's competitive position so that you can gain a deeper understanding of what your own business is trying to achieve and how it is trying to do it. As a result, you will be able to see the strategy that your IT function must align itself behind and prepare itself to support.

Touching

As a result of the last chapter you will now have some understanding of:

– Where your business is located in a strategic sense

– The key considerations that determine a business's choice of strategy

– The environment in which it operates.

Therefore, we now need to focus more specifically on the ways in which businesses compete and, in particular, we need to gain a detailed appreciation of the competitive components of your own business's strategy.

Where, and how do businesses compete?

Competitive advantage

One of the consistent themes you will hear your business partners discussing is the concept of competitive advantage. In theory, this is about getting yourself into a position where you enjoy a performance advantage over other players. Ideally this would be sustainable over the long term, but with other competitors continually at your heels this is difficult to achieve, and the reality is that often your advantage is short lived, and at best represents something that you can achieve over the medium term.

The purpose of this book is not to provide a detailed analysis of competitive business strategy; I will simply cover the key elements of where competitive advantage may be derived and how it can be measured.

Starting with the question of how competitive advantage is measured (so that we have an objective to work towards), we can say that in a commercial sense this is about enjoying growth in market share and profitability. In other words, if you benefit from this thing called 'competitive advantage' you should win more customers and higher levels of profit. In turn, this should show through to higher levels of performance in terms of return on capital and the overall value of the business.

If you are going to achieve market share and profitability growth, you need to be successful in winning, satisfying and keeping valuable customers. By the way, valuable customers are those that you want to do business with profitably. Regrettably, many businesses forget this and do business with customers at a loss. Indeed many businesses continue to pursue, serve and support customers who not only are unprofitable, but who also stop the business from focusing its resources on projects and activities that could deliver higher returns.

This would appear to be madness and as an outsider to the commercial world you may not believe that any business would be so foolhardy. Unfortunately, there are many who do operate in this way, and a couple of the reasons why are:

– They do not have the ability to measure the profitability of customer groups or products and services.

– They do not have the mental resolve and strategic focus to end unprofitable relationships and focus their resources (people and money in particular) on the more important things.

I am sure it will not take you long to realize that you have a role to play in helping your colleagues to access the information which enables them to determine the profitability or otherwise of customers' products and services. Additionally, I hope your enhanced understanding of strategy will enable you to participate actively in the board level discussions that challenge those business tactics that permit your business to continue to serve unprofitable customers.

Returning to our discussion of competitive advantage, it is necessary to consider what you need to put in place in order to enjoy the growth in profits and market share to which organizations aspire. The diagram below provides a simple series of steps that may lead to the achievement of competitive advantage.

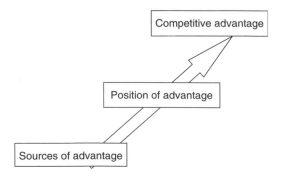

Figure 1: Creating competitive advantage

From this you will see the need to establish some sources of advantage which you then use for impact in the marketplace to gain a position of advantage, and hopefully you then leverage this to achieve competitive advantage in the long run. Let's look at each in turn.

Sources of Advantage

The sources of advantage are the building blocks on which your success is based. Generally, there are two core components of advantage, namely superior capabilities and superior resources. Chances are that your company needs to develop and improve both of these to enjoy the sustained success which you desire.

Superior capabilities

Superior capabilities are represented by skills that others don't have or possess. In other words, you may have an ability to design something or the ability to market and sell a product to the marketplace in ways that outstrips that of your competitors. You may have knowledge of technologies, marketplaces or legislation which presents you with an insight on opportunities that are not available to others.

– Porsche has developed some outstanding engineering and design capabilities.

– Audi has developed skills in four-wheel drive engineering that they utilize across the whole of the VW Audi group.

– The big four accounting firms have unrivalled skill and experience in auditing the books of the largest companies in the world, and in consequence the mid-size accounting firms cannot find a meaningful and sustainable position in that marketplace.

– Boeing and Airbus have superior capabilities in terms of the manufacture of large airplanes.

– McKinsey's have built relationships with the heads of the largest companies and governments around the world.

– Google owns outstanding internet search capabilities.

– Southwest Airlines and Ryanair have perfected the low-cost airline model in their respective markets.

– Procter and Gamble has marketing skills and knowledge which enable them to maintain the performance of hundreds of brands over the long term.

– 3M can be innovative and bring new products to market more reliably and more predictably than their competition.

If you look across this list you will quickly realize that these companies have massive experience in each of their sectors and chosen markets, and they use this experience, and the superior capabilities that result, in order to achieve dominance and to do things the others don't believe possible.

In this respect, it should be clear that the development of superior capabilities is closely linked to the company's ability to learn from their experience and deploy this knowledge for impact in the marketplace.

Equally, it should be clear that if this is a way in which your business competes, then IT has a key role in helping the business to collect the lessons from past failures and successes in order to improve their chances of success in the future. And the quicker you can do this, and the more accessible you can make the information to senior management, the quicker your business can learn and apply the lessons in order to accelerate your company's success.

Superior Resources

The two dominant features that we need to consider are the size of the balance sheet and the equity in your brand.

Clearly, if you have a larger pool of funds than your competition, you have the opportunity to muscle your way into positions that are not available to others:

– You may be able to acquire a competitor and remove them from the marketplace.

– You may be able to enter the marketplace by offering lower prices than your competition. And while they may be able to match you in the short-term, eventually the damage to their profit and loss account will force them to put up their prices. If you have more funds available, you can withstand the pressure of low prices for longer.

– You can invest more money in advertising and promotion, allowing you to reach more people and grab more market share.

– You can pay more to the supermarkets so that you get a more prominent position on their shelves.

It is not always the company with the biggest balance sheet that wins, but it is a case of how effectively you can use the resources available to you. The Royal Bank of Scotland was much smaller than NatWest, both in terms of branch network and balance sheet, but that did not stop it from buying and absorbing the much larger bank. It was also helped by its experience and the capabilities developed in earlier acquisition and integration programs.

Separately, superior resources can come in the shape of a superior brand. Whilst under modern accounting conventions brand equity or value can have a positive impact on your balance sheet, this has little bearing for the business strategist. More important are the opportunities that brands bring in the marketplace. They enable you to:

– Launch products more quickly.

– Charge a premium price.

– Build a relationship with your customers that encourages repeat buying.

These opportunities arise because customers use brands to shortcut their decision-making processes. When working well, a brand provides reassurance, it reduces risk, and it appears more dependable and more trustworthy. As a result, customers use the reassurance provided by brands to choose products from a company they know and discount those from the unknown supplier. I am sure you will recognize this behaviour in yourself in terms of items you purchase for your own home.

Let's say that a few years ago you were thinking of buying a new washing machine. If you were presented with a range of options including Bosch, Zannusi, Hoover and LG, there was a good chance that you would have ignored the offer from LG (the largest company in South Korea) because you didn't know the name. Today, you will be much more willing to consider their products because the name has become more familiar to you. To overcome this, LG initially used price discounting to attract buyers and alongside built brand awareness in the minds of the public.

A word of warning here. It is easy to fool yourself that you have something better than anybody else. But unless there are valuable customers out there who are willing to pay for these superior resources and capabilities, they are valueless in a commercial sense.

A Position of Advantage

This leads me on to the second box in the diagram that which I have called 'position of advantage'.

Here, I have to highlight that you need to use your 'sources of advantage' in such a way that they bring you success. In other words, it is not what you have, but how you use it.

Lower costs

For example, many of the resources and capabilities you develop will enable you to deliver your products and services at a lower cost. And here I use the term 'lower cost' rather than lower price for a reason. If you use your superior capabilities to deliver at a lower cost, then you have the *option* to sell at a lower price. But this is only an option. You may not wish to sell at a lower price, rather you may wish to maintain a high price and benefit from larger profits. Whatever, the ability to produce at a lower cost provides you with options, another key aspect of strategy.

For example, the UK supermarket Tesco has built a logistical capability that is superior to its competitors. This means that it can get its stock out of its warehouses, through its stores and into the boot of your car more cheaply than anybody else. As a result, they have the *option* of using the money they have saved to lower their prices, invest in advertising and promotional activities, improve their service (offering bag packers for example) or investing in new complementary business models such as online shopping, loyalty cards, insurance and banking. Additionally, these funds can also help support land acquisition, new branch openings and investment in overseas markets. Because they can manage their supply chain so much more cheaply than anybody else, they have all these options available to them.

Delivering greater value

The availability of superior resources and capabilities also needs to be applied to deliver superior customer value. In other words, you use your skills and resources to deliver more of what your customers want, so that they buy more from you, and ideally at a higher price.

You may well be wondering what is meant by 'value'. I find it easiest to describe this in three ways. I know there are more sources of value than the three areas I describe below, but I believe this approach will capture the essence of the value delivered in most businesses. The simple groupings I use are:

TOUCHING

- Simplicity

- Profit, and

- Emotional engagement.

Simplicity

In terms of simplicity, think of Direct Line, the car and motor insurance service which is delivered over the phone and online. You may recall the days before Direct Line existed. In those days we had to use a broker and complete long and complicated forms, which often demanded that we attempted to describe in detail our most recent accident. It was a long and tortuous process, and was the primary reason why we remained with the same insurance company for many years. Direct Line offered us an easier, quicker, and more responsive way by which we could organize our insurance cover. Alongside, through a very effective use of economies of scale, and processes pinched from the manufacturing sector, Direct Line were able to offer us simplicity at a lower price, and we grabbed it with both hands. As a result, Direct Line won substantial market share and became a profitable business.

It is interesting to note that the advantages they gained through first mover advantage have in part remained, and they retain the largest share of the UK market despite many other companies copying their model. Additionally, the purchase of Direct Line by The Royal Bank of Scotland has provided them with the financial resources to go alongside their brand resources and operational capabilities. Those financial resources have also been used to buy out a competitor, Churchill.

Profit

This is obvious but it needs stating. One point of value that a service can bring is to make customers more profitable. So a marketing consultant can make her client more profitable by helping them to grow our market share. A company director will use an accountant to reduce his personal tax bill and will pay for the service as a result. And the greater the saving, the greater the perceived value, the greater the fee that can be charged.

Emotional engagement

We will also pay for the pleasure and stimulus brought by the services and products offered to us. Whilst this is the last of my three headings, it is also the most important. One only needs to look at the size of the computer game, film and theme park industries to know how much money we will spend on electronic games, going to the cinema, buying DVDs, and travelling to Florida to enjoy Disneyland.

And don't think that emotional engagement only attaches to these specific examples. The whole process of purchasing any product and service is now bundled up with and packaged in emotional stimuli. Walk into any store of CVS Pharmacy, or a Tesco, or benefit from the reviews on Amazon and one of your many emotions is being triggered to encourage you to buy.

A further thought when considering emotional engagement is the importance of brands. It can be no coincidence that the power of brands is not only growing but accelerating as our desire for emotional stimulation has been increasing. Psychologists tell me that we have something like 328 emotions that can be stimulated, and it strikes me that we increasingly seek to have everyone of them tickled in some way or another when in buying mode. The internet, high-definition television, iPod, XBox360s, and my hairdresser (who offers a head and neck massage before each cut) are responses to our demands for greater stimulation, personally delivered exactly when we want it, and how we want it.

Alongside, we are willing to pay increasing sums for this personal gratification, and this presents the opportunity for premium pricing. But to do so we must ensure that our services or products are closely targeted on our customers needs, and are sufficiently differentiated from the competition.

Given the dominance of emotions, we need to recognize that customers can be very fickle and can quickly turn away from a brand and change their expectations and their behaviours. This demands that businesses must be able to leverage their capabilities and resources consistently, or otherwise their unpredictability will undermine the trust and reliance placed in them, regardless of promotional spending and activities. As they say in Tesco's, "a brand is made up of a million moments". Every time somebody touches your business, they should get a consistent experience that fits with the brand that you are endeavouring to exploit.

These 'touches' can come in the most obscure ways. Part of Ferrari's success on the forecourt over the last seven or so years has come about from the reliability evidenced by Michael Schumacher and his team on the Formula One track. Prior to Michael Schumacher's arrival, the unreliable track performance told a story about a brand which made buyers nervous and caused them to choose alternatives. Yes, Schumacher enabled Ferrari to shout about their success, but equally, his performance also shouted 'consistency, reliability and predictability'. Yes, customers love fast cars, and they love the Ferrari prancing horse, but they also hate poor build quality and breaking down.

TOUCHING

Thus, Ferrari highlight very neatly the point I have been making. You can develop sources of advantage in the form of superior capabilities and superior resources, but you must then leverage them so that you can operate on a lower cost basis and deliver superior customer value, consistently and reliably. If you can, then you have the chance of achieving a position of advantage over your competition and benefiting from the long term competitive advantage which you seek.

A last thought; given that people today buy in an emotionally driven way in response to emotional triggers, what are you doing in your IT function to enable your business partners to enjoy an emotional uplift as a result of their engagement with you?

Putting some meat on the bones

As a result of this understanding, we can now consider in greater depth some of the key strategic questions that individual businesses will be seeking to answer when determining and framing their strategy.

Therefore, this section is about the range of issues that need to be considered when constructing a strategy; it is about understanding what you are trying to achieve, what will encourage large numbers of customers to buy your products and services, and how you will deliver consistently and reliably over the long term.

The strategic hierarchy

First, though, we just need to understand that in a business, strategy operates at three levels; corporate strategy, business strategy, and functional operational strategy as shown in the diagram overleaf.

Corporate strategy

In corporate strategy, the board are very much acting as an investment manager. They have a finite sum of money to invest to maximize the returns to their shareholders. As a consequence, they may decide to invest in a new product or a new business, acquire another company, or they may decide to withdraw their funds from one of their existing businesses to invest elsewhere.

However, they are not just operating as an investment manager. They also have some operational responsibilities, and at corporate level they have the role of ensuring that the col-

Corporate level strategy	Determining the businesses we wish to be in and the results we wish to achieve for our stakeholders and investors Identifying businesses to buy and sell Allocating cash to different business units Managing the relationship between different businesses
Business unit strategy	Defining the strategic objectives of the business, such as: Growth targets, Return on Investment, Cash generation Stating the way that the business wishes to compete in its markets Coordinating team activities to achieve strategic objectives
Functional & Operational strategy	Determining the role functions play in contributing to the business strategy Translating business and competitive objectives into team objectives Managing team resources so as to achieve functional objectives Identifying improvement priorities

Figure 2: The strategic hierarchy

lective performance of all the business units is maximized. This means that they should be looking for ways of combining and utilizing the joint resources, and skills and capabilities of their businesses for the benefit of the whole group.

Business strategy

At a business unit level, we can readily recognize from our earlier discussions the issues that we have to address. Here we are concerned with the way the business competes, the markets and customers it is targeting and its performance in relation to its competitors.

Alongside, business units have responsibility for the next layer down, and hence they need to give consideration to how they will combine the activities of the various departments and functions within their business so that a cohesive and competitive team is built which attacks the market and has that impact necessary to achieve the targeted goals.

When considering strategy in this book, I am going to be particularly focusing on this level.

I also recognize that in some businesses, corporate and business strategy is combined and considered by the same board at the same time, but this is not always the case, hence my desire to describe them individually.

Functional and operational strategy

The functional and operational strategy level applies at the point where the country managers, product managers, and support teams such as human resources, central marketing, finance, and IT come into play. At this level lies the responsibility of these teams to deliver the strategic goals of the business. They need to work jointly to support each other to deliver, and they must ensure that they, focus their energies; what they do and what they deliver is tightly aligned with the business unit strategy.

The components of business unit strategy

Now that we can clearly see how organizations compete and the focus of different levels of strategy, we can identify the sorts of questions that should be answered at the business level in a coherent strategic plan.

In this regard, I am going to consider these questions at four levels:

• What strategic results must we deliver?

  – What are the performance outcomes that our stakeholders (e.g. shareholders, parent companies, strategic partners, funders, or public bodies) need;

  – What are the goals for business growth and productivity gains that are necessary to meet the demands of these stakeholders?

• What do we offer our customers?

  – This is the description of the proposition that we make to our customers which we hope will attract them in sufficient numbers to achieve our growth targets.

• How can we deliver this offering efficiently and effectively?

  – How will we run the business so that we can deliver our proposition reliably and consistently whilst meeting our productivity goals?

• What do we need to develop in the way of skills and technology?

  – What are the gaps in our capabilities, culture and systems that will need to be addressed in order to enable us to perform at the levels required to achieve our strategic goals?

You will quickly see the overlap between these questions and those posed in the first chapter. However, I must point out that these are different. In the first chapter, we were looking at strategy in the round; now we are considering the specifics of the strategy in relation to specific businesses and, more importantly, the place where you work.

In each case, I will highlight some key questions and expand them, so that you are aware of the sort of issues that board members should be considering when deciding their strategy. I must warn you that not all of these issues will have been addressed by your board. So when considering your own business, do not expect or demand an answer to every question. However, you should look out for the obvious gaps and seek explanations and answers if you are not satisfied.

What strategic results must we deliver?

What returns are we looking to achieve? At the end of the day, every strategy must have some measure of financial performance that is the ultimate determinant of success.

What is the ultimate measure of our success?

This may be 'return on capital employed', or something like 'growth in the overall value of the business'.

What do our stakeholders (e.g. shareholders, parent companies, strategic partners, funders, or public bodies) need from us?

In many cases this will overlap with the financial returns described above. But this is not always the case, and many businesses have to deliver specific returns to meet the needs of specific stakeholders, for example:

- Bankers may require a certain sum of cash to be generated or may stipulate that profits have to be above a certain level.

- Parent companies may demand that their subsidiaries deliver a certain amount of profit or achieve a position in the marketplace – for example number one or number two in their markets.

- Local councils have to deliver value to their communities, by way of improvements in the environment, health care and policing, etc.

- Charities must achieve something for the communities for which they were established

What are our revenue growth strategy and targets?

The strategy should clearly define the basis by which the business is going to grow and where new sources of revenue are going to be generated. Will they come from existing or new customers, or existing or new products?

In respect of new customers, how is the business planning to achieve this, and in what way are they going to deliver greater value to their customers?

In each of these elements. The volumes of growth must be clearly stated, both in monetary or percentage terms

What are our targets for improving efficiency?

By what amount will we deliver improved profitability by improving our internal productivity? In other words, how will we ensure that we are continually improving our break even, overhead, and direct cost performance?

What are our plans for making better use of our assets and resources? Will performance gains be achieved through better management of the fixed assets or the working capital of the business?

If we are a people business, then how will we improve the capability of our staff so that they can deliver more?

What is our approach to risk?

What is our strategy for managing and minimizing the key risk areas, be they organizational, operational, financial, environmental, social or political?

What do we offer our customers?

What is it that our customers are actually buying and what is it that we are offering them?

Here, the strategy would describe the proposition the business is making to the customer. This will include a description of the key components of the product or core service, complemented by a description of the relationship and added value services offered to the customer.

What are customers buying? Do we understand what the core benefit to customers is?

In what way are their lives different as a result of doing business with us?

Why buy from us? What is the unique selling point for this particular business?

What needs are we satisfying? Does the business have a clear understanding of the specific customer needs that they are satisfying?

How do we measure this? Are there any measures in place that represent the value that customers gain from doing business with us?

What do we mean when we talk about the quality of our proposition?

Which aspect of quality is the business focused on and how will it be delivered? For example, is quality about reliability, accessibility, or responsiveness?

Customer satisfaction measures? Do we measure satisfaction, and does it relate to the value that we offer?

How do we handle complaints? Are these handled centrally or are all complaints passed through to relative departments?

Service recovery philosophy? Does the business use complaints as an opportunity to generate loyalty?

Learning and improving? Is there a robust mechanism by which we ensure non-repeat of quality failures?

Flexibility; how responsive and adaptable is the product or service?

What flexibilities will be needed? In an increasingly fragmented marketplace with ever more demanding consumers (consumer or industrial) flexibility is an important competitive tool. Therefore, an understanding of how this flexibility translates into the customer offering is likely to be strategically very important.

What inflexibilities exist and what might need to be improved? In all large organizations there will be inertia to change and inflexibility. Do we understand what these are and how to manage them to minimize the effect on the customer offering?

Price; a description of our pricing strategy.

What is our position in the market? Are we a premium player? Are we a niche player? Are we a price-driven player?

What is the pricing strategy? Are we deploying a premium pricing strategy or is the business about low cost to achieve market share?

How does this compare to the value delivered? We have to ensure that the pricing strategy is linked to the value delivered.

Innovation; what is our approach to the ongoing development and improvement of the product or service?

What are the plans to introduce new services, and do these link to the ways in which we need to be offering increased customer value in the future?

New delivery methods – how will customer value be delivered using different distribution formats.

In what respect is the business recognized as innovative? Is it purely through the product or is it through the way that it does business?

What competitive innovation pressures exist? Is the business innovating at the pace of the competition, and how will it match or overtake the competition?

How will we relate to the customer?

The strategy should also describe how value will be added to the customer through the relationship that is built with them:

– Here we are simply looking to describe how the business manages the relationship with customers, and for specific evidence that the business is listening to and responding to their needs, so that we can identify potential areas to add value for the customer.

– Is the business using our relationship with our customers to identify new business opportunities and to maximize the value of our existing business with them?

What services will we offer?

What are the key components of the service that the business is offering to its customers?

– Customization – will the business treat each customer uniquely and allow the service to respond to their needs?

– Tangibility – how will the business make the service accessible and tangible for its customers?

– Reliability – how will the business measure, monitor and ensure complete reliability at all times in its service?

– Emotional stimulation – how will the business stimulate the customer's emotions by the delivery of its service?

How will we manage the customer perception of our image and us?

It should be clear what the brand stands for, and how it supports the product, service and relationship:

– What value does the brand add?

– How does the strength of the brand add to the value delivered by the business?

– How will the customer recognize the value represented in doing business with our brand?

– How can the brand be developed to add to the customer value offered?

– How is the brand keyed into your strategy? Is the brand being utilized for good effect, and also in a locally sensitive way?

– How will the brand be leveraged to enable higher profitability?

How can we deliver this offering efficiently and effectively?

Within this section we are looking to identify the necessary organizational activities, processes, and capabilities that are going to be required in order to deliver the products and services that we are offering.

What is our operational strategy?

How will the way we operate the business enable the customer proposition to be delivered consistently?

TOUCHING

– How do our processes deliver value to the customer?

– How will the quality promised in the proposition be delivered through the operational performance of the business?

– How will the business deliver the customers' needs every time?

How flexible is the operation, and how will it respond to the changing needs of the market?

What are the costs of providing the product, service, relationship and support?

The strategy should also address knowledge, data and information flows and how these can be used to leverage value. How will the business do this effectively and efficiently?

How can we manage better?

To support any form of business growth there is clearly a need for management and leadership skills. Therefore, what management capabilities must be in place that will bring about delivery of the strategy?

The strategy should also describe how the business undertakes the core management roles of:

– Communications

– Planning

– Performance management, and

– Learning.

How will we build the brand?

For the brand to effectively support and add value to the customer offering, it must be actively managed to ensure the correct image, perception, awareness. Therefore we must have a strategy that delivers the right mix of messages and media to ensure brand penetration and awareness in our target markets.

– How will customers experience the brand?

– Ideally there will be a fit between the brand and the product and service, where both will be of mutual advantage to the other. How is this achieved?

– In what way does the brand live within the business – are we making the most of our brand values to build an internal culture?

What do we need to develop in the way of skills, culture and technology?

By its very nature, strategy involves developing new skills, resources, capabilities, etc. that will enable us to compete differently in the future, and to ensure that our staff have the means to support and deliver the customer offering.

What capabilities do we need to develop?

As a result of all the issues identified so far, there will clearly be some capability developments across the staff group as a whole. The strategy should identify the key developmental needs and state what will be done to develop these capabilities. These needs are likely to be in the following areas:

– Management Development – The strategy should identify the key development needs and how they are being addressed.

– Staff Skills and Behaviours – What staff skills and behaviours need to be developed, and how will this be achieved?

– Structures and roles – In what way will the structure or people's roles need to change?

– Retention and recruitment policies – What plans are in place to ensure we have the right talent in the future?

– Innovation – What new product development skills are needed and how will they be developed?

– Relationship management – What capabilities must be developed to deliver the planned customer relationships?

TOUCHING

– Training and development – What training and development programs will exist to support these needs?

How do we need to develop our culture?

The strategy will only be delivered if there is a good fit with the culture. Therefore we must be clear about the way in which the organizational culture will facilitate and enable delivery:

– Values – What are our core values and how do they fit with the customer proposition? What needs to be developed here?

– Behaviours – What is it like to work within this business, and how will we behave in the future in support of our strategy?

– Structure – How is the business going to be structured, and as a consequence, where will the power lie and what is the effect of this? How bureaucratic or empowered will the business be?

– Control systems – What are the key controls within the business; what is their purpose; and how will people behave as a consequence of those controls being in place?

– Market sensing – How will the business gain feedback from customers and the marketplace; what channels will be used; how will the information be collected and used within the business?

What role can systems, processes and technology play?

In what way will technology, processes, and systems need to be developed to support the efficient operation of business? What initiatives may need to be created to deliver these?

– Delivering operational excellence – To reliably deliver the customer offering, what operating processes do we need to develop?

– Delivery/IT systems – What are the main delivery/IT systems required to support these processes, and what are the systems that may need to be developed or integrated?

– Supply chain – How will the business streamline its supply chain? Are there ways that the business can re-engineer its processes or systems to enable them to more simply and more effectively deliver the customer offering?

– Performance Management – What systems and reporting processes are required to manage performance? What specific aspects of performance do they need to drive and monitor?

As you will see, there is a lot that needs to be considered in a coherent strategic plan. The important thing is to see how the answers to the questions fit together and support each other. In other words, you are looking for coherence and joined up thinking.

I am sure that you will also recognize that IT has a major part to play in the delivery of the strategy. Therefore, you will now start to see how important it is for you to be able to understand your own business strategy so that you can to determine what it is IT needs to be doing.

In closing

In the first chapter we saw the importance of the strategic context in which the business operates, and the implications that arise for IT as a result. In this chapter, we have looked at competitive strategy and how it provides you with much greater detail and the clarity that you need to enable you to align your IT function behind the business strategy with a real sense of purpose.

Indeed, I would go as far to say that you cannot even start to align your IT team behind the business unless you understand the answers to the questions I have posed throughout this chapter. If you develop a good understanding you will be able to identify the future role of your IT function.

TOUCHING

Looking

In this part of the chapter, I would like to look at the way in which a wide variety of companies are competing around the world, and consider the implications for IT functions in terms of supporting those competitive aspirations and goals.

Tesco

The UK retailer Tesco was once a simple supermarket. Through the development of incredibly powerful and effective capabilities, it has transformed itself from being a supermarket, then a logistics company and now a marketing company, which happens to sell baked beans, insurance products, banking, and an enormous range of household goods.

Along the way it has managed to move from selling products with low margins (bread and milk) to high margin products such as pet and car insurance and personal loans. Looking at this another way, it has moved from selling products that contain very little information (and therefore little margin), to products that contain lots of information (and therefore lots of margin).

It has been able to do this by building very specific capabilities which have been embedded across the company, and by maintaining a very high degree of focus on a relatively simple and focused strategy.

Logistics were the first capabilities to be developed, followed by the marketing ability that is shared by everyone in the business. This is not just about an ability to communicate, it is more about an obsession with the customer. In a tangible sense, this started with the Tesco Clubcard, and the 'one in front' cut-the-queues drive. More broadly, Sir Terry Leahy, Tesco's Chief Executive, takes a simple, but customer-focused approach. "What I always do is to take the opportunity to look at the business the way the consumer looks at it. So I am always taking the opportunity to see what the customer is seeing, and I am thinking, what is it like to be in Tesco this week? I genuinely think the consumer is the most powerful person in Britain. They have got the power to give to you, and they can take it away by shopping elsewhere."

In terms of the strategic aspirations, Tesco's also keep this simple:

– Increase the core UK market.

– Develop the non-food side and retailing services.

– Expand into international markets.

This they have done with remarkable success, by doubling their turnover in the UK super-market sector and moving from third place to first place in terms of market share, whilst at the same time increasing the turnover from non-food, so that it nearly equals turnover from food. More recently they have entered Eastern Europe, Asia, and California. In the UK they are the number one food retailer, will soon be the number one non-food retailer, and are the number one online retailer. Not bad.

So what?

So, what would this means to the CIO in Tesco? In the first round of development which involved logistics, the IT function would need to be able to provide processes and re-sources to support the implementation of a company wide, world leading logistics system that could speed up the process of supply, reduce stock holding whilst at the same time ensuring stock availability on the shelf, and also substantially reduce the cost of the whole supply chain. This would demand both the ability to quickly provide information on stock-holding to a wide range of managers to enable them to make decisions, but also to be able to link with Tesco's suppliers.

In the marketing stage, the focus of information moves from being internal to external. First, capturing information through the Tesco's loyalty card, and then managing and manipulating the information so that the buying behaviour of customers can be identified. As a result, promotions can be targeted and the company can make decisions about what it wants to offer, in which store and to whom.

International expansion demands an ability to support a business operating in a wide variety of time zones, with different cultures, as well as the capability of integrating exist-ing systems, technology and cultures into the Tesco's way of doing business.

Wells Fargo Bank

Over the past 20 years Wells Fargo has generated annual total returns of over 20%, almost double the level of Standard and Poor's 500 Index. It has a simple strategy: to sell as many financial products as possible to its customers. The average retail customer in Wells Fargo has 15 of these, of which nearly five are provided by the bank. The average UK bank provides about two products per customer and the average US bank, approxi-mately three products per the customer.

It is fair to say therefore, that on its own strategic measures, Wells Fargo has done very well indeed. As a result, its main stakeholders (the shareholders) have done very well on the back of the company whose share value has outperformed the Standard and Poor Index by a multiple of five.

Some detail behind these headline strategic thrusts provides very useful direction for the CIO of the bank:

– Wells Fargo calculate that the cost of selling a product to an existing customer is 10% of the cost of selling to a new customer. Therefore, you will quickly understand that Wells Fargo seeks both growth and cost control through a focus on their existing customers, rather than winning new customers. Of course, they would not say 'no' to new customers, but the energy is clearly directed towards encouraging existing customers to do more business with them.

– The company believes in what it calls 'economies of skill'. If one of their outlets can find a way to boost sales by 5% more than anybody else, they want to be able to use that skill across the business.

– In respect of acquisitions, the bank will buy, but not to produce cost savings. Acquisitions are only pursued where the company believes they will drive faster revenue growth. This is partly because they do not believe in the benefits of economies of scale in banking, but more importantly, the whole focus of the company is about growth built on a customer focused approach.

So what?

The challenge for the CIO is clear; provide systems and technology to provide a complete picture of the customer and their needs and make that accessible to everybody in the bank. Therefore, when anyone is facing a customer or making decisions about customers they have the information to hand to make the right decision, which results in customers buying more financial services products.

RAC Roadside Services

Every seven seconds a car driver somewhere in the UK calls the RAC because their car has broken down. They are often in distress and want someone to repair their car quickly so that they can continue their journey.

LOOKING

The RAC has 8 million members, and is committed to providing the very best service in handling calls, dispatching an engineer to the broken down vehicle and undertaking faster diagnosis and repair. They have 1500 patrols around the country and to deploy them effectively in a customer focused way, they need to be able to quickly identify where the motorist is; provide a reliable estimate of the engineers likely arrival time; and then have the skills and knowledge to be able to diagnose and find a solution to almost any type of vehicle problem.

To deliver, the RAC has invested in a very sophisticated engineer dispatch system centred on their control centres in three sites throughout the UK. More importantly, though, this dispatch system is linked to in-van technology used by the engineers.

To do this, the in-van systems provide the engineer and the contact centres with the same view of the customer, satellite navigation, and a diagnostics system that can connect with the customer's car to undertake fast diagnosis.

At the end of the job, customers can provide instant feedback through the same system so that the engineer and the company as a whole have an immediate understanding of customer satisfaction.

So what?

The IT director supporting the RAC business must not just focus on the technologies of remote support and satellite navigation. Any chosen system clearly has to be reliable, but it must also speed processes and be focused on increasing customer satisfaction.

This demands a very strong understanding in the IT team of the role of the RAC engineer and the wide range of customers, circumstances and challenges they face in serving customers anywhere in the country from late-night inner-city breakdowns to remote mountainside assistance in sub-zero temperatures.

This means that IT don't only need strong technological skills, but also an ability to engage with and understand the engineers and their role so that they can find practical solutions that work. This demands that IT spend a lot of time out in the field learning, exploring and testing – indeed, being close to their customers

Container Store

Container Store, the US provider of personal storage and organization products, is unusual. In the retail sector, sales people on average receive less than 10 hours training in their first year of service. In Container Store, new entrants receive 230 hours of training before being let loose on their customers.

Why? Because they want to "get their customers to dance every time they go into their closet because the product they bought has been designed and sold so carefully." They can only do this if their staff are highly trained so that they can both understand and explain the shelving systems that they use, and are able to relate to the customer to understand their needs and translate them into practical solutions that will in time 'Get the customer to dance'.

Supporting this approach is a number of other coherent strategic activities:

- A highly selective recruitment policy involving telephone screening, group interviews, and as many as four further meetings.

- The company has appeared on *Fortune Magazine's* list of 'Top 100 US companies to work for' for seven consecutive years.

- Above average pay rates and payment of health-care insurance premiums covering families and part-time workers.

- Employee turnover kept below 10%.

Has this worked? It would appear so, with sales growth of between 15% and 20% annually, and recently 5000 people applied for 180 positions in a recent store opening in Manhattan.

So what?

The IT team in Container Store need to both provide systems that facilitate flexible, customer focused solutions at the point of sale and IT needs to support a strategy that is focused on winning, developing and retaining high quality, highly skilled and highly motivated staff.

On the one hand, you could say that this comes from how those staff are managed, but it also comes from having internal systems and processes which staff can rely on to simplify their lives. Staff get incredibly frustrated by unreliable, inflexible and bureaucratic systems and processes which stop them doing what they want to do, namely serving customers, achieving sales and being productive. IT has a key role to provide this platform for success.

Scion Cars

Scion is a brand within the stable of Toyota cars. It exists because of a problem relating to the main Toyota and Lexus brands, which appear to be attractive to older customers; the average buyer of Toyota and Lexus cars is 54 years old.

Scion is based in California and sells funky cars to young people; it is seen by Toyota as a stepping stone into the Toyota group for younger buyers. It has a tiny staff of 17, and Toyota builds the vehicles and handles their distribution through their existing show-rooms.

However, Scion compete in an interesting way. The car company sells many more cars over the Internet that any of its competitors, but more intriguing is that they try to sell their cars by aligning tightly with the lifestyle of its target customers. There are almost 40 accessories available, including items such as gold and chrome license plates, various types of sound systems, and most interestingly, amber or blue interior lighting.

Instead of selling cars by way of car magazines and television stations, dealers use alternative approaches which often involve promotional events. These include activities at nightclubs, linking with DJs and appearances at music stores. Alongside, Scion has launched a record label and has a clothing line.

The link into Toyota could be seen as a liability, but customers seem to take reassurance from Toyota's reputation for quality.

Is the concept working? Toyota hope to sell something like 160,000 Scions in the US this year, and the average age of buyers is just over 30. Longer term, it is Toyota's hope that their customers will trade in their Scion for a Toyota or a Lexus, but given the newness of the Scion brand it is too early to tell whether this part of the strategy is being fulfilled.

So what?

A fascinating story, and one that poses a number of challenges of the IT team.

Firstly, the need to provide the company with access to information and knowledge surrounding the behaviour, attitudes and expectations of customers with whom the parent company has limited selling experience.

LOOKING

Secondly, the need to provide web sites oriented at the target market, providing ordering facilities and supporting a wide and growing range of accessories. It also demands integration with the parent company, its systems and dealer networks.

In respect of the promotional activities, there is the need to gather information regarding events and activities attractive to the target market, so that dealers are aware of them to take advantage of the opportunities presented.

Finally, there is the need to monitor the ownership experience and trade-in patterns, so that the opportunities to cross sell into the main Toyota brand are realized, and the parent companies aspirations satisfied.

Harley-Davidson

Harley-Davidson has suffered some ups and downs over the years, and it came close to bankruptcy in 1985. Since then it has enjoyed 20 years of record revenue and profits. Total revenue is $5 billion, leading to a net profit of $900 million, largely through the sale of over 300,000 bikes.

However, Harley-Davidson's success has not so much come from the quality of its manufacture (although this was an important foundation stone), but from making the most of its brand and the loyalty of its customers.

It has leveraged the fact that in reality it is seen as a cult American brand related to a lifestyle first loved by 1950s and 1960s bikers who have since grown up and got respectable jobs. However, they still wish to enjoy the memories of their youth and their aspirations are for the Harley-Davidson brand. Arising out of this, Harley-Davidson created HOG, the Harley Owners Group, which now has one million members, and which provides a substantial part of the company's income through Harley-Davidson accessories and clothing.

As a result, Harley-Davidson enjoys the benefits of selling high margin products on the back of high value brands. Its financial performance, and the growth in the value of the company and its brand equity is testimony to its strategic success.

So what?

Once again, customer attitudes and behaviours (and this time) aspirations dominate. It is critical for Harley-Davidson to understand how their brand plays out with their target market, so that they can translate this insight into new products, brand development and promotional activity, and then into the cross selling of high margin, branded accessories and clothing.

Harley-Davison customers are repeat buyers, and therefore there is a critical need to maintain a dialogue with them throughout their ownership of a bike, using HOG and other relationship activities to reinforce their aspirations and to encourage and accelerate the next purchase. For example, Harley-Davidson sponsor, initiate and run many bike rallies across the country to make the owners of their bikes feel as though they belong and are part of the family.

Underpinning all this is the need for systems and technology to support lean manufacturing and continuous improvement techniques, cultures and systems.

Many more of the same

I hope that these little vignettes have helped you to see the range of strategies which organizations adopt, and in turn the implications for IT functions in respect of their role supporting and enabling successful delivery of those strategies. There are many more that we could have looked at, for example:

Kodak

Kodak is trying to undertake a transformation to respond rapidly to the digital age. Three years ago, film accounted for 70% of its business. This number is falling rapidly and by as much as 30% last year. Soon Kodak will phase out film sales altogether.

Gibson Guitars

Like Harley-Davidson, Gibson plays on the heritage brand concept, and has also improved the quality of manufacture, and made sure that big name guitarists endorse the brand.

Procter and Gamble

A focus on product innovation, customer service, brand management, and long-lasting success by getting the basics right, and keeping customers happy with quality products and good service.

So what?

It does not matter how many we look at, they all underline the need to use information, technology and systems to support delivery of the strategic plans of the company. Unless IT intimately understands the strategy and the implications of the strategy, then they cannot provide specific answers to the specific questions and challenges that strategic plans raise.

Whilst the strategy can be delivered with a generic and poorly aligned response by IT, the chances of success are diminished and the ultimate results are reduced. IT has not only to understand what is required, but it also has to be capable of delivering focused and sustained support over the long term.

The rest of this book considers how we get IT into shape to achieve this degree of alignment and impact.

LOOKING

Doing

With the benefit of an understanding of the key strategic themes and the competitive issues facing businesses generally, you are now in a position to consider and identify the strategy that your own business is pursuing.

You cannot do this in a darkened room on your own. To be successful you need to engage with the key players in your business, and I would suggest interviewing them in a structured manner to identify the key strategic issues that they are pursuing. Below is a simple approach that you can use as the main point of reference for your meetings with them which will help you to identify the key strategic thrusts for your business in the years ahead.

Determining your approach

Before meeting with them identify the level of strategy that you are going to discuss with each member of the board and senior management team.

☑ Are you going to explore corporate level, business level, or functional level strategy issues with them?

☑ Based upon this analysis, decide which of the three sets of opening questions shown below you will utilize.

Corporate level strategy	What business do we want to be in? What businesses do we plan to acquire and what to divest? How do we allocate cash to different businesses? How do we manage the relationships between different businesses?
Business unit strategy	What are the strategic objectives of the business, such as: Growth targets, Return on investment, Cash generation? In what way does the business compete in its markets? How does the business coordinate team activities ?
Functional & Operational strategy	How does your function contribute to the strategic objectives of the business? How do business and competitive objectives translate into team objectives? How do you manage your resources so as to achieve functional objectives? What performance improvement priorities have you established?

Figure 3: The strategic hierarchy

☑ It is very likely, that you will use two sets of these questions with each member of the executive and senior team, because they will have responsibility for the company's performance at two levels.

Exploring the business strategy

In terms of those directors and managers responsible for business units and functional strategy, you need to go beyond these opening questions and explore the following additional issues:

What are your key 3 year goals?

Describe 5–6 headline key issues.
Delineate between the external market-based goals and internal, development-based goals.

What are the growth challenges you face?

If success is going to be achieved in the external market, what are the key issues that will have to be overcome as an organization – internally and externally?

How will you measure strategic success?

How will you know when you have arrived and what measures will you use to quantify that success?

Revenue Growth Strategy

How are we going to grow the business? Is it from new businesses, existing or new products, or from existing or new customers?

How do you manage risk?

How risk tolerant are you? What are the key risks you face?
What is your strategy for managing & minimizing the potential effects of key risk areas?

Productivity Strategy

What are your plans for continually improving breakeven/overheads, direct costs and asset productivity?

Deliver more value to our clients

An additional way of increasing income is to offer more value to the existing served market. What is your strategy here?

Figure 4: Understanding the business strategy

☑ In most instances these questions and the discussion that follow will provide you with sufficient information to understand the business and what it is trying to achieve, and hence the role of IT.

☑ However, where appropriate, or where you feel the responses are of insufficient depth, utilize the additional and more detailed questions I described in the Touching section of this chapter under the headings:

What strategic results must we deliver?
This section will have been covered by your earlier questions

---

What is our customer offering?
What is our offering?
What elements make up the value of our offering?
How will we relate to the customer?
What service will we offer?
How will we manage customer perception of our image and us?

How can we deliver this offering, efficiently and effectively?
What is our operational strategy?
How will we deliver the customers' needs?
How will we do this effectively and efficiently?
What innovations are we planning?
How can we manage better?
How will we build the brand?

What do we need to develop in the way of skills and technology to do this?
What capabilities do we need to develop?
How do managers need to develop in order to support the plans?
How do we need to develop our culture?
What role can technology play?

DOING

Figure 5: The components of business unit strategy

☑ Please don't accept answers from just one director or business head; you need to meet with them all, including your CEO, to gain a broad picture.

☑ Don't be frightened to challenge the business heads regarding their strategic aims and aspirations. Many of them will be poorly thought through, and you should feel confident to challenge their thinking by using these questions.

Summarizing your findings

☑ Having met with them all, pull together the key and common elements together in a summary document

☑ At this juncture, discuss your findings and test your conclusions with your managers in your IT team:

- Indeed, to enhance buy-in and commitment from your IT managers, you may have included them in this interview process, either by getting them to join you for the meetings or asking them to carry out the meetings on their own with selected senior managers and directors

- This will demand that you get them to read this book first, so that they understand strategy, the questions they are asking, and why they are asking them

☑ When you prepare your summary document, a good way of structuring it is along the lines of the four boxes used above; strategic results, customer offering, delivering the offer, and capability development. You will find this a simple way to structure your findings and to play them back to the business and explain them to your team.

Testing your thinking

Check your conclusions with the CEO and other key directors:

☑ Check that the picture you have gained is accurate, and is a fair representation of what the business is trying to achieve.

☑ A word of warning. Don't be surprised if you hear disparate views; boards are never as cohesive as you would like nor as strategic textbooks like to suggest. If only they were, life would be simpler for us all and organizations would achieve so much more. Therefore, you will need to accept a degree of compromise, but I am sure you will be able to extract the main strategic issues as a result of these interviews.

Outcomes

As a result of these further meetings. You should:

☑ Share a common view with those of your directors and senior management regarding the direction of the business, its goals and aspirations.

☑ Be able to identify three, or possibly four main strategic themes that your business is pursuing. These will not just be headline bullet points, they will also benefit from a brief description; sufficient to enable you to talk to your own team and provide them with clear guidance on the strategy in a way they can understand, and which is sufficient to enable them to have a good grasp of what the business is trying to achieve, and how it is going to go about it.

In closing

☑ Gain an understanding of the strategy through structured interviews with the business heads and directors.

☑ Pull the answers together in a summary document.

☑ Identify the top three or four strategic themes the business is trying to pursue. These are like buckets in which everything else is placed.

☑ Test your understanding with the CEO and other directors and let them fill gaps and omissions.

☑ Finalize the summary document.

☑ Tell the story of the strategy to your own management team.

☑ Use it to test your understanding, and to inform them, and to engage them in the process of delivering value from IT.

☑ You will now have a picture sufficiently detailed and accurate to enable you to start to align your IT function behind your business strategy.

DOING

3 The setting for strategy

- The individual user

- The challenge of teams

- Different types of organization

- Living with lifecycles

This chapter will take you outside of the IT function and force you to look at the needs of the different types of users that you will serve. This will build and develop your understanding of the context in which the IT function has to operate and the specific needs that you need to satisfy.

Touching

This relatively short chapter serves to highlight and remind us of the differing needs of the audiences that you serve, in different organizations in which you work. Therefore, and whilst most of you reading this will work for profit-making, private sector companies serving shareholder needs and expectations, not all of you will be. Some of you will be working for small enterprises, others for charities, and others in the public sector and government departments.

I fully recognize that the focus of this book appears to be on private sector companies and their aspirations, but the principles discussed throughout apply whatever your sector and environment, and wherever you are located globally.

Accordingly, this chapter will address the expectations and needs of a wide range of users, groups, organizational types, and sectors. This is not intended to be a detailed and complete analysis of every business sector, but serves to remind you of the need to stop and consider your particular circumstances before you proceed with the rest of this book.

The individual user

Despite the views of some managers, most people get up in the morning wanting to do a good job, and also they like to work in an environment that is conducive to doing so. IT has an important role in helping these people to perform and to create a positive workplace context.

Firstly, and at a basic level, users expect to work with systems and equipment that are reliable and responsive, and which don't get in the way of them doing their job. Staff are frustrated by slow response times or systems that are continually crashing. Either weakness makes them both unproductive and results in less positive feelings towards the workplace, making them harder to manage and more likely to leave.

At a higher level, they have a desire to achieve and improve their performance, and therefore require IT systems that reduce repetitive work and increase their productivity. This demands that systems are flexible, and provide easy access and use.

IT, however, is not just about technology, it is about the use of information and therefore you may need to consider the implications of supporting what are known as 'knowledge workers'. If you do, then you need to deeply understand what information they specifically need and why. You also need to be able to provide information in a timely manner, ensure it is accurate and offer the necessary flexibility so that data can be manipulated and used in a variety ways.

Users will make some other demands upon you. Firstly, be invisible. It is a strange irony of corporate and IT life that people want all the benefits that you bring but they don't particularly want to see or know that you and your equipment exist. Indeed, the mindset is that if they are seeing lots of you then something has gone wrong. So somehow you have to have a massive impact (the whole purpose of this book) in a discreet way. Now there's a challenge.

Secondly, when you do an upgrade or replace a system, you need to minimize the impact on people's day-to-day lives. Ironically, even if you are replacing a system that users have moaned about for years, any disruption to their daily work patterns will suddenly result in them saying how good the old system was. But then people are strange creatures.

One last thing that you must do, and that is providing effective support when things go wrong. People do not react well to disruption nor to interference to their plans. So, make sure that you have systems in place that respond quickly and in a supportive manner when the inevitable happens.

The challenge of teams

There are two fundamental aspects of teams that you need to bear in mind; first, they are meant to be about people working together to achieve an objective; and second, they reflect our natural desire to socialize and be with others.

Both of these aspects demand collaboration, even though the first one demands collaboration with a little more purpose. So put simply, the role of IT is to facilitate that collaboration within and across teams. This may mean that you need to help people to connect with each other or to share and use information and knowledge. Given the nature of global operations, you also need them to do these things across time zones.

Oh, and don't forget that the informal teams (social groups, people gathering around coffee machines, sports teams, etc.) are just as important as the formal ones created by the organization (project teams, departments, workgroups, etc.). I know your company won't give you as much to resource these informal groups, but helping these as well as the formal groups has a positive effect on morale and motivation, as well as enhancing the reputation of IT.

Really that's all there is to think about with teams, except that there are some special types of teams that you need to bear in mind.

The finance department

A strange bunch by any measure. In behavioural terms, they are most probably the closest type of people to the IT function that you will get; but strangely enough the two rarely seem to get on that well. This weak relationship is exacerbated because IT often reports into the finance director, circumstance which frequently reflects a historical perspective of IT rather than a focus on the potential impact that it can bring.

However, this reporting and hierarchical relationship tends to make Finance feel superior to IT, and I find it quite strange how often finance staff think they can do the job of IT. Indeed, they are the most likely part of the organization to start building their own IT systems, and if given the chance, their own mini IT function.

On the other hand, there is the potential for an incredibly close relationship because of the proximity of shared interests. Both functions are about the use of knowledge, both functions use technology more widely in their roles than anywhere else, and both functions have a strong interest in reducing costs and improving productivity.

Your focus should be on trying to move yourself away from the parent-child relationship through the provision of timely and accurate information that can be manipulated and used in a wide variety of ways. In this sense, the demands of Finance are pretty basic; they are not looking to use information for competitive advantage, but for effectiveness and efficiency. Make sure you satisfy those needs, and don't try to get too clever as generally they are not interested.

HR

HR is a very different animal and like IT they are often subject to criticism, and business units enjoy questioning their very existence. They too are a support function whose role and potential is not fully understood. Like IT, if focused and harnessed in the right way the value that they can bring is enormous.

HR's needs are principally twofold; processes and systems on one hand, and creating value on the other. The processes relate to their responsibilities in respect of staff records, compensation and benefits and legal matters. Here once again, their requirements are for timely, accurate and readily accessible information from a system that is reliable and responsive.

They create value through their organizational development work, which is focused on building the capability of the people in your organization. This should improve productivity and your competitiveness. In respect of the former, there is a strong overlap with your role in the IT function as they too will be looking to improve the reliability of the staff in the organization, and one way of achieving this is through the availability of reliable IT systems.

Equally, though, their focus will be on the development of staff and leadership competencies, and they will need support in managing processes such as competency-based training and assessment, leadership assessment, personal development program planning and delivery. In all these areas, and many others, they will both need to be able to manage the processes, gather and use information and knowledge, and measure performance.

Marketing and Sales

Of all the areas where IT should have a close relationship, the Marketing and Sales function should be top of the list; unfortunately it rarely is.

Yes, I appreciate that in many ways Marketing is about the management of communication and brand management, and Sales is about the deal, but at its heart, marketing is about understanding the needs of customers and enabling the company to respond and satisfy those needs. Ideally this should involve marketing in getting all parts of your company closer to the customer.

The ability to fulfil this market and customer-centric approach demands the use and manipulation of large quantities of data regarding the business environment, customers, potential customers and competitors.

Unlike finance, traditionally marketers neither profess great IT skills nor do they really have any great interest in the creation and management of databases and systems. Therefore they welcome the type of value adding support that IT can bring to enable them to use information, and turn it into knowledge which can be used to advance the performance of the company. However, the increasing use of e-marketing means that they are becoming more skilled with IT and more demanding of IT functions. You need to ensure that you step up to the mark, and don't let them start to build their own IT function.

Alongside, IT are in a unique position in that they can see the flow of data across the company in a way that cannot be achieved by any other function; IT can see data at the most granular and, if it wishes, also at the highest level; IT can see the flow of data into and across the company; and IT can see who is using what data and when.

Appropriately managed, this data can be turned into knowledge that will be invaluable to marketers to help them provide the company with a customer centricity. It is regrettable that most CIOs and IT functions do not recognize the value that they can bring to marketing and do not seek the type of relationship with marketing that would result in a powerful partnership that would benefit the company in multiple ways.

Also, it should not be forgotten that IT can support the sales function to improve sales effectiveness, develop new distribution and sales channels, reduce sales expenses and support the development of new product and service lines.

The board

IT's role in respect of the board and their needs are multiple. At a basic level they will receive information from a variety of functions. However, to meet the challenging reporting timescales normally set by boards will demand reliable and responsive IT systems.

At the other extreme, the strategic opportunities arising from evolution of information and technology are massive and will only increase. Hence, the board needs and deserves an IT function that is aware of the world at large and emerging technologies. It also needs to provide the board with a window on customer behaviours and the activities of competitors in a way which can stimulate insight and strategic debate so that the company can identify and choose appropriate strategic options.

In between, the board needs to know that IT is capable of:

– delivering the key strategic programs;

– helping to improve business processes;

– aiding governance, compliance and risk management processes and systems,

– facilitating links with key business partners both through contractual arrangements and open systems development.

Different types of organization

As I noted in the introduction, the world isn't just made up of private sector, profit-driven companies, and many of you reading this book will also work for other types of organizations. We need to look at your needs and the focus of IT's role.

Small businesses

Generally, these enjoy a narrow focus which certainly aids the task of the IT function. On the other hand, the experience of using IT, particularly in the way described in this book, is likely to be very limited, and the demands placed on IT are likely to be about efficiency and the operation of technology.

The influence of senior managers (who are often owners) will be strong, and the approach towards IT will be influenced by their experience. Therefore IT functions should ensure that they understand what is important to management. Equally, though, there is a strong role for education and helping people to understand the value that IT can bring.

By nature of their size, flexibility is often a trait within these businesses, and the opportunities to implement innovative IT solutions to business problems should be actively and continuously explored.

Professional partnerships

Many professional partnerships are small businesses as well, and need the same supportive approach. However many, especially in the legal and accountancy worlds, are also multinational organizations with enormous scale. Despite the range of size of businesses that are seen in this group, a factor common to them all is the power of the partners. In this way, IT should take a similar approach to that suggested for the senior managers of small businesses.

Alongside, knowledge is central to the way they compete, and therefore there is a massive need to manage and deploy knowledge throughout the organization. IT must be at the centre of facilitating knowledge transfer in these types of businesses.

The global nature of many of these businesses also demands cross-border working and the integration of resources. Often this is not easy in an environment where people often work happily in their own silos.

Charities and the voluntary sector

In organizations where personal beliefs and passions often dominate it is often hard to discern the central purpose of the charity and the challenge is one of understanding the strategy and the role that IT has to play.

In these organizations, IT can become marginalized or wholly ineffective because its resources are simply being pulled in too many directions at once and nothing is really achieved that has real impact.

TOUCHING

In this regard, the skills required by the IT function are those of gathering and analysing multiple views of strategy, and managing multiple relationships to determine and deliver the IT strategy and priorities.

In this environment, your frustrations may cause you to want to lead a boardroom discussion regarding the direction of the charity. If you can do this successfully, well done. But it is likely that you will not be given the opportunity to do so or you will find that you do not have the facilitation skills necessary to successfully manage this complex environment. Therefore, in practice you will find that you are running something akin to a federal IT strategy whereby you agree key priorities with a different factions and functions, and then identify the best allocation of your resources across these projects to maximize the impact. From there it is all about negotiation, communication and relationship management.

The public sector

This is a wide and diverse grouping which includes government agencies, local authorities, health services, NGOs, nationalized industries and a wide range of other public services. Each has a complex mix of products and services, projects, set in the communities they serve and where politics dominates.

This demands the ability to support the delivery of these products and services, once again through the provision of reliable and effective systems and processes.

More broadly, these organizations have to maximize the use of resources and evidence value for money. Hence the ability to demonstrate the delivery of outputs is vital. This means that managers focus on performance indicators, resource allocation and planning; all areas where IT can play a key role.

Many of these organizations also have a role in respect of community leadership. IT has the, as yet unrealized, potential to aid the operation of those communities in ways that mirror the communities already being built amongst the young through MySpace, YouTube and BeBo, etc.

The public sector is subject to massive change driven by political agendas (both national and local) and therefore needs to be able to respond quickly and frequently to new demands and expectations of performance. IT needs to be able to establish architecture, systems, processes and ways of operating which offer the organization the necessary agility and flexibility.

Global networks and multinational corporations

These are intrinsically complex organizations where the need to integrate activities, support rapid growth and compete in a variety of countries and cultures, drawing on both local and national resources are great.

In reality, success cannot be achieved without a highly effective IT function which is tightly aligned with the business strategy. Being able to respond at speed, shrinking cycle times, reducing costs and improving consistency will be demanded and expected. Alongside, a wide variety of portals will operate to coordinate activities and deliver the sales and distribution processes:

- Employee portals

- Including personal performance dashboards, access to information, internal marketing and training, appraisals, executive briefings as well as management information around company performance.

- Supply portals

- Integrating suppliers, logistics management and stockholding, and driving out cost savings.

- Customer portals

- Facilitating the sales and distribution process through a wide mix of media and channels.

Beyond this, IT will need to integrate systems and coordinate activities across alliances, acquisitions and joint ventures which will draw IT into cost-saving, setting standards, changing and creating processes, educating and informing, simplifying coordination and control.

Living with lifecycles

It is worth recognizing that regardless of the size and sector of the organization in which you work, the role of IT will be impacted by the maturity of your organization and your IT function.

TOUCHING

Childhood

In this initial stage, the organization is learning about IT, often driven by enthusiastic users rather than any meaningful systems planning. There maybe a list of priorities, but little senior management understanding or involvement resulting in inflexible systems and often incompatibility across systems.

The main focus is on efficiency and that is achieved through sourcing externally.

Adolescence

The need to share information has now been realized and management are concerned that we are not getting value for money from our IT investments. As a result, formal reviews of existing systems and their effectiveness is undertaken and some joint planning is now evident between business managers and the IT team.

The focus is now on improvement and the dawning recognition that some competitive advantage can be gained through the use of information, and the effective use of company-wide systems.

Middle age

The organization now readily recognizes the need to share knowledge and for strong relations between the business and IT, so that the right information is available to the right people at the right time. Systems now support the core activities and systems and strategic planning are now formal activities which are improving flexibility and speed of development. An external focus allows integration with third parties and the board are seriously interested in the potential value of IT.

As a result, opportunities to use information technology to build barriers and increase market power are being explored as well as finding ways to build alliances and change the nature of the industries in which these companies operate.

In closing

There are some common themes that run through all of these organizations, and in many ways these relate to the core demands of demonstrating and delivering efficiency and effectiveness. The challenge, however, is to go beyond these entry points and satisfy the specific needs and requirements of your various customers.

For many IT functions this will be demanding, but without the initial and conscious recognition and exploration of their expectations you cannot hope nor expect to perform at the levels demanded.

Looking

Priorities, politics and personal agendas

Why is it so difficult for the public sector and government agencies to deliver the results we all need? From the public's expectations of the public health services, there remains much concern about the ability of these organizations to deliver the value that we increasingly demand and expect.

I propose that there are some common themes that really prevent these organizations from delivering the benefits that they are set up to achieve.

I believe that the key difficulties revolve around the issues of 'Priorities, Politics and Personal Agendas.' And in turn, I suggest that unless urgent focus is given to the issues of 'Purpose, Performance Management and Potential' then little will change, despite the sums of cash now being pumped into the system by central governments.

Priorities

The difficulty for most public service bodies and government agencies is the number, variety and nature of the priorities with which they are bombarded. And it is not just the volume that impacts so heavily, it is the often conflicting nature of these priorities and tasks.

In the commercial world, we enjoy a sense of purpose that can be quite clearly articulated through the measurement of profit. This helps us to focus our energies, and it is relatively easy to see the steps that go towards delivering this outcome; target and understand the customer; identify and develop the offering; deliver the offering.

In the public sector it is much harder to identify the cohesive theme that pulls everything together and provides the appropriate focus for everybody's energies and activities. When this is compounded by multiple and conflicting priorities a number of things often result:

– Confused staff

– Wasted resources

– Unnecessary investment in the wrong projects

– Ineffective delivery

The failure to implement and deliver serves to undermine the public's belief. This then serves to further damage the confidence of the teams operating within the organizations, reinforcing negative thinking and creating a damaging rift between the public and the organization concerned. All together, these factors often act as catalysts for a downward spiral in performance.

Politics

So why are there so many priorities?

In part, they can be explained by the continually changing demands and influences of the political environment at both local and national levels. As national and local governments democratically change political persuasion, hue and colour, so the demands and pressures on public bodies similarly change. Compound this with the politicians' need to be seen to be responding to public demands, and one shouldn't be surprised about the profusion of priorities, many of which will be conflicting and often created without recognition of existing demands on resources.

Personal agendas

An environment in which multiple priorities and oscillating political views abound provides a wonderful climate in which personal agendas can be pursued and cultivated. Such an environment permits the opportunity for the ego to rise above public need, and personal aspiration to dominate over the public good.

This is not to say that all these issues are evident in all public sector organizations and agencies, but these are the main dangers faced by these organizations and they have to be actively neutralized.

So what?

So what can be done to frustrate these dysfunctional effects?

In the simplest terms, I believe that the three negative 'P's of Priorities, Politics and Personal Agendas can be counteracted by the three 'P's of Purpose, Performance Management and Potential.

LOOKING

Purpose

As I said earlier, purpose is easy to identify in the private sector. We have to satisfy our shareholders by generating sufficient profit. We have to develop a proposition that is tightly aligned with the needs and wants of our customers, and then deliver it more effectively and efficiently than our competitors.

However, in the public sector the organizational purpose cannot be so easily articulated. Therefore, public sector managers have to be even more effective in establishing absolute clarity of purpose and focus. They have to strive for a coherence and consistency of perspective that provides a filter for decision-making and prioritization up and down the organization. Achieving this degree of clarity is not easy, but it is the essential foundation by which the resources within public sector organizations can be deployed to real effect. Unfortunately, in an environment in which 'task' dominates, insufficient time is allocated to this vital role.

Performance Management

For the purpose of the organization to be cascaded throughout and translated into action, strategic performance management systems, processes and behaviours are required. These must seek to reinforce the behaviours and the development of skills and capabilities that will enable the organization to deliver on its core and critical purpose.

Alongside, performance management has a key role in leveraging the delivery of performance. Strategic performance management is a difficult skill to acquire and develop, but in the environment in which public sector bodies have to operate, it is a critical element in the successful delivery of the right outcomes.

Potential

It is necessary for public sector workers and managers to recognize the skills and capabilities that they have, and leverage them for real effect. Too often, I believe they spend their time looking over the fence at the private sector. This is an exercise that only serves to undermine their confidence in their own managerial capability and competence. They do have excellent skills, but they also need to recognize that what is demanded of them is different from that which is demanded in the private sector. Hence, they should focus on building the skills necessary to achieve in the public sector.

And whether they like it or not, the environment in which they operate will always create multiple and conflicting priorities; it will always be subject to political pressures and the outputs will always be more diverse than in the private sector. This environment will always demand different skills than those needed in the private sector.

It is therefore important that public sector management are building the ability to cope with this unique set of variables and find ways to effectively manage the organizational flexibility that is demanded as a consequence.

Building this set of capabilities takes time, but once established provides the bedrock upon which managers and staff can deal with the competing and conflicting pressures, and get on and be able to deliver the results demanded of them.

In conclusion, there is no point in pretending that the difficult environment of the public sector will become easier, it won't. The challenge is to ensure that clarity and purpose are achieved and that the skills and mechanisms of strategic performance management are implemented. But most of all, management have to build the organizational capability to cope with fluidity, and still deliver the results that we need.

LOOKING

Doing

The focus of this chapter has been on understanding the type of organization in which you work, and the teams and people you work with. You need to do this in order to gain a broad understanding of the focus of the organization so that you can consider the specific issues arising out of your organization's strategy.

The Touching section of this chapter described many of the organizations and teams with whom IT interact, but of course life is not as simple as my 'pen pictures' portray.

Therefore, you need to undertake your own analysis of your organization so that you can see the general thrusts which you will need to pursue and support. To do this, demands a three stage process:

☑ Analyse the organization by using a number of core dimensions and characteristics.

☑ Identify from each characteristic the likely implications in terms of the expectations and demands that may arise for the IT function.

☑ Identify the common themes that exist so that you can clearly see the major issues that IT must address.

1. What are the core dimensions and characteristics which help you to understand and describe your organization?

Who are you?

☑ How big is it?

☑ How old is it and what is its history?

☑ How far does it spread – how many countries, how many cultures?

☑ Who owns it and what influence do the owners have on the organization and what you do?

☑ Is the management of the business centralized or decentralized?

☑ Do hierarchies or networking dominate?

☑ What impact does politics have on the direction of your organization?

What do you do?

☑ What sector are you in?

☑ Are you about manufacturing products, delivering services or managing knowledge and information?

☑ What are the 'value' points of your proposition?

☑ Do you tend to focus on the short or long-term?

☑ When it comes to technology and innovation, do you lead or do you follow?

Who do you serve?

☑ Who are your customers, and how many segments do you serve?

☑ Why do customers buy your products or use your services?

☑ Where are your customers?

☑ What 'value' are they wanting you to deliver?

☑ What is the range of products and services that you supply?

☑ What distribution channels do you use to reach your customers – do you go direct, or through third parties?

2. Identify the implications for IT

Having done this, complete the table below.

☑ List each of the characteristics identified.

☑ From each of the characteristics that you have described identify the possible implications for IT.

DOING

Organizational dimension and characteristic identified	Resultant expectations and demands	Likely systems and services needed

Table 1: The organizational context and the implications for IT

☑ Identify the likely systems, services, support and capabilities that will be expected of you.

3. Identify the common themes

Looking across all the issues identified in the table you have just completed:

☑ Specify the three or four main themes that you will need to address to satisfy the needs of your users.

☑ Specify the infrastructure requirements needed to support these demands.

As a result, you now have the necessary understanding of the organizational context to enable you to start to develop the IT strategy itself.

DOING

Section 2

Aligning IT with the strategy

4 The potential value of IT

- Does IT matter?

- IT strategy versus business strategy

At the heart of this book is the need to get IT directors and managers to deeply understand what your business is trying to achieve and your role in making that happen. To do this you have to understand the potential of IT to really have strategic impact and the differences between an IT strategy and that of the business.

Touching

Now that you have an overview of the strategic context, and more importantly an understanding of where your business is pointing, you now need to determine the strategic direction of the IT function.

This section of the book focuses on the issue of IT strategy in particular, rather than business strategy. In this regard, the issues are slightly different from those outlined in the previous section, but many of the principles regarding value, understanding customers, what we offer and how we act remain pertinent. The big difference is that IT is a support function to the business and hence the IT strategy must support the strategy of the business.

This may seem a statement of the obvious, but regrettably many IT departments carry on life in a direction that seems completely disconnected from the rest of the business. (But then again, so do many HR and finance functions.)

Alignment therefore is the key word here, and hence the value of the meetings with the business heads that were discussed in the Doing section of Chapter 2. If you have an understanding of where the business is headed, then you have a chance of pointing your IT function in broadly the same direction. Whether you can actually get the IT function to run with purpose in that same direction is an issue we will focus on later in the book.

Does IT matter?

However, before we get carried away with ourselves we ought to ensure that we understand the ways in which IT can add value to the business and pose the core question, 'Does IT matter?'

If we don't understand this, we are unable to present a strong picture to the business, change their negative perceptions, or get them to use us to achieve their goals. Equally, unless we understand the value that we can bring, we cannot tell the story to our people in IT so that they appreciate their role, understand their importance, and prepare them to deliver consistently, and with impact.

In the first section of the book we saw a number of examples of where IT can be involved in supporting the business strategy. In this chapter I would like to look at this in greater depth and in a more structured way. Firstly, I consider how IT can help the company in terms of its pursuit of:

- A position of competitive advantage

- Greater productivity

- A transformed organization

Achieving competitive advantage

There are a number of ways in which IT can support the business's goal of achieving competitive advantage. In particular, IT is about information and adding value to the customer through the use of information.

Supporting

Firstly and at a basic level IT can provide the technology and systems to support the core business activities so that processes work more effectively, reliably, and in ways which are more accessible, enjoyable or more stimulating for the customer.

In some ways, I see IT as the function within your business that exists in order to 'search for simplicity'. By simplicity, I mean both internally and externally; making it easier and more cost-effective for the business to deliver so that it becomes more reliable, and a better place to work. Externally you have a role in making your customers lives simpler so that they enjoy doing business with you.

To be able to support your business in this way, IT should be the function that continually asks the question 'how can we do it better?' To do this you need to be good at learning from success and failure and simply looking at problems in a different way. Mastery of the internal processes permits IT teams to create new ways of operating so that the business can achieve more with less.

Value adding IT functions also support business growth by identifying or facilitating ways to restructure the business or by changing management processes. Alternatively, high performing IT functions enable the business to respond faster and more flexibly.

Linking

IT can link the various activities that the business uses to deliver value to its customer. In other words, it can link different systems, so that they appear to be one and are seamless to the outside world. This can be an internal role or undertaken across organizational borders.

For example, a bank will draw on a number of systems to support savings, mortgages and loans products, relationship management activities and outsourced call centres to deliver to its customers. IT has to pull all these together in a cohesive and effective way.

Equally, I think linking is also about collaboration. The ability of IT to facilitate organizational learning across boundaries or to provide the organization with the insight that enables it to find new ways of doing things or better solutions.

Alongside, IT can offer new ways to operate in partnership with partners, and establish a way of operating that becomes an industry norm. This can become a barrier to the entrance of new competitors to your marketplace, or make it difficult for customers to switch to a competitor.

This is not a book about outsourcing, but clearly IT must be alert to the opportunities that are presented and should be leading the discussion within the company about the options, benefits and problems. With your enhanced understanding of how your business competes you should be in a strong position to show how outsourcing can provide opportunities to simplify, reduce costs, or allow the business to focus its resources on those activities which really provide a competitive edge.

I do not see that your remit in this regard is constrained to the IT function. Yes, there may be outsourcing opportunities within the IT function, but IT is the custodian of knowledge, information and processes across the business and therefore you must look at the whole business, not part. Indeed taking this company-wide perspective provides even further opportunity for IT to add value.

Reducing competitive pressures

In a related way, IT can help to reduce the pressures your company feels as a result of the competitive environment in which it operates.

As noted above, IT can help to establish new industry standards so that it becomes harder for new players to enter; the fewer competitors you have, the easier it is to succeed. Similarly, by changing the way in which you use IT to manage the relationships with your suppliers you may be able to alter your relative bargaining position, and hence provide the opportunity for your purchasing department to get better prices or more flexible contracts.

You can also distance yourself from the competition by simply raising the levels of efficiency and effectiveness of your systems, either through re-engineering or improved simplicity or reliability.

Adding value through information

Alternatively, IT can improve the value of a product or service by increasing the amount of information, either within the product itself or in its supply. For example, a library contains high levels of information in its product (the books) and very little information in terms of the process of supply. By contrast, there is very limited information in the product of an oil refinery (petrol and diesel etc.), but there are substantial volumes of information within the supply chain from the oilfield through the refinery, through transportation, and then distribution and supply.

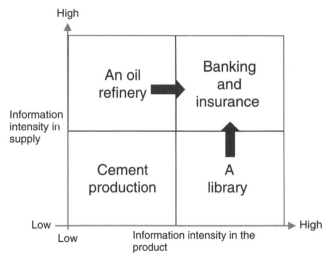

Figure 1: How Information Gives You Competitive Advantage (Porter and Millar, 1985)

This chart lays out the different ways in which a library and an oil refinery use information.

However, better still are those products and services which evidence high levels of information and hence value in both the product and the supply chain. Banking and insurance are examples of this. I say 'better', because the greater the value and use of information in the product and supply, the greater the profitably of the business. Additionally, IT enjoys greater importance in those companies that compete in this way.

This discussion of information has so far been externally focused, yet IT would be more readily recognized in terms of its role of managing information inside the organization. After all, IT is the function that stores, processes and distributes data. If management of that data is effective, it will also create new knowledge and understanding.

TOUCHING

To fulfil your potential in this regard, you need to understand the uses to which information will be applied and therefore the ways in which you need to present it to the business:

– Operational data is used for, day-to-day activities such as transactional processing and financial control. It tends to be structured and needs to be highly accurate, reliable and delivered at speed.

– Tactical information is more concerned about improving the performance of the business and allowing management to take day-to-day decisions. In that sense it will include performance reporting and again needs to be accurate and delivered in a timely fashion. However, it may also allow management to make some predictions. Systems will need to contain filters, so the only important material is immediately accessible, and managers are provided with what they need, rather than what is available.

– Finally, there is the information provided to facilitate strategic debate, exploration and decision-making. This information will be more unstructured, derived from a much wider range of sources and will not necessarily be as accurate of the as the former. It also needs to be provided in a way that can be readily manipulated and investigated by management.

Innovation and new technologies

Clearly, IT has a role in alerting the board to new and evolving technologies. Equally, IT must open the board's mind to how existing and new technologies are being used in other industries and how they can be applied in your own business.

Just because iPod's started out supplying music to the youth market hasn't meant that this is the only application. Other businesses in other sectors are taking advantage of its capabilities in a wide variety of ways:

– The sale of audio books by way of download has multiplied many times over.

– The BBC and business schools download educational broadcasts.

– The ABC channel is creating new commercial opportunities through downloads of *Desperate Housewives* and ESPN through abbreviated broadcasts of the Rose Bowl.

When considering innovation it is therefore important that IT not only looks at the product or technology itself, but also at new ways of using it. You should seek to identify how it can be deployed to improve the performance of your company at various stages of the supply chain, including the interface between your company and your suppliers, your company and your customers or even your customers' customers.

Equally important to the company is the capability of IT to implement those technologies better than the competition; success is not always about being first, or having the best or newest technology; it is about what you do with it.

Sometimes, however, it is about being first, and hence an IT function that can take a concept and turn it into operating reality on the ground faster than the competition provides real advantage for its company. Given that so many product and service innovations derive from technological advances, and many (if not all) rely on IT systems to deliver them your importance cannot be overstated.

Improving productivity

Whilst IT has an incredibly attractive role in enabling the business to compete more effectively and grow, it should not forget its responsibility to improve the productivity and cost base of the business. In part, I touched upon this when considering the issue of 'Supporting' and 'Linking' above, but there are some other considerations.

From its cross-organizational perspective, IT can see the company flows of data, information and knowledge, and it can see how all the processes and systems within the business link and interact including duplicate and unnecessary activities that deliver little to the business.

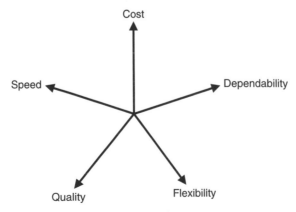

Figure 2: The drivers of operational success (Slack _et al.,_ 2005)

It is IT's role to identify these and drive the necessary changes to deliver improvements in productivity and reduce the cost base of the business.

This will mean that as an IT function you need to understand the principles underpinning operations strategy. At its highest level this tells us that by managing the following component elements, we can reduce our costs and improve our efficiency and effectiveness.

Dependability, flexibility, quality and speed individually and jointly impact on the costs of running your business:

• Dependability

Dependability is about being on time, internally and externally, and being reliable. This will deliver benefits such as low inventory and reduce cost to the business by avoiding the need to have 'buffer' stock.

• Flexibility

On the other hand, flexibility is about your business's ability to respond to changes in product and service mix, volumes and timescales so that you can respond more quickly to the needs of your customers and partners.

• Quality

There are a wide variety of views on what quality means, but it is sufficient for us to consider it as our ability to conform to specification. The benefits are increased speed and dependability, higher levels of performance and customer satisfaction.

• Speed

Speed is about throughput efficiency so that we can deliver faster and bring new products to market quicker, with benefits in terms of both customer satisfaction and competitive advantage.

IT functions that understand these issues and can manage them, are able to deliver much greater value to the business in terms of driving down costs. IT functions with these capabilities also tend to have closer relationships with the operations and finance teams. As a consequence of these allegiances and the value delivered, IT enjoys greater credibility and in turn, greater freedom to pursue avenues which support the goal of competitive advantage.

However, IT doesn't just deliver productivity gains as a result of managing operational processes more efficiently, it can provide productivity benefits in a wider range of ways:

– IT functions that evidence real value have the capability to deploy and leverage enabling technologies such as teleworking, groupware, communications systems, intranets, and decentralization that leads to higher levels of autonomy across the business.

– Alongside, more effective use of limited resources can be achieved by IT functions that have the ability to understand and define user needs accurately. As a result, these IT functions apply their resources to projects, functions and features which users need and less time is wasted at the point of implementation through unnecessary revisions and improvements.

– Equally, IT functions that can introduce new technology and systems with limited disruption to the operation of the business markedly increase productivity. If only because it results in members of staff engaging positively with technology upgrades with learning how to use and deploy them more rapidly. Once again, the quality of relationships across the business will improve as a result, preventing time being wasted on backbiting and political games.

– Value driven IT functions will see the opportunity for business process re-engineering, across all the internal and external boundaries of the organization, ensuring that the interfaces between departments, suppliers and the customer work effectively to deliver value.

– IT can also improve internal management processes and systems by providing the technology and processes by which managers and leaders can direct, monitor, control, plan, advise and communicate.

Transforming the organization

Already we have seen the potential for IT to deliver substantial value in a number of ways, but there is a further aspect that needs to be considered and this relates to IT's ability to transform the organization.

In one respect, this arises as an outcome of its role in introducing new technology and systems.

TOUCHING

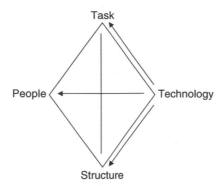

Figure 3: The broader impact of technology change (Leavitt, 1965)

The dimensions of task, people, structure and technology are inexorably linked; change one and you have impact on the others. In our particular case, the decision to change a piece of technology will most likely result in people being asked to do a different task, which in turn, may demand that we recruit a different sort of person with different skills. This may also mean that we need to change our structure to cope with the impact.

For example, if a customer service centre decides to introduce call centre technology with algorithms to guide their staff through the telephone call process, the task will change from that demanded of the existing staff operating in a free-format environment. In turn, the people you need to handle the calls will no doubt require a lower level of skills and less experience. As a result of the controls exercised by the technology, perhaps the business will require fewer managers and supervisors.

However, the changes wrought by IT in this regard may still be limited, and are only incidental to a separate objective. There are other ways in which IT's impact is much greater:

– IT provides the vehicle through which global economic shifts and trends are recognized and realized in the business. This might include the transition to e-commerce, responses to recessions, implementation of Japanese manufacturing techniques or the accelerated growth of the service sector.

– IT enables the business to respond to the shifts in the competitive environment and the structuring of businesses through the facilitation of partnering arrangements, alliances and acquisitions, and by enabling the business to cope with increasing complexity and speed.

- IT allows the business to leverage the opportunities of new technology so that the organization can operate in a world without geographic boundaries.

- IT can permit the organization to utilize worldwide project teams to bring new concepts to market faster and respond more quickly to customer needs, whilst at the same time reducing cost.

- IT is able to substantially shift the structure of the organization with the result that power can shift to new departments and managers. Skills and capabilities can become redundant as they are replaced by new performance imperatives, which in turn lead to new organizational cultures and behaviours.

- IT provides the vehicles by which managers can control, but equally can delegate and empower their teams to change fundamentally the way in which the business is led and managed.

- IT provides the opportunity for the business to establish and operate completely new types of relationships with its partners, to the point where it is difficult to tell where the business starts or where it finishes.

- IT provides the opportunity for businesses to change the rules of the game and opens up the possibility that the business can move into new sectors and industries.

At the beginning of this chapter, I asked 'Does IT matter?' I believe you will see that the potential of IT is massive and far reaching, both internally and externally. IT has the capability and the potential to deliver more in every organization. Our task now is to realize that potential.

IT strategy versus business strategy

Now we have a strong understanding of the potential of IT to deliver substantial value to the business, it is worth exploring the differences between business strategy and IT strategy.

In the first instance it is worth reminding ourselves of the hierarchy of strategies, as shown below. IT is, of course, one of the business functions with the role of supporting delivery of the business strategy.

Corporate level strategy	Determining the businesses we wish to be in and the results we wish to achieve for our stakeholders and investors Identifying businesses to buy and sell Allocating cash to different business units Managing the relationship between different businesses
Business unit strategy	Defining the strategic objectives of the business, such as: Growth targets, Return on investment, Cash generation Stating the way that the business wishes to compete in its markets Coordinating team activities to achieve strategic objectives
Functional & Operational strategy	Determining the role functions play in contributing to the business strategy Translating business and competitive objectives into team objectives Managing team resources so as to achieve functional objectives Identifying improvement priorities

Figure 4: The strategic hierarchy

These layers highlight the role of the IT function in supporting the delivery of the business strategy. By working in tandem with the other functions and determining how best to utilize the resources available to you, you need to find the best route to achieving the objectives that have been allocated to you from the business strategy.

Beyond that, and utilizing the structure deployed in Chapter 1, the notable differences are as follows:

• The Why. There should be no doubt in your mind that you are here to serve the rest of the business and enable it to achieve its strategic goals

• The Who. These will be internal customers, and unlike a business strategy you will have no choice of who you serve.

• If your business strategy demands that you look beyond the business at the links between the parent company and other subsidiaries, or across the supply chain involving your company's suppliers, then these too are the customers that you will be serving.

• The What. These are the systems and services you provide that enable the business to achieve its strategic goals. They will principally encompass the aspects which I have described throughout this chapter:

  – Ensuring the operation works efficiently and effectively.

- Providing the technology systems and processes that support the core operation of the business.

- Driving up productivity.

- Enabling management to direct and control the business.

- Supporting the delivery of the business objectives.

- Supporting strategy formulation.

The How. This is about delivering these systems and services in a manner that fits with the needs of the business whilst operating within the obligatory budgetary constraints.

Fundamentally, there will be a demand from the business for reliability and responsiveness; in other words, getting the basics right, repeatedly and on time. This represents your point of entry – unless you can do this, you will progress no further.

Your role in the business

We can talk about value, but delivery is the passport to a place on the board and the decision-making table. Unless you are recognized for delivering value, regularly and in a way that enables the business to achieve its goals, you will continue to be an outsider rather than a key player.

In this sense I see three stages of development in strategic terms for the IT function:

Following

- The first and lowest level whereby you follow the business and react to its needs. However, you are capable of delivering consistently and reliably, and can manage the costs, effectiveness and efficiency of IT systems.

- Regrettably, many IT functions are failing to deliver even at this basic level. Often responses are too late, they find themselves leaping from one crisis to another. These IT functions are ineffective and perceived as such.

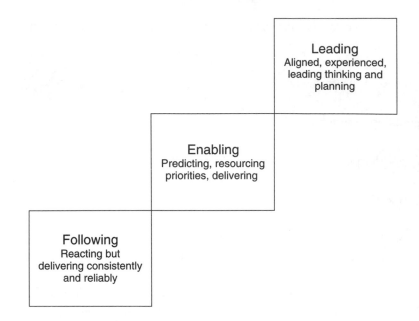

FIgure 5: Following, Enabling, Leading

Enabling

– With the benefit of an understanding of the businesses strategy, the IT function is able to predict likely needs and is able to resource priority and strategic issues in order to maximize the performance of the business. In this way, IT has the role of enabling the business to enjoy strategic success.

Leading

– A well aligned IT function, which is experienced in enabling the business to deliver and which then builds a broad understanding of the environment in which business operates and the technologies that may have impact on it. You are able to lead the board's thinking and become a key player, not only in delivery but also in terms of creating strategic opportunities for the business.

Where are we now, where do we want to be?

Therefore, part of your strategy must be to identify where you are now in this ladder and determine where you want to be in the future. Mapping your current position on the following grid may help you to understand where you are now and see the degree of change required.

TOUCHING

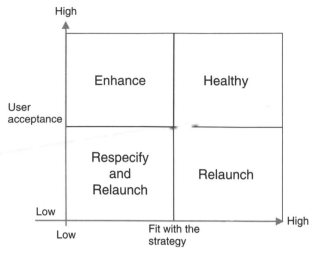

Figure 6: IT – fit for the business?

When considering your fit with the strategy, you should use the work you have already undertaken to understand and to assess your performance. If you are still not certain, you could assess your fit in terms of our fit with the strategy:

– Competitive advantage and business growth

– Productivity gains

– Business transformation

– Effective and efficient organizational processes and IT systems.

In terms of user acceptance, you can measure that against the credibility or otherwise that IT enjoys within the business. Are you?

– On the board

– Part of the strategy development team

– Invited early into major projects and new product development programs

– Jointly running projects with other functions, and especially marketing, operations and finance

– Seeing your success reported widely and positively across the business

– Seen as a partner of the business and appreciated for the value you bring the decision-making

– Recognized for the reliability and responsiveness of your systems, projects and delivery.

As support function, the management internal relationships and the business stakeholders will be a more important part of your role than you would normally see within a business strategy. Therefore, in terms of determining your IT strategy, you will wish to be clear about your aspirations for your function within the business across the following dimensions:

Board relationships

– What will be your relationship with the board?

– Will you be an active player, ever present and a key partner in the decision-making process?

– Or will you be an occasional visitor providing support and clarification where necessary?

Board relationships	Delivering the strategy
What will be your relationship with the board?	What will be your role in delivering the business strategy?
Power and influence	New strategic options
What influence and power will you have in the business?	What will be your role in generating new strategic future options?

Figure 7: What is the role of IT in your business?

Delivering the strategy

– What will be your role in delivering the business strategy?

  – Will you be Following, Enabling or Leading?

Power and influence

– What influence and power will you have in the business?

  – This question is interesting in that it not only seeks an answer to the question asked, but also begs the question 'how will you gain the power and influence that you seek?'

Developing strategic options

– What will be your role in generating new strategic options future?

  – For many, this discussion will have to be delayed until you are known for reliability and delivering value, and have built the credibility that merits your admission to this forum.

In closing

There are also areas of overlap between IT strategy and business strategy, and like your business partners you must be clear about the value that you are bringing to your customers. Unless you and your team can clearly state the value that you deliver and promote the benefits that you have brought, you will find yourself dismissed, misunderstood and much maligned.

Therefore, it is important you and your team can articulate the value that you bring to the business and ensure that you tell the story of your success to the business many times each day. In other words, you need to make sure that the business understands why they work with you and the benefit they gain from their relationship with you.

As a result of this book so far, you now have:

– An understanding of what the business wants to achieve.

– An appreciation of the key issues within the business strategy upon which you can have the greatest impact.

TOUCHING

– An understanding of the ways in which IT can generically deliver greatest value to the business.

– An appreciation of the ways in which you and your function, within your business, can have the greatest impact.

– An understanding of your relative strengths and weaknesses in terms of the use of information.

– Knowledge of what you are doing at the moment, and how you are perceived by the business.

– Identified your aspirations regarding your place and your role within the business.

As a result, you are now in a position to align your IT function so that it delivers the desired results, and receives the recognition it deserves.

TOUCHING

Looking

IT – following, enabling or leading?

Is the role of the IT department limited to responding to the needs of the business or is there a role at the centre of the company that enables the business to be more competitive?

Have you ever felt that there is more that IT can do in your business than just take the punches? Perhaps you feel that there must be something better than simply responding to the requests for new technology or systems and being forced to deliver them ever more quickly, at a lower cost and with greater risk of failure because of the short cuts that you are taking. And then having to suffer the continuous body blows of users grumbling and groaning that systems are not reliable, help desks are not available nor well informed, and being called 'the pointy heads'.

I guess you know that there must be something better; in the same way that a person who holidays in Spain knows that the Caribbean has to be better even if they haven't been there.

So is the concept of IT enabling the business to be more competitive, or IT leading the business to new highs of performance a real possibility?

Yes it is a reality, yes it is possible, and yes it is within your ability and your remit to grasp it.

But it does demand that you take control of a number of factors in company:

– Understanding the business; its strategy, its goals and the value it is trying to deliver.

– Linking your activities, goals and behaviour to the really big organizational objectives.

– Enhancing the capability of the business to use information.

– Managing your stakeholders and the culture.

Understanding the business; its strategy, goals and value

Do not believe that you can play a dominant part in your business unless you really understand current thinking about business strategy and the value that the business is trying to deliver. You cannot expect to have credibility and a place at the top table if you do not have the ability to question, challenge and understand the business managers and leaders.

And today's strategies are not about analytical tools and constraining plans, they are about a fluidity and flexibility of thinking that reflects the dynamic and unpredictable environments in which businesses operate. It is about creating an organizational agility, passion and customer focus that is second to none. It is about sensing customer needs and responding – quickly.

And don't delude yourself that you operate at this level now; even many business managers can't and if you really want to add value then you need to be able to think ahead of them and lead them to new possibilities.

But, if you truly understand strategy and how value is created, you have the opportunity of partnering with marketing, operations and finance to find new competitive and value creation opportunities for your business.

Linking your activities, goals and behaviour to the really big organizational objectives

When you understand the principals of strategy, you need to be able to understand the corporate plan and translate it into aligned themes and objectives for the IT Department. But it is not enough to see those objectives in tightly defined single project goals; they need to reflect and deliver against the overall strategic themes.

No longer is it good enough for you to consider one of your projects a success just because it met its specific project goals. If other related projects have not delivered, then your IT project will fail to deliver the overall value expected by the business. So, you have the opportunity to manage and lead your colleagues in the business to ensure that all the related projects jointly perform and deliver the desired uplift of your company's performance.

Indeed, it is likely that in your company no one is really taking the lead in coordinating projects; this is your opportunity.

Enhancing the capability of the business to use information

Even if you understand strategy and have keyed the IT department into the business goals, this is no good to you unless the business as a whole can use the information that flows around your business for real impact.

This demands building capabilities across the organization in three main areas:

– The way the technology is used.

– The way information is managed.

– The values and behaviours that attach to the use of information.

Today, most IT departments still focus on ensuring that the technology does its job of supporting the business. Some may address the management practices across the business. But very few really get at the core values and behaviours that underpin the truly competitive and value creating use of information.

And if the IT department doesn't take a lead in these areas, who does? Perhaps your CEO, but if you allow her to do this, IT just slips back down the ladder again to be another support function. So, the challenge has to be for the IT function to lead the way in these areas.

To drive issues such as these demands a totally different set of skills and capabilities within the IT function: leadership, change management, relationship management, and stakeholder management skills.

For many, this is a big task, and a big shift. But if you truly want to be seen for the value you deliver in enabling your business to compete in the future, then you have to be able to respond to the big challenges and not just stay in your comfort zone and manage technology projects.

Managing your stakeholders and the culture

You have to manoeuvre yourself into a position of influence where you have the freedom and opportunity to deliver the sort of value that only IT can supply. This demands a structured approach to the issue of stakeholder management so that you can target the right people and win the opportunity to change agendas, and shift the quality of thinking and performance across the company.

This will demand that you are able to understand the differing cultures that exist in different departments, in different sites and in different countries.

LOOKING

All in all, this represents a sizeable challenge for any CIO and the IT team. But unless the nettle is grasped and these issues addressed, then your IT function deserves to be what it is today, simply a support function.

Stay there if you will, but you stand guilty of allowing your business to perform below its potential and will subject your IT team to the ever-lasting role of corporate punch bag.

It's your choice.

LOOKING

Doing

This chapter is about understanding the potential value that IT can bring to your business. This means that you need to be able to identify the key strategic thrusts of the business and in turn the priorities of the IT function which will be realized through the:

☑ Projects that you undertake

☑ Focus you give to your team

☑ Resources you build

☑ Capabilities you develop, and

☑ Processes and systems that you operate and manage.

To do this, you need to draw on the information that you have as a result of your actions in the earlier chapters and identify the strategic imperatives for IT that arise as a result.

You could structure your thinking by using the following approach:

	Strategic thrust 1	Strategic thrust 2	Strategic thrust 3
What is the business trying to achieve?			
How will the business measure its success?			
What must IT do?			
Delivering competitive advantage and growth			
Delivering productivity gains			
Transforming the business			
As a result:			
What are our key priorities and areas of focus?			
What systems and processes will be required?			
What capabilities do we need?			

Figure 8: Identifying strategic imperatives for IT

This approach will enable you to see clearly the direction of the business and the role that IT needs to fulfil.

At this stage you are only looking to identify the headline issues so that you have clarity of the direction for your function and the context in which it is set. We will address the detail in later chapters.

In terms of the table, these are the issues you should be considering when completing it:

Strategic thrusts

These are the big themes that the business is seeking to pursue as a part of its strategy. You will have extracted these from the interviews and discussions that you have engaged in with your fellow directors and senior managers.

For example, I was recently in a business where they had three thrusts, which were:

☑ Being customer centric

☑ Delivering exceptional customer service

☑ Driving continuous improvement.

In another they could

☑ Understand the customer

☑ Deliver value through innovation

☑ Be efficient, be effective.

What is the business of trying to achieve?

Here, you should be describing the aspirations of the business and what success would look like for the business.

☑ How will the business measure success?

• What objectives has the business set to measure their success?

- You need to be specific and ensure that you have a good understanding of what board and senior management will use to report and manage performance.

- These measures should extend beyond financial parameters and are likely to encompass elements of:

  - Customer responses, behaviour and actions

  - Internal organizational performance, and

  - Organizational capability.

- You will have impact on each of these elements, and therefore need to understand what the business is trying to achieve in each dimension.

Delivering competitive advantage and growth

As a result, you will have clearly mapped out the business goals and can now start to see what is required from IT. You need to be specific about the value that you will bring and need to be able to articulate it clearly. In other words, in what way can IT have impact and deliver value through:

☑ Supporting

- Providing the technology and systems required by the business

- Simplifying and doing things better

- Changing business processes.

☑ Linking

- How will you link systems to create seamless delivery, both internally and externally?

- How will you facilitate collaboration and learning?

- Can you establish new ways of operating?

DOING

- What outsourcing opportunities exist?

☑ Reducing competitive pressures

- Can new industry standards be established?

- How can the relationship with suppliers be changed?

- What opportunities arise from new technologies to introduce new products and services?

- How can you make life simpler for your customers?

- How can you make it harder for your customers to switch to your competitors?

☑ Adding value through information

- In what ways can you increase the intensity of information in the product and supply chain?

- What information is required by the business in order to process transactions and manage the business?

- How can you deliver information so that it meets the business's needs and improves and accelerates its decision-making?

☑ Innovation and new technologies

- What new technologies does the business need to be aware of?

- How can you help the business to explore the opportunities arising out of these new technologies?

- What is IT's role in accelerating and improving the implementation of new technologies, products, and systems and processes?

Delivering productivity gains

☑ What areas of duplication and unnecessary activities exist in respect of processes and systems, and the flow of the data and information? How can they be removed?

☑ In what ways can IT facilitate improvement in dependability, flexibility, quality, and speed?

☑ What opportunities exist to deploy enabling technologies to improve communication, increase autonomy and reduce costs?

☑ How can IT better understand users' needs and what benefits will result?

☑ What opportunities for system improvements exist across internal and external boundaries?

☑ How can internal management processes and systems be improved?

Transforming the business

☑ What are the implications of the changes in technology that are currently under way and how will we manage the implications for our business model, our structure and our people?

☑ What global economic shifts are occurring; what are the technology, systems and information implications; and what are our responses as a business?

☑ In what way can IT accelerate the integration of partnering, alliances and acquisition plans?

☑ How can we substantially enhance our businesses ability to cope with increased complexity and speed?

☑ What organizational structure changes are underway and what is our role in enabling them to deliver their planned results?

☑ How can we facilitate organizational skill development and cultural shifts?

☑ How can we help the business see and realize new opportunities for partnering arrangements in our supply chain?

☑ What opportunities exist to change the rules of the game?

DOING

What are our key priorities and areas of focus?

I do not expect that you will have answers to all the above questions; some will not be relevant to your circumstances or business strategy. However, as a result of considering these issues you will have identified the key priorities for the IT function in terms of its role of delivering the business strategy.

What systems and processes will be required?

As a result you should be able to identify the critical processes and systems that you need to support delivery.

Some of these will already exist and simply need improvement. Others will demand that totally new approaches to be introduced.

What capabilities will be needed?

You now need to identify what skills and capabilities you will need within your IT team so that you can deliver your key priorities.

You now have a broad, but coherent and aligned picture of the role of IT in the business.

Your role in the business

In terms of articulating your strategic aspirations, you need to understand and state your intentions regarding the influence that you will have in the business.

Use the following grid to articulate your goals:

Board relationships	Delivering the strategy
What will be your relationship with the board?	What will be your role in delivering the business strategy?
Power and influence	New strategic options
What influence and power will you have in the business?	What will be your role in generating new strategic options in the future?

Figure 9: What is the role of IT in your business?

Test, these aspirations with your chief executive and other members of the senior management team to check for reality and the degree of support available to you.

IT health check

How healthy is your function in terms of strategic alignment and where do you need to make improvements?

Fit with the strategy

☑ Does your function understand its role and does it have the capability to deliver in the following areas?

- Competitive advantage and business growth

- Delivering productivity gains

- Accelerating business transformation

- Effective and efficient organizational processes and IT systems.

User acceptance

☑ How strong is your relationship with the business and how is IT perceived? Are you?

- On the board

- Part of the strategy development team

- Invited early into major projects and new product development programs

- Jointly running projects with other functions, and especially marketing, operations and finance

- Seeing your success reported widely and positively across the business

- Seen as a partner of the business and appreciated for the value you bring the decision-making

• Recognized for the reliability and responsiveness of your systems, projects and delivery.

Utilizing your answers to map your position on the grid shown below.

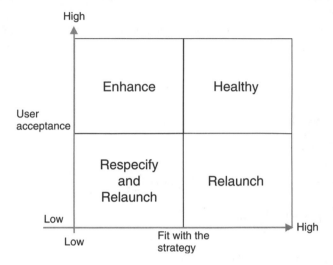

Figure:10 IT – fit for the business?

With your team, identify the headline actions that you need to take in order to move your function into the 'Healthy' box.

At this stage, you do not need to go into detail regarding these actions as they will be explored later in the book.

As a result of these activities you will now be able to see:

☑ What your IT function has to do

☑ What it has to deliver, and

☑ What it needs to build so that it does deliver.

It is now necessary to put some meat on the bones of these key strategic themes and these headlines.

5 Aligning IT

- Planning – who cares?

- Planning – some approaches

- Strategy mapping

- IT strategy maps

- Aligning IT

This chapter is about enabling you to translate the business strategies and needs into clearly articulated IT strategies and plans that are cascaded throughout the IT function. On the way we explore some key principles around business planning and understand various tools and approaches that you could adopt.

Touching

Up to now we have been exploring the broad concepts of strategy and the generic role of IT. As a result you have:

- An understanding of what the business wants to achieve.

- An appreciation of the key issues within the business strategy upon which you can have the greatest impact.

- An understanding of the ways in which IT can generically deliver the greatest value to the business.

- An understanding of your relative strengths and weaknesses in terms of the use of information.

- Knowledge of what you are doing at the moment, and how you are perceived by the business.

- Identified your aspirations regarding your place and your role within the business.

Our task now is to turn these fairly high-level concepts into the plans against which your team can transact and deliver. The role of this chapter and the next one is to show you how you can do this and how you can focus your IT strategy. Chapter 6 will consider how you can measure your success.

In a diagrammatical form, what we are doing is shown overleaf:

In other words, we now moving from concepts to specifics and at each layer of the cascade shown above, the information and detail becomes more granular to the point where individuals can look back up through the model shown above and say 'Ah, now I can see where I fit in and why I'm doing what I'm doing'.

To achieve this, I am firstly going to take a quick look at the concept of planning to lay out some principles and objectives, and then I will consider some of the approaches we could adopt to the principles of articulating our strategy and cascading it through the business. Following this, I will describe how you can go about the cascade and the tools you can use to make clear your plans.

Strategy and how businesses compete Chapters 1 and 2

Understanding how *your* business competes and the core initiatives that it is pursuing Chapters 2, 3 and 4

The IT functional strategy - What is it your IT function has to do? - What does it have to deliver? - What does success look like? - What do you need to build so that IT can deliver? Chapters 4, 5, 6, 7, 8, and 9

IT departments and teams' strategies and tactics - What is the role of the teams within your IT function? - What do they have to deliver? - What does success look like? - What do they need to build so that they can deliver? Chapters 5, 6, 12, and 13

IT teams and individuals - What is the role of the teams and individuals - What goals have we set them? - How do they need to develop? - How we manage their performance Chapters 10, 11,12 and 13

Figure 1: The strategic cascade

TOUCHING

Planning – who cares?

Have you ever found yourself on a journey where you were very late for an appointment and very low on fuel? If you have then you will recognize the conundrum whereby you cannot decide whether it is better to stop for fuel and therefore be even later, or keep going but run the risk that you run out of petrol.

Planning in the workplace is a bit like that. You are already incredibly busy and really don't have time to stop because you know that there are a host of tasks and activities you must complete by the end of the morning, or the end of the day, or the end of the week. However, at the same time you know that things would be better and less risky if you stopped what you were doing and planned ahead.

Also, there is the problem that people see strategy as being something out there in the distance; something that doesn't relate to the day job. However, strategy should be able to link today's immediate needs and tasks to our long-term goals in a way that provides a clear path that people can follow.

In reality you are always going to compromise, so we need to find a way that enables you to plan without it becoming too onerous or too enormous a task. And yet it must also involve people so that they understand what is required and are engaged with making it happen.

Similarly this planning process must also ensure that what is created relates to people, their jobs and what they are expected to do on a day-to-day basis. If the plans are at too high a level then your staff will dismiss them as not relevant, but if too detailed you will create massive documents which are not used. Often I have seen business plans amounting to fifty or even a hundred pages, beautifully bound and prepared but which sit on a shelf or in a drawer for the whole year and which do not come alive or are not used by the business to guide people's actions and decisions, nor informing them on what is or what is not important.

And then the danger is that people become cynical about the whole planning process and this negativity translates to their approach to delivery. This presents you with the danger that the mindset of your people is completely inappropriate, and there is no way in which they are going to share your desire and passion to successfully deliver your beautifully crafted aspirations. As a result change is much less likely to succeed.

So we have to find a way to balance these conflicting issues and achieve the following:

– Step back and identify what it is that we want to achieve and how we can achieve success, both at the IT functional and individual team member level.

– Specify measures that help to clarify our understanding and which help us to see whether we are still on the right road.

– Provide a framework in which your teams can operate; which ensures effective use of your resources; keeps everyone focused on the needs and wants of the IT strategy and the business that we support.

– Which provides a sense of purpose and which enables you to build a function that is flexible and able to respond to the jolts and shocks we will surely suffer on the road to success.

More tangibly, the planning process must result in:

– A clear direction that is linked to the business strategy and goals.

– Specified goals, measures and critical success factors.

– Clear understanding of our priorities.

– Agreement on the opportunities available to us and an understanding of the constraints and risks that apply.

– Desire for the benefits that success will bring.

– Identification of what we have to change, and how.

– A plan of what is going to happen, who is going to make it happen and by when.

– A critical mass of people who understand what is required, what we are trying to achieve and are committed to making it happen.

I cannot overstate this last aspect. Without it, you have little chance of success, and therefore you should continually ask yourself whether or not the approach you are adopting is helping or hindering buy-in of your people. This doesn't mean that planning is a democratic process. The challenge you face is one that normally demands that you (you and your management team) set the direction for the function, but at the same time set a direction which is informed by the organizational context (i.e. the business strategy, the skills, knowledge and experience of your staff, existing systems, processes and capabilities) the environment in which you operate, and the customers you serve.

TOUCHING

I have seen effective planning processes described as the culmination of the 'Five I's':

– Involve – involve management and staff in the development and implementation stages.

– Insight – draw on the knowledge, skills and perspectives of everyone in the team to identify possible options.

– Intent – be clear about what it is you want to achieve and where you are going to invest your limited resources.

– Imperatives – be clear about your priorities and business goals.

– Initiatives – state the actions that you are going to take to deliver success.

Planning – some approaches

I acknowledge that there are a host of ways in which we could structure, capture, and articulate strategies and plans. I do not propose to describe them all here, as there are more appropriate places for such comprehensive analysis. My aim, however, is to provide you with an approach that I believe you can readily deploy to address the issues and goals that I have highlighted above. I acknowledge that I may appear to be a bit of a 'one club golfer' in this respect, but life and strategy demands that we make decisions and choices. And in writing this book I have had to make such a choice. However, I have done so having used the approach (or variants of it) on many occasions, in many circumstances and in many organizations and IT functions.

You will see that in the following pages I will take you through a number of versions of the approach, and will make the point that you will need to adapt it to your own circumstances. So, what you will find in this chapter is a foundation stone on which you must build and evolve your own approach to suit your own particular needs. These differing needs arise because of your organizational culture, the expectations of the business, the skills of your people, and your confidence.

In many ways I am going to provide you with the foundations and the timber framework of your house. It will be up to you as to how you lay out the floor plans, and furnish and decorate it.

Balanced Business Scorecard and Strategy Mapping

The approach that I am going to adopt is based upon something called Balanced Business Scorecard which was created by Kaplan and Norton to address the excessive bias towards financial reporting and management by companies in the 1980s. Balanced Business Scorecard asks companies and managers to identify goals and measures to complement the financial perspective.

```
              ┌──────────────┐
              │  Financial   │
              │ performance  │
      ┌───────┤              ├───────┐
      │ Customer     │    Operational │
      │ performance  │    performance │
      └───────┤              ├───────┘
              │ Learning and │
              │   Growth     │
              └──────────────┘
```

Figure 2: Balanced Business Scorecard (Kaplan and Norton, 2000)

In other words, the approach demands that we set additional performance targets beyond the standard financial goals (e.g. turnover, profitability, return on capital employed) in the areas of:

– Customer performance, e.g. customer satisfaction, market share, length of relationship.

– Operational performance, e.g. reliability, speed, system uptime.

– Learning and growth, e.g. skills development, culture change, staff turnover.

However Balanced Business Scorecard is only the foundation of the approach that I will use. As a 'scorecard' it focuses on objectives and measures. But people generally find it hard to engage with a set of numbers and measures. If we did, our parents would have put us to sleep in our cots by reading multiplication tables rather than fairy stories. They didn't do this because like Aesop and Walt Disney, they know that we like to hear a story rather than being subjected to a list of numbers. This was also recognized by Kaplan and Norton, and others who have worked with Balanced Business Scorecard with the result that an approach called the Strategy Mapping has evolved.

TOUCHING

I will admit, however, that most strategy maps do not paint a story as interesting as that achieved by Hans Christian Andersen, and perhaps even he would struggle to make strategy interesting in some organizations. The point is that strategy maps are more about the story of strategy so that people can understand what we are trying to achieve, and why.

Some exponents of the approach have managed to use maps to tell the story of strategy in extremely interesting ways and others use them as a foundation on which to create very visual and pictorial approaches to explaining the organizational goals. However, this is not a book about strategy mapping and I do not propose to explore all the different approaches that could be adopted. However, I will provide you with the understanding that is necessary to make the approach work in an IT function.

Business Excellence Model

Before I explain the strategy mapping approach, it is worth a quick detour to consider an approach that is often adopted as an alternative; the Business Excellence Model. This will be recognizable to many of you by the following layout:

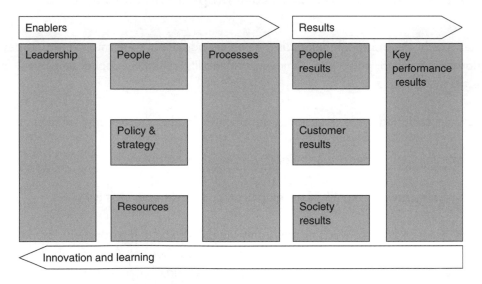

Figure 3: Business Excellence Model (Introducing Excellence: The EFQM Model)

I mention it because it is worth understanding the different benefits that the two approaches bring so that you can decide which is more appropriate to your organization and need. In this respect, I hope that the following table is useful:

PURPOSE	CHOICE OF MODEL
To perform regular 'Health Checks' of all business processes identifying strengths and weaknesses	The Business Excellence Model
To initiate and drive a continuous process improvement program	The Business Excellence Model
To enable external benchmarking of company processes	The Business Excellence Model
To develop a 'checklist' indicating "Good practice" used for business planning and evaluation	The Business Excellence Model
To improve understanding of cause and effect to improved management decisions and actions	The Balanced Scorecard
To align operational activities with strategic priorities	The Balanced Scorecard
To prioritize strategic initiatives	The Balanced Scorecard
To facilitate two way communication of strategy and strategic issues across large organizations	The Balanced Scorecard
To focus management agenda more on future strategic issues than on historic financial issues	The Balanced Scorecard

Table 1: Business Excellence Model or Balanced Business Scorecard? (Andersen *et al.*, 2000)

In a simplistic way I often see the Business Excellence Model as ensuring that 'we do things right', whereas the Balanced Business Scorecard is more focused on 'doing the right things'.

Many of you will be thinking 'but I need the benefits of both' and if so, perhaps the following will help you:

Now we can see the roles these different tools have to play:

– The Strategy Map is central in articulating your strategic goals and purpose, but it also captures the strategic objectives of the business.

– On the other hand the Balanced Business Scorecard is very much about strategic objectives, but has a role to play as well in business planning.

TOUCHING

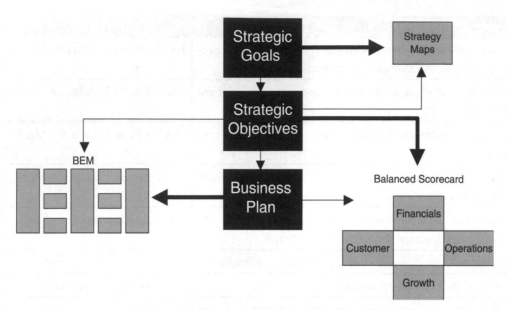

Figure 4: The differing roles of planning tools (Andersen *et al.*, 2000)

– The Business Excellence Model though, is primarily about business planning whilst also providing clarity in respect of your strategic objectives.

Here I will focus on the use of Strategy Maps and I will return to the Balanced Business Scorecard when we consider measures in Chapter 6.

Strategy mapping

The principles

Coming from the same stable as the Balanced Business Scorecard, the principles underpinning strategy mapping are very similar. The other key principle is that of endeavouring to articulate a complete view of your strategy on one page. To achieve this, it will be obvious to you that unless the font is very small it will only be possible to identify the main strategic thrusts rather than the detail.

You will also see strategy mapping is an organization-wide activity demanding that strategy maps are completed for the organization as a whole and also functions, departments and teams. At each level the detail within the map becomes more granular and specific. In this way, strategy maps collectively describe the strategy of an organization as well as individually describing the strategy of a function, department or team.

Firstly, we will see the overlap with Balanced Business Scorecard, by looking at the four areas that a strategy map focuses on. These are:

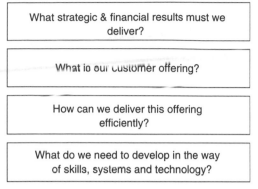

Figure 5: The components of a strategy map

The language is slightly different but the dimensions very much overlap with the Balanced Business Scorecard of:

– Financial performance

– Customer performance

– Operational performance

– Organizational learning and growth.

In the top (strategy and financial) layer, which focuses on the strategic and financial perspective, the type of issues we are seeking to address are:

– What returns are we looking for?

– What returns do our stakeholders need?

– What are our revenue growth targets?

– What are our targets for improving efficiency?

– How will you best use your assets?

- Which markets are we looking to exploit?

The customer layer answers the questions:

- What is our offering?

- What elements make up the value of our offering?

- How will we build relationships with the customers?

- What type of service will we offer?

- How will you manage customer perception of our image?

The third layer deals with operational effectiveness and covers:

- What is our operational strategy?

- How will we reliably deliver to the customers' requirements?

- How will we do this effectively and efficiently?

- What innovations are we planning?

- How can we manage better?

- How will we build the brand?

And the final layer addresses the development of the organization:

- What capabilities do we need to develop?

- How do managers need to develop in order to support our plans?

- How do we need to develop our culture?

- What role can technology play?

These are only a sample of the questions that need to be considered but they give you a flavour of the aspects that are being addressed at each level.

The principle underpinning strategy maps is that you start to write the strategy by completing the top layer (strategy and financial) and work down to the bottom (organizational development).

Firstly, therefore, you articulate the strategic goals you are trying to achieve.

From there you need to be able to answer the questions relating to the proposition that you make your customers (layer two). In other words, if you are going to achieve your strategic goals, then you need to offer your customers something they are going to want to buy repeatedly.

However, they cannot, and will not buy repeatedly if you can't produce the product or service consistently or reliably and hence the need to focus on the third (operational) layer. Similarly, you need to ensure that you can produce your products and services for a cost that results in the business making a profit and this third layer should also say how you're going to achieve this.

None of this will be possible unless you have the skills and capabilities necessary and hence the need for the fourth (learning and growth) layer.

By approaching the creation and description of strategy in this order you start to build the necessary coherence and alignment of thinking that is necessary to ensure that the organization is appropriately focused on delivering the goals that you have set.

The Application

To help you understand, I am going to provide further detail and provide examples so that you can see how these maps work and how the various pieces fit together. In the first instance I will look at this from the organizational perspective and then focus particularly on IT.

So at this juncture it is worthwhile to show you a style of format of a strategy map so that you can see where I am heading:

Alongside, I think it is worthwhile seeing a version of the map which poses some basic questions so that you can quickly see what it is we are trying to achieve in each layer.

TOUCHING

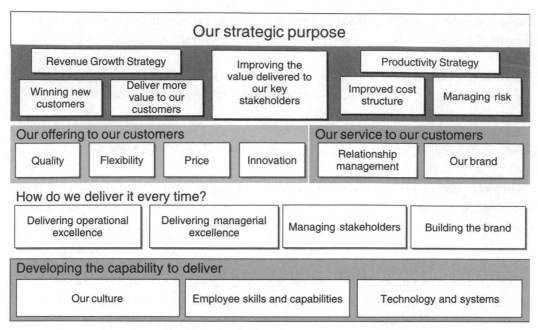

Figure 6: A strategy map – an example layout

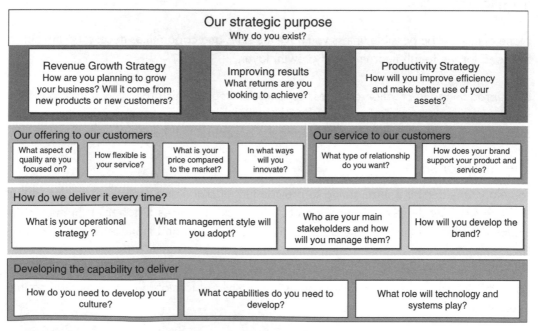

Figure 7: A strategy map – issues to consider

In these examples I have shown some of the key issues that need to be addressed. However, they may not be appropriate for your business and so you may wish to remove some or add others. I don't have a problem with this, but before doing so please stop and check that you are not removing a critical piece of the jigsaw. For example, I think it would be very rare for you to remove the section entitled 'Employee skills and capabilities' as I can think of very few businesses that do not need to develop the capabilities of their staff in order to deliver their strategic goals.

Also, you will see that I have used a format that deploys boxes and to some is quite angular. I know of the other people who use circles and ovals, and other shapes. I really cannot get hung up on this and it is very much down to your own personal and organizational preference. The more important point to me is not the formatting, but the discussion and debate that goes on across the management team that results in you agreeing on the contents.

In the Looking section of this chapter, I have provided some examples of completed maps. If we look at each of these layers in turn we can see:

– Strategic and financial perspective: Centrally is a statement of what we are trying to achieve and what we are trying to deliver to our main stakeholders. In a commercial company this will be the return to our shareholders by way of dividends and capital growth. In a not for-profit or charitable one it will be the rewards that we deliver to the communities that we serve.

– On the left hand side is a description of our plans for growth; namely the rate of growth and the basis by which we will achieve it. On the right is the approach we will adopt to productivity and risk.

– Combined, this layer provides us with a type of profit and loss account. On the left is our income, on the right are our costs. Take one away from the other and you are left with a profit which is available to our stakeholders whose expected returns are captured in the centre.

– Customer perspective: At this level we are describing the proposition that we are making to our customers and in this regard I have broken this into three principle elements. Firstly customers buy the hard product in the shape of a PC, or a car. Alongside, they expect this product to be wrapped in a service and then they also buy the brand. In most cases customers do not buy just one aspect alone, but buy them as a complete package.

– Operational perspective: In answering the question 'how do we do this every time?' we need to manage a mix of operational and managerial excellence that keeps the business operating at peak performance, whilst handling the diverse needs of our customers and building a brand which complements the customer offering.

– Learning and growth: Every strategy demands change or otherwise we would just be standing still. Therefore the demands of the three layers above mean that we have to evolve in some way and it is likely that this will demand some form of shift in our culture or an improvement in the skills and capabilities of our staff and our systems and technology.

– In this regard, this last layer is slightly different from the other three. The other three are a statement of where we want to be in the future, say in three or five year's time. This fourth layer however states how we are going to get there.

Some of you will now have recognized the approach that I adopted in the Touching section of Chapter 2 where I adopted a strategy mapping approach without telling you. I don't apologize for being deceitful as it was not appropriate to complicate matters with technical jargon regarding strategy mapping at that point. However, the questions that I posed in that section are very pertinent, and complement the headline questions that are shown on the strategy maps in this section.

IT strategy maps

The approach to strategy mapping that I have described provides you with a useful tool when thinking about strategy at the organizational level. However, I do not believe that it is sufficiently specific to the IT function. As a result, and if you were to use it in IT, you would find yourself with some empty boxes, or trying to force answers into the format that I have discussed above. This clearly isn't good enough so we need something more suitable for the IT environment.

Additionally, any approach that we adopt should incorporate the concepts that we have discussed regarding productivity and creating value, and moving the IT function from just 'Following' to a point where it is 'Leading'.

I have therefore adapted the standard strategy map so that it encompasses these issues and an example outlined is provided below:

As you will see, the format in terms of the layers is the same, but the questions and issues being addressed are very different. However, they cannot be answered without an

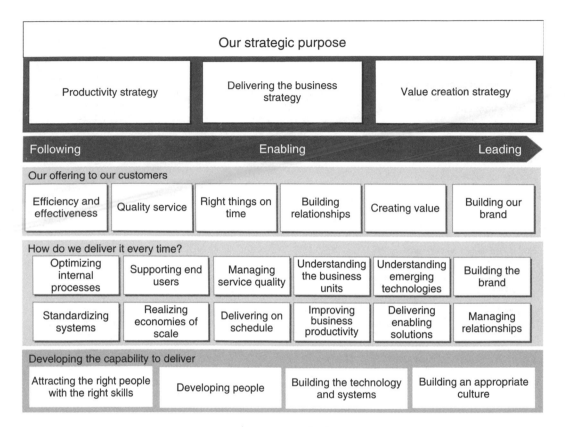

Figure 8: An IT strategy map – an example layout

understanding of the business, its strategy and the environment in which it is operating as we have discussed in the earlier chapters.

Most notable on this map is the arrow which traces the concept of moving from 'Following' through 'Enabling' to 'Leading'. In this respect, the format of the map follows this general concept, so the issues addressed on the left-hand side of the map are about productivity, reliability and basic levels of performance, whereas the right-hand side is about value creation and finding innovative solutions so that you become an integral part of the strategic management team.

As with the organizational strategy map earlier in this section, I have provided a version of this IT strategy map with the core questions that can be considered in each box (see Figure 9 overleaf). Again, an example is provided in the Looking section of this chapter.

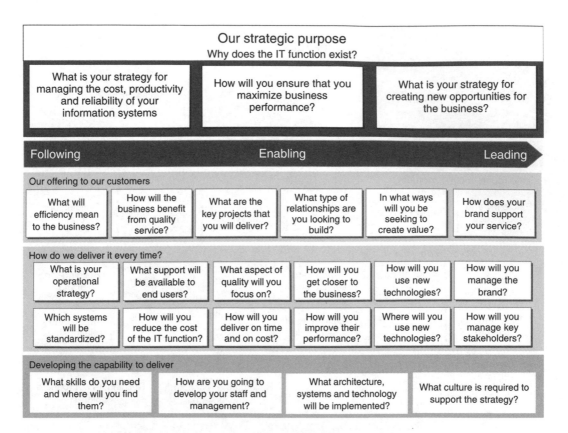

Figure 9: An IT strategy map – issues to consider

A final thought in respect of the concept of strategy maps relates to the idea that I have mentioned previously regarding strategic thrusts or themes. In this regard it is possible that your business or your IT function has identified some key themes that you wish to pursue. If this is the case, it may be important to make these themes explicit in your planning. If this is the case, you may need to adopt an alternative approach to strategy maps (see Figure 10 overleaf) that focuses on these themes, rather than use the structure that I have used previously in this chapter.

Over the years I have adopted a number of approaches and you should feel free to find a format that works best for your circumstances. However, even when utilizing these alternative approaches, I utilize the concepts contained within the core strategy maps that I have described above to test and structure my thinking. Therefore you may also find it helpful to initially utilize the core maps shown above and then restructure your thinking into a themed approach.

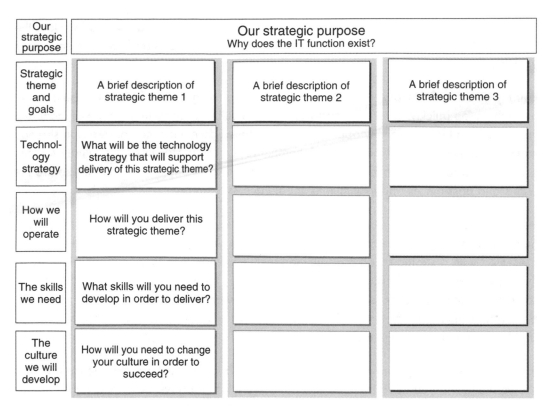

Figure 10: A themed IT strategy map – An example layout

Aligning IT

You now have a number of approaches by which you can articulate and capture your IT strategy and plans. The challenge now is to use these approaches to align the plans, activities, behaviours and thinking of your whole IT team so that you are collectively delivering what the business needs and creating and delivering real value.

Issues to consider

You must remember that strategy maps are just a way of capturing thinking and understanding. In other words if you were to just complete a map and hand it out to everyone in the team you would not achieve the degree of clarity nor commitment that is necessary to deliver success.

Yes, I recognize that the boxes provide a useful check to ensure that you have taken a comprehensive approach but it is important that you are not hamstrung or constrained by

TOUCHING

the maps, their structure or their approach. You should use them as a lever to facilitate the type of discussion and understanding that leads to shared thoughts and commitment across your team.

Equally, you may find that some people are put off by strategy maps if you force the concept on to them too quickly. Over the years I've learnt to utilize strategy maps in a way that prevents this from happening. My approach is one where I do not mention or describe strategy maps at the outset, but use the thinking inherent in the maps to structure my facilitation of the group with whom I am working. In this way, I use the questions to get them to explore the issues and possibilities and to stimulate debate across the room.

Having done this and worked with the group to achieve agreement upon the key components of the strategy, I then capture their thinking in a strategy map format. When they are presented with a strategy map that summarizes their work, they firstly see their language, their words, and their decisions captured in what they now see as a simple and complete summary of their discussions and debates. In other words they take ownership of it, and positively receive the structure and approach. It is at this point that I explain the workings and background to strategy maps.

In terms of the contents and the agreements that need to be reached, experience has also shown me that if you have involved them in the work that I have described earlier in this book, then they will come armed with a deeper understanding of what is required form the IT function and where you need to improve. In this way, the preparatory work in the earlier chapters is both about understanding and winning a commitment to change.

You should also be wary of the dangers of expecting an immediate result. You are asking your team to think in a different way, lift themselves out of the day-to-day tasks and think strategically and tactically about the future of the function. At the same time, you are asking them to use an approach with which they will not be familiar. As a result it can sometimes be some two to three years before they become really competent at utilizing the approach and performing as a strategically focused team.

In this regard, I find that in the early stages of using approaches such as this it is often useful to use the themed strategy maps rather than the full ones as they are slightly more accessible and less daunting.

Who do you involve?

At this early stage in the alignment process you need to consider who you want to involve in the program and your discussions.

In most cases this will be fairly obvious, and it will be your management team and colleagues. However, you may have doubts about the capability or mindset of some and you may not wish to involve them. There may be others elsewhere in the organization who you know will be able to bring experience and perspectives to your discussions. Others you will want to include because of their knowledge and capability.

Equally there may be a case involving people from the business and perhaps even your CEO or the board director to whom you report so that you win the necessary sponsorship and support. There can be no right answer offered in a book, and all I can do is prompt you to stop and think about what is appropriate and whose involvement will best enable you to achieve success.

Raising these issues will also make you consider the format and approach that you wish to adopt so that you achieve more than just a completed document.

Building the strategy

In practice you will find that the whole approach is an iterative process that is not resolved at the first attempt. As a team you will reach initial agreement on the main components of the strategy and as I suggested above you will then capture this in a strategy map format. This first cut could then be reviewed and reflected upon by the team:

– Is this what we understood, discussed and agreed?

– Does it tell a story?

– Is it realistic and achievable?

– What are the main barriers?

From there you and your managers should get back together to explore these issues and to build the detailed version which will also include initial thoughts on performance measures and implementation planning. The circulation of this second version will stimulate further debate, discussion and clarification.

It is also useful after this stage to test the thinking with the business and against the business strategy. You will find that there will be plenty of managers in the business who will be more than happy to express an opinion and tell you whether or not your plans meet their needs.

TOUCHING

The team can then get back together to further refine and eventually finalize the strategy, the map, the measures, priorities and implementation plans.

In reality however, you will need to consider in greater depth the contents of the strategy. To do this you will need to refer to the contents of Chapters 7 through 9. You will also need to determine the performance measures by which you will assess your success. I am not going to cover them here even though they are an important element in this stage of discussions because they act as an important tool to ensure clarity and commitment. They do this by testing the differing assumptions and perspectives that people adopt during these types of discussions. Their importance means that they demand a chapter of their own and therefore I will cover them more fully in Chapter 6.

Cascading the strategy

As a result of your discussions you will have a strong understanding of your IT strategy and built a strategy map for the IT function. More importantly you will have a shared view as a group of what it is and will have started to consider how you are going to deliver it.

You now need to make sure that this understanding amongst your small group of managers is extended across the whole IT function so that everybody can start to transact against your plans. Here, my interest is simply in the concept of cascading strategy rather than the change program itself which we will consider in greater depth in Chapter 12.

As I said at the outset of this chapter, you need to ensure that the strategy is explained to people in a way that relates to their day-to-day roles and jobs; not at too high a level, nor too detailed. You will find that strategy mapping facilitates this and provides an appropriate degree of detail at each level; indeed I find that this is one of the biggest attractions of using strategy maps when I am managing change,.

The simplest way of describing the cascade process is to provide a visual representation:

The challenge is to make sure that the activities, thinking, behaviour and objectives of individuals within the function are pointing in the same direction as your strategy. To achieve this you need to work from the top of Figure 11 to the bottom.

You will now have prepared a strategy for the IT function which you have captured in your IT function strategy map. The content and responsibilities of this map now needs to be shared amongst the departments. For this to be achieved the department heads should be

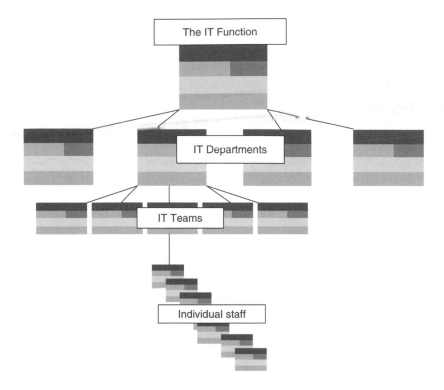

Figure 11: Cascading your strategy through the IT function

working with their managers in order to build their own strategy map whereby they take responsibility for the elements of the IT functional strategy that relates to them.

To achieve this, they should be adopting similar approaches and thought processes that you adopted to develop the IT functional strategy and related strategy map.

From there, managers and team leaders need to be working with the individuals in their teams to create their own team strategies. In many ways these are really tactics not strategies, but if you use the words 'strategy' and 'strategy maps' throughout, you will find that alignment and commitment is easier to achieve because everybody starts to see that they have a role in delivering the strategy.

The final step in the cascade process is the translation of team plans and objectives into individual objectives and development plans through your normal appraisal process. There are other issues to consider in this respect and I will cover these in Chapters 6, 10 and 12.

TOUCHING

You will find that the detail in the maps becomes more granular and specific at each layer of the cascade because of the roles and focus of the individuals involved and their desire to discuss issues that relate to them personally. So department managers will happily (you hope) talk and think strategically and will construct a map that reflects this perspective. On the other hand, team leaders are much more operationally and task focused and so their map will reflect their view of the world and will be more detailed as a result.

In consequence, each map relates to the level for which it was created and individually each map only has a limited amount of detail within it. But collectively the maps will provide a detailed and complete strategy for the function as a whole.

Some checks and balances

It is important during this cascade process that you check for good alignment at each level before you progress to the next. In this regard you need to ensure that the totality of the maps on each level add up to the stated aspirations of the map at the level above.

– The problem of 'Too little': For example, as the CIO with responsibility for the IT functional strategy you will want to know that the combined maps of the IT departments will jointly deliver everything contained within your functional strategy. If they don't and there are gaps, these need to be addressed or you won't deliver your strategy.

– The problem of 'Too much': Equally you want to ensure that your departmental heads are not putting things in their strategy maps that are not included in the IT functional strategy. If they are, then it will result in them applying resources to programs and activities that are not strategically important. As a result these resources will not be available to deliver your strategy.

Therefore, you want to review the maps for each of the departments and check that you are satisfied with them before you allow your departmental heads to start creating maps at the next level down.

One approach that I find useful at this stage is to create a type of shadow board on a wall (like a mechanic uses for storing tools and equipment) where I stick up copies of the strategy maps as they are completed. By the end of the cascade process I have all of them in one place and on display so that I can easily check for fit, omissions and unnecessary activities.

You also need to ensure that you maintain a customer and business focus throughout the program. Often people get so engrossed in the process that they forget that we are here to deliver to our customers. You can address this taking the customer perspective yourself, and by getting individuals to check the contents of their maps with the business units with whom they work.

In closing

As a result you will find that you will have created an alignment of thought and aspiration, and of plans and performance measures that will guide the IT function from top to bottom. You will also find that people understand what they are trying to achieve and their role in successful delivery.

I fully appreciate that achieving clarity such as this is different from getting people to do things differently on the ground, but you will have a foundation on which to build and against which you can manage performance.

Alongside, you will also have a vehicle by which you can explain your role to the business. This is an important aspect in managing their expectations of what is and isn't possible, what you are here for, and what you are not here for.

And you will have aligned your function with the needs of the business.

TOUCHING

Looking

In this Looking section I have elected to provide you with some example strategy maps so that you can visualize the format and contents in order to make the creation of your own maps a little easier.

The following maps were included within the touching section and are repeated here for completeness:

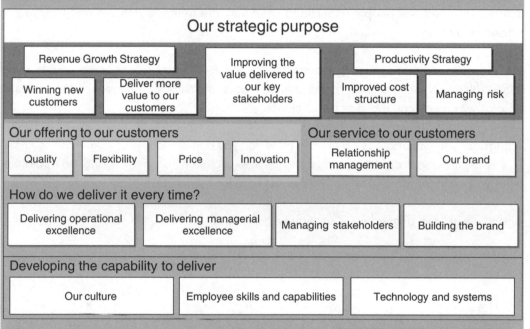

Figure 12: A strategy map – an example layout

Our strategic purpose
Why do you exist?

Revenue Growth Strategy
How are you planning to grow your business? Will it come from new products or new customers?

Improving results
What returns are you looking to achieve?

Productivity Strategy
How will you improve efficiency and make better use of your assets?

Our offering to our customers

What aspect of quality are you focused on?

How flexible is your service?

What is your price compared to the market?

In what ways will you innovate?

Our service to our customers

What type of relationship do you want?

How does your brand support your product and service?

How do we deliver it every time?

What is your operational strategy ?

What management style will you adopt?

Who are your main stakeholders and how will you manage them?

How will you develop the brand?

Developing the capability to deliver

How do you need to develop your culture?

What capabilities do you need to develop?

What role will technology and systems play?

Figure 13: A strategy map – issues to consider

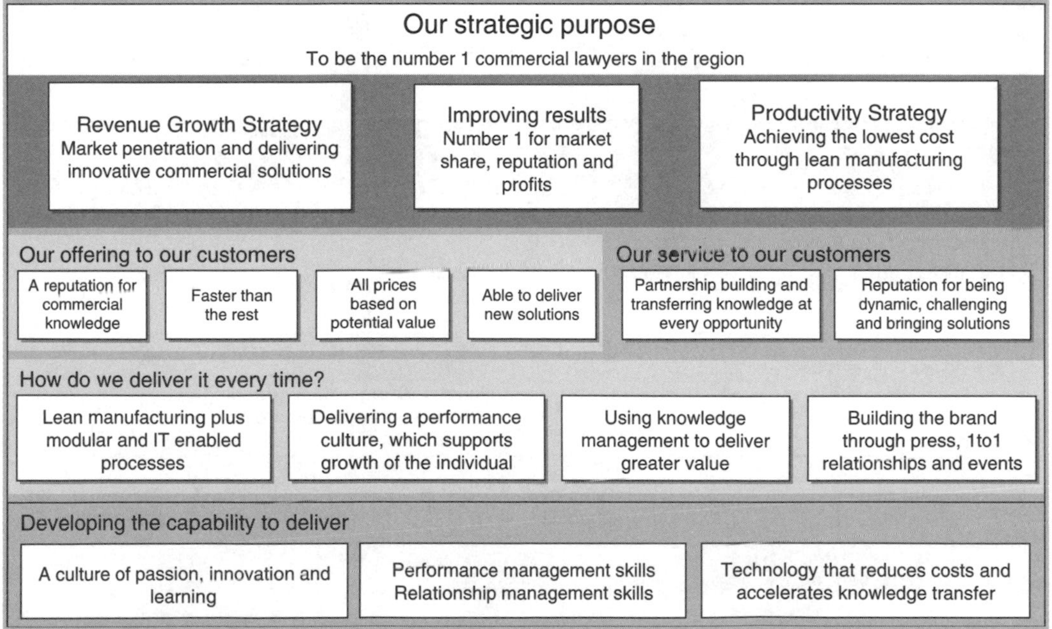

Our strategic purpose
To be the number 1 commercial lawyers in the region

Revenue Growth Strategy
Market penetration and delivering innovative commercial solutions

Improving results
Number 1 for market share, reputation and profits

Productivity Strategy
Achieving the lowest cost through lean manufacturing processes

Our offering to our customers

A reputation for commercial knowledge

Faster than the rest

All prices based on potential value

Able to deliver new solutions

Our service to our customers

Partnership building and transferring knowledge at every opportunity

Reputation for being dynamic, challenging and bringing solutions

How do we deliver it every time?

Lean manufacturing plus modular and IT enabled processes

Delivering a performance culture, which supports growth of the individual

Using knowledge management to deliver greater value

Building the brand through press, 1to1 relationships and events

Developing the capability to deliver

A culture of passion, innovation and learning

Performance management skills
Relationship management skills

Technology that reduces costs and accelerates knowledge transfer

Figure 14: A strategy map – a solicitors' practice

LOOKING

LOOKING

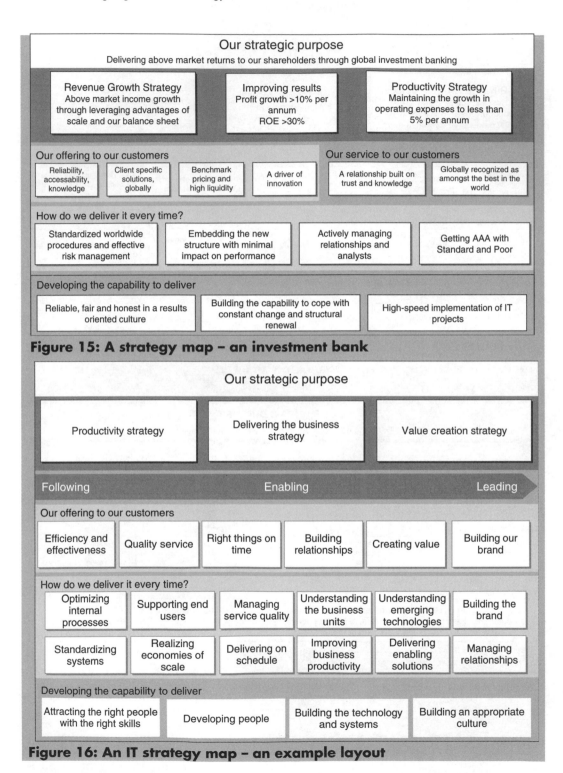

Figure 15: A strategy map – an investment bank

Figure 16: An IT strategy map – an example layout

Our strategic purpose		
Why does the IT function exist?		
What is your strategy for managing the cost, productivity and reliability of your information systems	How will you ensure that you maximize business performance?	What is your strategy for creating new opportunities for the business?

Following	Enabling	Leading

Our offering to our customers

What will efficiency mean to the business?	How will the business benefit from quality service?	What are the key projects that you will deliver?	What type of relationships are you looking to build?	In what ways will you be seeking to create value?	How does your brand support your service?

How do we deliver it every time?

What is your operational strategy?	What support will be available to end users?	What aspect of quality will you focus on?	How will you get closer to the business?	How will you use new technologies?	How will you manage the brand?
Which systems will be standardized?	How will you reduce the cost of the IT function?	How will you deliver on time and on cost?	How will you improve their performance?	Where will you use new technologies?	How will you manage key stakeholders?

Developing the capability to deliver

What skills do you need and where will you find them?	How are you going to develop your staff and management?	What architecture, systems and technology will be implemented?	What culture is required to support the strategy?

Figure 17: An IT strategy map – issues to consider

LOOKING

Our strategic purpose					
To enable the business to achieve rapid growth through deep customer knowledge					

Delivering what is promised on time by managing our legacy problems and simplifying systems	Becoming business and end customer focused and delivering a service not a box	Creating a modular architecture that can deliver flexible solutions at speed

Following   **Enabling**   **Leading**

Our offering to our customers

Improved helpdesk support	Implementing a knowledge management system	A relationship built on joint problem-solving	A modular architecture focused on speed	A new portal framework to link the supply chain	Building a reputation for flexibility and resilience

How do we deliver it every time?

A base of service oriented architecture	Implement an extended hours support service	Responsive and reliable everywhere	The same pace as the business	Customer behaviour visible thru IT	IT = knowledge about customers
Reduce the number of data centres	Replacing legacy systems to reduce cost	SLA's for top 20 systems	Providing knowledge for decision-making	IT triggering customer emotions	New RM team created

Developing the capability to deliver

Knowledge management and customer behaviour analysis skills required	Need to develop SOA and processing speed skills	SOA, knowledge management system, extended support required	Culture focused on learning, sharing and fast decision-making

Figure 18: An IT strategy map – supporting a company competing through proximity to the customer

LOOKING

Our strategic purpose	Our strategic purpose Why does the IT function exist?		
Strategic theme and goals	A brief description of strategic theme 1	A brief description of strategic theme 2	A brief description of strategic theme 3
Technology strategy	What will be the technology strategy that will support delivery of this strategic theme?		
How we will operate	How will you deliver this strategic theme?		
The skills we need	What skills will you need to develop in order to deliver?		
The culture we will develop	How will you need to change your culture in order to succeed?		

Figure 19: A themed IT strategy map – An example layout

Our strategic purpose	Our strategic purpose — Proactively providing the IT systems and support that accelerates the delivery of the business strategy		
Strategic theme and goals	Improve the efficiency and effectiveness	Responding to the business needs	Predicting business needs
Technology strategy	Going back to basics – getting the core systems stable, maximizing standardization and simplification, finding reliable partners	Built on internet-based infrastructure to provide online and real-time systems	Utilizing portals to link the business with customers, partners and suppliers to provide flexibility and responsiveness
How we will operate	Establishing performance and governance systems to ensure we are focusing efforts on the right things for maximum impact	Empowered and flexible teams which are focused on and aligned behind business units	Becoming much more commercial, agile and strategically oriented
The skills we need	Implementing the necessary project management skills, process control and governance systems	The management, communication and relationship skills to operate within the matrix environment	The ability to absorb emerging technologies and environmental changes in order to provide solutions before they are asked for
The culture we will develop	Not being blamed for everything – feeling good about ourselves	An enthusiastic team that listens to its customers and has a can-do attitude	An entrepreneurial team that can turn thinking into action, and which enjoys challenging and innovating

Figure 20: A themed IT strategy map for an IT function that needs to get the basics right first

Doing

In this section I have laid out a short and sharp overview of an approach that you can take to identifying your IT strategy and capturing it by way of strategy maps and determining your action plans. The main components are:

– Immersion and preparation

– Launch workshop

– Playback & check

– Testing with the business

– Revising the plan

– Delivering the plan

Immersion and preparation

The main steps are:

☑ Selecting the team to be involved

☑ Outline briefing and objective setting

☑ Gather environmental information

☑ Undertake interviews with the senior management team

☑ Sharing experiences and lessons

So that you achieve:

– Reassurance and direction for team members

– Understanding of the company background

– Starting to win commitment

– Increasing focus on the customer

This first stage is about preparing the ground; identifying who you want to work with in your strategy team, who you want to work with in the business, and gaining the understanding of the business environment and business strategies and plans as described in the first four chapters.

This will involve members of your team going out and interviewing senior management in the way that I described in the Doing sections of Chapters 2 and 4.

Whilst your managers are doing this they should be encouraged to share their experiences with their colleagues and their staff so that they initiate business focused discussions right across the function.

This will mean that when they arrive at the Launch Workshop they will have already clarified and tested their thinking and will be better prepared to discuss and debate the key strategic issues.

Launch workshop

The main steps are:

☑ Introduction and objectives

☑ What is strategy and is it important?

☑ Sharing experiences & key themes

☑ Identification of key priorities and the implications for the IT strategy

So that you achieve:

– Clarity over our objectives

– A shared view about what has to be delivered and how it may be achieved

– Understanding of how we have to improve

The Launch Workshop is about initial exploration and discussion. It is about bringing out into the open personal views and perspectives, as well as the ideas, priorities and issues that have arisen from the discussions with the business. It is about opening up a range of possibilities and letting people test their thinking in a positive environment so that you can all identify a wide range of options and possibilities for the IT strategy.

From there it is about drawing together the key themes and issues that arise and identifying the central thrust of the strategy.

In this regard I suggest using the strategy maps in the main part of this chapter to help you to structure your thinking and ensure that you have taken a coherent approach. As I said in that earlier section, you may or may not wish to introduce the concept of strategy mapping at this stage. This is up to you, all I am suggesting is that you use the issues raised in the strategy maps at this stage to facilitate the discussions.

Playback & check

The main steps are:

☑ Prepare first draft strategy map

☑ Explain first draft to the team

☑ Introduce the broader concepts of strategy maps

☑ Review, revise, challenge and rework

So that you achieve:

– An ability to use strategy mapping

– An outline IT strategy

– Winning clarity and commitment

– A working copy strategy map

As a result of the Launch Workshop you were in a position to capture your strategic thinking and planning in a first draft of the strategy map.

DOING

This can then be presented back to the team so that they can challenge it and rework it. When presenting this first draft of the strategy map I would first focus the team more on the words in the boxes rather than the structure of the map. This is because the words are their own from the Launch Workshop, and they will have some attachment to them and recognition.

Following this, you can go on to explain the concept of strategy mapping in greater detail.

This would then allow you to work as a team to undertake further revisions to the map and agree the actions of the next stage, Testing with the business.

Testing with the business

The main steps are:

☑ Presenting our thinking to the business and testing our conclusions

☑ Getting feedback and checking understanding

☑ Getting senior management to identify gaps, and highlight their priorities

So that you achieve:

– Alignment with the business

– Stronger relationships with business heads

– Support from business managers

– A strong foundation for our final plans

It is no good generating IT strategy in isolation from the business. You are a support function and everything you do relates to what the business is trying to achieve. Therefore you need to take your early draft of the IT strategy and IT strategy map back to the business and test it to ensure that your thinking fits with their needs.

Responsibility for having these discussions should be allocated amongst the team so that everybody is involved and participating.

DOING

The idea is to engage business management in free-flowing conversation about the proposed IT strategy, their responses and reflections and whether or not the planned approach will be delivering what they need.

The type of response you will receive will depend on whether you are already operating in the Following or Enabling mode as an IT function. If you are struggling to Follow, they will be very cynical about your ability and the nature of the conversation will be very different from an IT function that is already reliably in the Enabling role and looking to step up to become a key business partner.

You will therefore need to gauge how to best structure these conversations and help business managers to understand that you fully appreciate the need to get the basics right, but equally there is a need to progress to higher levels of performance so that the business can benefit from the possibilities that IT can deliver.

Whatever the stage you are at, this is a core opportunity to build closer relationships with the business.

Revising the plan

The main steps are:

☑ Sharing experiences & key themes

☑ Revise the strategy, the map, priorities & plans

☑ Prioritization of key pieces of work

☑ Identification of performance measures

☑ Development of the outline action plan and tactics to be adopted

So that you achieve:

– Making sure that we know what we are going to do, where we all fit in how we are going to deliver

– Understanding of how we have to improve as a team

DOING

– Shared understanding and ownership

– Support from business managers

This is a strong foundation for our final plans. The team now comes back together to pool their experiences and learning from their discussions with the business managers.

This, together with their reflections following the earlier sessions should enable you to refine and finalize the IT strategy and the strategy map. You will also need to agree performance measures (see Chapter 6).

As a result you will be in a position to identify and prioritize key pieces of work and agree an outline action plan.

I have not found it is particularly helpful at this stage to get into detailed action planning using project tools, Gant charts, critical path analysis, etc. as this tends to dissipate energy, and encourage people to argue over silly bits of detail rather than focus on strategic imperatives.

My suggestion is a much simpler one with the aim of ensuring agreement over the key priorities and process:

– Drawing from the strategy map and your discussions, identify the key activities and actions that need to be put in place to deliver the strategy.

– Capture these on post-it notes and stick them up on a wall.

– As a team, gather round and put them in sequence.

– Agree broad timescales.

– Take a digital picture and e-mail it to everyone in the group.

Delivering the plan

The main steps are:

☑ Cascading the strategy throughout the function

☑ Turning our thinking into action

☑ Managing performance and delivery

☑ Developing the capability and culture

☑ Reporting our progress and relationships with the businesses

So that you achieve:

– A successful IT team enabling and leading the business

Now it is a simple task of managing the performance and delivery of the team so that we deliver the results that we have targeted and the success and support that the business demands. Easy!

If only it was. Unfortunately, this is the hardest part, and the rest of the book is focused on this. However, you now need to take the initial actions that will bring your IT strategy and strategy map alive throughout your departments, teams and individuals.

This demands that you cascade functional strategy down throughout the IT departments, teams and individuals. I have explained how this can be done in the Touching section within this chapter.

Thereafter, you will need to set the performance measures (Chapter 6); manage the change (Chapter 12), manage performance and lead the team (Chapter 10) and develop the culture (Chapter 13).

DOING

6

Focusing on outcomes

- Performance measures – some principles

- Performance measures – some approaches

- Creating performance measures

Sound business disciplines demand that the rigour of measurement is attached to a strategy. This chapter reinforces this principle and guides you through the development of strategically aligned performance measures.

Touching

Execution is what counts

"Far away there in the sunshine are my highest aspirations, I may not reach them but I can look up and see their beauty, believe in them and try to follow them".

Louisa May Alcott

Strategy is not about a plan. It is about a way of thinking and behaving both individually and organizationally that focuses the whole organization's energies on the delivery of your aspirations.

And yet, a *McKinsey and Company* research program on why executives fail concluded that the most common reason was their inability to execute strategy. Whilst common sense itself dictates that it is the ability to execute and deliver your strategy that counts, only one in ten companies do so. Why? Consider these research findings:

– 60% of organizations do not link strategy to budgeting

– 75% of organizations do not link middle management incentives to strategy

– 86% of executive teams spend less than one hour per month discussing strategy

– 95% of a typical workforce does not understand their organization's strategy.

With statistics like these, the failure to deliver strategic success is not surprising. Another challenge is that the source of value has shifted from tangible to intangible assets such as human and information capital, and creating value from intangibles presents a new strategic management challenge. The fact is that most organizations do not have a strategic management process that puts strategic thinking and behaviours at the centre of what they do.

On the other hand, organizations that do succeed are strong in the following areas:

– Mobilizing change through executive leadership

– Translating the strategy into operational terms

– Aligning the organization around its strategy

– Making strategy everyone's job

– Making strategy a continual process.

In the last chapter I focused on the use of strategy maps in order to align the IT function behind both the business and the IT strategies. But for maximum effectiveness, not only should the strategy maps for all parts of your function be aligned so must be the objectives. In this chapter I am going to look at the ways in which you can ensure the performance measures and objectives are aligned and do indeed 'translate the strategy into operational terms', and 'make strategy everyone's job'.

To that end, I am the going to consider some of the principles underpinning objective setting and then propose approaches that you can adopt with your own team, with the result that your strategy not only benefits from clarity of direction, but also performance measures that focus energy and ensure that you are keeping to the path that you set out on.

Performance measures – some principles

This is not a performance management book and therefore it is inappropriate to go into great detail regarding the theories underpinning measures, systems and management processes. However, it is appropriate to highlight some principles that will be helpful to you as you endeavour to attach measures to your strategy and cascade them down through the function.

What are we trying to achieve?

So, first some objectives. In simple terms you are trying to make it clear to people what it is they have to deliver:

– An administrator in the program office should be able to look at their own personal objectives and see how they connect and link to the strategy of the function.

– There should be an explicit link between what people do, the objectives of the teams to which they belong and the IT strategy.

– People should be able to say 'I now see where I fit in, and why I do what I do'.

Equally, your measures should light up the path you are on towards successful delivery of your strategy. In other words, they should act as lights at the edge of the path to illuminate the way forward, but also to signal when you are going off-track and leaving your intended route. And the brightest beacons will be at the end of this path to provide you with the ultimate direction and aspiration.

Your measures should also serve to aid understanding and to trigger action. Therefore, they work well when they inform people and action is taken because of that additional knowledge.

In these respects, performance measures have three principal roles:

Providing focus

– Measures need to be focused on your strategic objectives

– Measures must create alignment with strategy to direct daily activities

– Measures need to be meaningful to individuals throughout the organization

– Measures need to be consistent throughout the organization

– Measures need to provide a balance between financial and non-financial aspects of performance

Creating clarity

– Measures need to provide accurate and credible results

– They need to be clear and simple supported by definitions and calculations that are understandable

– They need to be observable and countable

– More than six measures to each person can serve to create confusion

– Measures should not overlap

Driving action

– Measures should give results that are actionable

- Measures need to be available on a timely basis so that they provide the opportunity for action to be taken

- Measures should help people to predict future outcomes

- Measures need to identify where improvement is needed

- There needs to be a balance between the cost and benefits of gathering and using the information

Performance measures and behaviour

However, performance measures are not just about outcomes. They are also about how people behave and act on the journey. In this regard measures need to be chosen which encourage and reinforce the right behaviour.

For example if you are running a helpdesk to support users across the company the use of a measure such as 'number of calls are handled' is more likely to drive the wrong behaviour than a measure such as 'number of highly satisfied callers' or 'issues resolved at first point of contact'.

So, when designing measures you need to think about the perverse ways in which people will behave as a result of the measure that you have set. Similarly, you need to put measures in the context of the:

- Values of your business

- Culture that you are trying to create, and

- The service that you are trying to offer.

Given that we are a support function endeavouring to align ourselves with the business, the business strategy should also influence the measures that you set.

To achieve this, you need to establish measures across the two dimensions shown in Figure 1 over the page.

In this regard, imagine that you have identified your strategic purpose and the outcomes that you are looking to achieve. In many businesses the focus then switches to setting objectives and identifying the competencies or skills which are needed to get you there. All I am saying is that you must equally focus on the values and culture in your company and make sure

TOUCHING

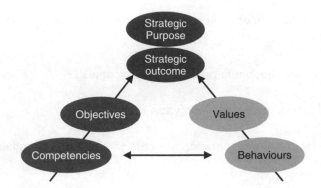

Figure 1: Setting objectives – focusing on skills and behaviours

that these are supported by measures that drive the right behaviours, so that you achieve the right results with the right behaviours.

For example, the UK retailer Marks & Spencer was incredibly successful for many years both as a result of having staff with the necessary skills, products and processes, but also because their behaviour and culture allowed them to understand the British shopper and treat them in a way that met their needs.

As Stuart Rose, their current Chief Executive says, they lost sight of the needs of the shopper and their behaviour became arrogant and inward looking. This inappropriate behaviour (and a changing competitive environment) resulted in the British shopper voting with their feet and Marks & Spencer's losing market share and profitability.

Performance measures and motivation

Performance measures should also motivate your staff so that they try to achieve the goals they are set. As Hertzberg identified many years ago (Herzberg, 1968), two of the biggest motivators for people are a sense of achievement and recognition. If measures are set which fail to offer the opportunity of success (achievement), the likelihood that people will be motivated by the measures is much reduced. Indeed, it is equally likely that people will be demotivated.

However, when you look at the unrealistic goals that are set for so many people in the workplace, you are left wondering whether managers set out to demotivate their workforces. Sad but true. By the way, it is this aspect of achievement that underpins the 'R' in the much used SMART acronym, where it stands for 'Realistic'. (The others being Specific, Measurable, Agreed and Timebound.)

The other point arising from Hertzberg's work is that people are motivated by a sense of recognition. In most organizations, recognition results from success and the achievement of goals and targets. However, if those targets are so unachievable the people cannot enjoy success, they are unlikely to be recognized, further deepening the downward spiral towards demotivation, dissatisfaction and eventually disengagement.

An aspect of recognition that you can consider at this stage of the alignment process is the involvement of your staff in the setting of the performance measures. Not only will they know what will and what won't work, they can also give you a good understanding of the ways in which people will adapt their behaviours as a result of the measures being set. Adopting this approach will help to win the support of your staff, who at the end of the day are the ones who will deliver your strategy.

Similarly, and as a support function endeavouring to build stronger and more effective relationships with your colleagues in the business, real value can be gained by discussing your planned targets with them. In consequence, you will be able to understand whether or not the measures you are setting do indeed deliver the results that they want.

Returning to the broader issue of motivation through performance measures, you may wish to ask yourself these questions:

– If we are going to energize our people to dig deep and achieve more, what should we measure?

– Why will this goal stimulate and energize people?

– What is the story of this goal that others will relate to and engage with?

– In what way is this goal meaningful to the people who have to deliver it?

Three final thoughts in this introductory section.

'What gets measured, is what gets managed.' In simple terms, measure the results you want and reward those results.

> "It is very important, I think, that league tables or whatever measurement, should be used to improve and to learn rather than be the end in themselves." Lord Brown, Chief Executive of BP

TOUCHING

"Targets can never be substitutes for a proper and clearly expressed strategy and set of priorities. Targets can be good servants, but they are poor masters." House of Commons Public Administration Select Committee, 2003

Performance measures – some approaches

There are a host of approaches that exist, and my objective is to provide you with an overview of a few so that you have some options to choose from. In this respect I am conscious that it is much easier to create financial measures (turnover, profitability, costs, stockholding, etc.) than it is to create non-financial performance measures.

There are two main reasons. Firstly, there are thousands of accountants out there who've been creating financial measures for decades. They are practiced at it, they are good at it, and they have a long list of measures that you could use. Secondly, we grow up with numbers and are taught in homes and school. We use numbers to count the money which acts as a core currency and common language. However, we are not taught at home or in school how to assess customer satisfaction, or measure the value we have delivered to a partner, or how to assess the skill levels of our people.

As a result, I am afraid that you will have to accept that setting a broader range of measures is not easy and that there are no absolute answers. You will need to compromise and you will need to be flexible:

– You need to compromise because it is likely that you will not find the perfect answer.

– You will need to be flexible because it is unlikely that you will find the perfect answer first time and you will need to be prepared to find alternative solutions when it becomes clear that your chosen approach is not working.

Establishing non-financial performance measures

For a business, non-financial measures serve a critical role:

– Centrally, they provide a leading indicator of progress on the road towards a financial goal.

  – If our customers are increasingly satisfied with our service and recommending us to their friends and colleagues, or

- If our systems are becoming more reliable and responsive to our customers needs

- We may be able to predict that an improvement in turnover may result.

- In a world where approaching 70% of a developed country's GDP comes from the service sector, it is necessary to measure much more than just income and costs.

- In a function like IT we have limited direct impact on financial measures. Yes, we may be able to manage our costs, but it is much harder to say whether or not our actions have been directly responsible for an increase in turnover or profitability.

As a result, businesses need to be better at utilizing non-financial performance measures. Indeed, those of us in IT and other support functions need to be better than the rest of the business because of our reliance on them to evidence the quality and value of what we do.

In a very useful article in the *Harvard Business Review*, Christopher Ittner and David Larcker provided some really valuable and practical guidance. This can be summarized in the diagram shown below.

Figure 2: Establishing non-financial performance measures (Ittner and Larcker, 2003)

Link to your strategy

This is a statement of the obvious given in the earlier discussions in this book, but it needs restating. Not only is this about alignment, it is also about ensuring that you select the right measures.

Find the real drivers of performance

This next stage takes us beyond a simple matter of alignment and demands that we identify those areas of performance that really have impact on our success. If you know for example, that your program office can deliver new systems more quickly using Service Oriented Architecture, it is more important to assess the improvement in the skills of your staff in this using this approach than it is measuring their communication skills.

However this should not just be a guess or based upon personal opinion. Your managers should be checking and testing whether or not their assumptions hold true in practice. In other words, is it their skill in using Service Oriented Architecture that makes the difference to the speed of delivery? Or is it that program office staff have a deep understanding of the business strategy and are consequently able to anticipate likely requirements in advance? Indeed, neither of these may be the solution, but what is needed is for managers to identify and understand the real drivers of performance.

Setting the right targets

Having identified the aspects of performance which will deliver the greatest impact, it is necessary to identify targets in each of those areas; i.e. do you need 50%, 60% or 100% achievement, or do you need to do 10 or 20 a day?

Often inappropriate targets are set, particularly in the area of customer satisfaction. For example, some organizations chase survey results that reveal 100% of customers are satisfied. However, it might be that even if they only achieved a 90% customer satisfaction rating this might be sufficient to achieve all their other strategic goals in terms of customer retention and income generation. In this case, pursuing the additional 10% may be very expensive and yet fail to deliver any return to the business, so there is little point wasting resources trying to do so.

Conversely, for an IT system, the difference between 95% and 99% uptime is massive and have a dramatic impact on the performance of the business and the reputation of your function. And whilst you may be proud of 100% phone cover on your UK helpdesk during the hours of 9 a.m. to 5 p.m., this is no good if you are supporting staff in Mexico and Dubai as well as London.

Measure effectively and act

To enable you to be able to rely on your performance measures you need to ensure that the data you are collecting is valid and reliable – does it capture what it is supposed to capture, and is it statistically sound enough for you to make management decisions?

Equally, you may want to consider whether the data you are collecting is consistent across the function. Often businesses combine apples and pears and count them as oranges. This occurs because different methods of collecting data and analysing are used in different parts of the business.

If you address these issues you should have the right information available to you at the right time to enable you to make decisions. Regrettably however, the information you present isn't used effectively. People receive your management information packs but don't really take much notice and then move on to other matters. If this is the case, you might as well not measure anything and stop wasting limited resources collecting, manipulating and presenting information that is not used nor relied upon.

So the challenge must be to present the information in a way that stimulates debate, forces people to face the reality of circumstances and work together to find solutions that deliver a performance uplift. Partly this is about the culture of the organization and the way in which the performance management regime operates. But it is also about the way in which data is presented and used so that it engages people right across the function and not just at management level. This may mean presenting the information in different formats and using different media and approaches to stimulate debate. Given that our performance measures are about providing focus, creating clarity and driving action, we must put the same effort into ensuring its utilization as we do in creating the measures in the first place.

Balanced Business Scorecard

I have already described the principles underpinning Balanced Business Scorecard in Chapter 5, and do not propose to repeat those here. It is appropriate just to highlight the main component elements as follows:

If you are utilizing the Balanced Business Scorecard to structure your performance measures, you need measures in each of the four dimensions to ensure that the balance is maintained in all aspects of the business.

Examples of the types of measures that you use are included in the Looking section of this chapter.

Whilst the Balanced Business Scorecard approach is widely used and very effective in many circumstances, I find it difficult to use in a stand-alone way, especially in terms of aligning measures with the functional strategy.

TOUCHING

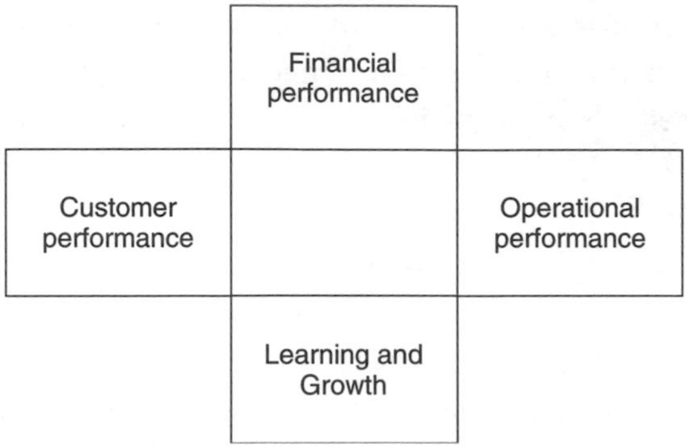

Figure 3: The Balanced Business Scorecard (Kaplan and Norton, 2000)

However, it is naturally aligned with the strategy mapping approach (it is its forefather after all) and helps us to structure our thinking when applying measures to the issues identified and captured within a strategy map.

In practice, therefore, I find that the process of creating the strategy map allows me to identify measures as I go along. I then need to test those measures against the principles outlined by Ittner & Larcker (as described earlier) to ensure that they are both appropriate and sufficiently rigorous.

In this way, the development of performance measurement areas is a natural development from the creation of the strategy map and is part of your strategic thinking. However, it is necessary to check and review in case you have missed important aspects or included measures that are inappropriate. This review should not be conducted alone; as I mentioned earlier, your measures should be explored with your management team, your staff and ideally your customers in the business.

As a result, you may have identified objectives, measurement areas and targets in each of the domains and can capture them as shown in Figure 4:

Be careful, as there is a danger with any of these approaches that you create too many measures in each layer. This is a common problem with all measurement systems and especially when dealing with non-financial measures in particular. In the absence of the certainty that is provided by measuring turnover or profitability, managers measure too many areas in the hope that they hit the mark. This is not a good use of resources, does not bring the necessary clarity or focus, and tends to undermine belief in the approach.

Financials			
Objectives	Measures	Targets	Initiatives

Customer			
Objectives	Measures	Targets	Initiatives

Operations			
Objectives	Measures	Targets	Initiatives

Growth			
Objectives	Measures	Targets	Initiatives

Figure 4: Translating your strategy into action using the four perspectives (Kaplan and Norton, 1996)

Themed strategy maps

You may recall that in Chapter 5 I discussed the option of using themed strategy maps and if you decided to go down this route, you will again need to create performance measures to support your strategic aspirations and goals.

In these circumstances I find the approach shown in Figure 5 is helpful for creating measures and enables me to reinforce the themes that have been chosen:

You will see that the approach I have adopted is one where in each theme we first of all articulate our aspirations; if we were a successful team, what will success look like?

Having identified this state, we are in a position to identify ways in which this aspiration can be measured. Once again, I would use the approach proposed by Ittner & Larcker (as described earlier) to identify the right measures to use.

I do this for each theme in turn.

TOUCHING

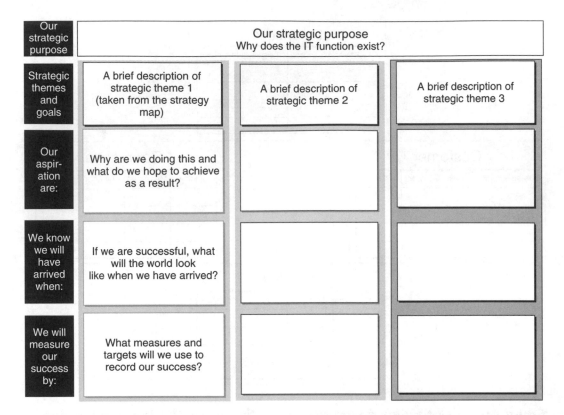

Figure 5: Creating measures for a themed IT strategy map

Benchmarking

Whilst IT may not be an area where you can easily use financial measures, it does lend itself to comparing your performance to the marketplace using benchmark survey material. This approach provides the opportunity to test the cost base and utilization of the resources of your function against other businesses.

It also provides a mechanism by which you can manage the concerns and challenges of the business. I am conscious that many IT functions find themselves facing a continual barrage of complaints along the lines of 'Too expensive, too slow, too many people, too unreliable, etc.' and having information like this available to you can be invaluable.

There is always a danger with benchmarking that managers and staff focus more on other organizations within the survey data rather than the needs of your business. In this sense, I do not believe that benchmarking is the only solution and performance measures aligned with the IT functional strategy can be the only appropriate way forward.

However, if you do decide to use benchmarking measures to complement your other strategic performance measures then the following list will provide you with an appreciation of some of the areas where comparison is usually possible and data is readily available from companies and membership organizations such as the National Computing Centre in Manchester, England:

IT spend overall
  % of turnover

IT Spend versus
  Number of end users
  Number of workstations

Breakdown of IT spend by %
  Capital & development
  End user
  Operations

IT Staff
  Numbers per 1000 users
  End user support staff per 1000 users

Breakdown of staff allocation by role %
  IT Managers
  Development
  Operations
  End user support staff

Salary costs
  Average IT salary

The service-profit chain

In 1994 James L Heskett and others outlined a concept called the Service Profit Chain (Heskett *et al.*, 1997). The approach makes very explicit the link between developing internal capabilities, delivering customer satisfaction and achieving the target in financial goals. It also presents us with an alternative approach to Balanced Business Scorecard and Strategy Mapping.

TOUCHING

In essence, the approach says that if we:

- Embed high levels of internal quality, we can provide an environment in which our staff can perform and be satisfied, and...

- We recruit the right staff and enhance their productivity by developing their skills and capabilities, then...

- We can deliver greater value and higher levels of service to all of our customers, so that...

- They become more satisfied with what we deliver, and as a result...

- They become more loyal, buy more from us and refer us to their friends and colleagues, so that...

- We achieve the growth in income and profits that we seek.

As you will see this approach provides a very clear and logical link from one end of the chain to the other. An example set of measures for IT are shown in Figure 6:

I recognize that in an IT environment, the final element relating to the generation of income and profits does not apply. However, there are some very strong pointers for the IT function in the rest of the model. Without doubt we need to:

- Get our internal quality right and our staff willing and capable of delivering at higher levels (Following), so that...

- We deliver high levels of customer satisfaction and end up with customers willing to use us and recommend us to other parts of the business, because...

- Our involvement enables them to achieve their business goals (Enabling).

The project lifecycle approach

Whilst this approach is more about investment appraisal, I believe it is appropriate to consider it here as understanding it will provide you with another vehicle by which to develop performance measures.

The approach is built upon initial work by the Boston Consulting Group (1977), Harvard Business School, Boston (1977) who considered product life cycles in the marketing environment. It was further developed for IT by McFarlan (1984), and I have developed it further

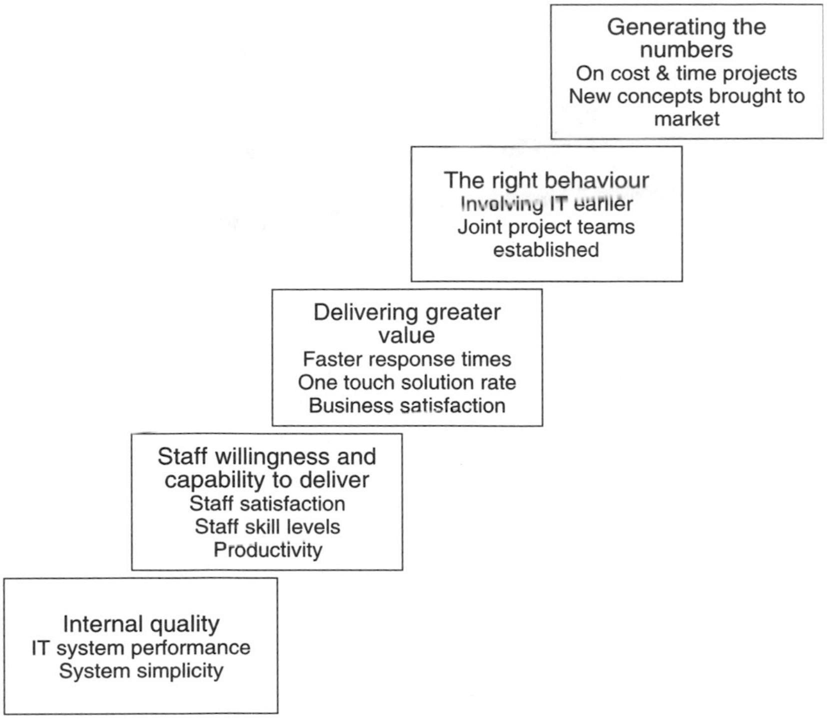

Generating the numbers
On cost & time projects
New concepts brought to market

The right behaviour
Involving IT earlier
Joint project teams established

Delivering greater value
Faster response times
One touch solution rate
Business satisfaction

Staff willingness and capability to deliver
Staff satisfaction
Staff skill levels
Productivity

Internal quality
IT system performance
System simplicity

Figure 6: The service to profit chain in IT

to provide me with a tool by which I can make investment decisions and determine appropriate management approaches. You will see that I refer again to this approach in greater detail in Chapters 7 and 8.

To understand the construct of this (which is shown in Figure 7) model, imagine a company developing a new product. During the development phase, the product sits in the top right-hand corner and nobody knows whether or not it is going to be a success. Boston Consulting Group described these products as 'Question marks' for obvious reasons. However where these new products are a roaring success, and provide the basis on which the company competes and succeeds they are described as 'Stars'.

However over time, these leading products are copied by other firms and the competitive edge is lost. Despite this, the company can still generate large volumes of sales. As the product is well known in the market and does not need substantial investment it can generate large volumes of cash and for this reason, products in this third box (bottom left-hand corner) are called 'Cash Cows'.

TOUCHING

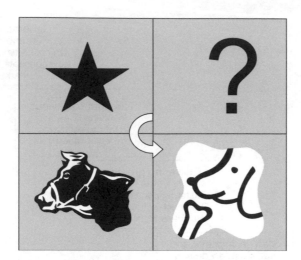

Figure 7: The BCG Growth-Share Matrix

Later, the product that was once a Question Mark and which became a Star, and then a Cash Cow becomes a 'Dog' as it fades into decline.

IT projects enjoy much the same sort of lifecycle. (Figure 8)

There will be those projects that are purely exploratory and which relate to potential opportunities from new systems and from which the benefits are not yet clear. These are the 'Pioneering' projects.

If adopted and successful, the systems and processes become strategically critical and enable your business to compete and 'Win the Race'. Over time, systems that enabled your business to enjoy growth and success are copied by others and simply become part of the suite of tools and processes that any competitor in the marketplace must possess to be a player. They keep you 'In the Game'.

Eventually these processes drift down to become 'Supporting' systems which simply help to drive up our productivity.

For example, Wal-Mart are still exploring the potential value they can achieve via the Internet (Pioneering), but they know that their marketing and market information systems are strategically critical in allowing them to compete in new ways, in new markets and to meet new customers expectations and needs (Win the Race). Their logistics and stock control systems that were once strategically critical and now simply key operational activities (In the Game), and their financial record-keeping is simply a support process (Supporting).

Winning the race	Pioneering
In the game	Supporting

Figure 8: The IT life cycle

Each of these four areas demands different criteria for the investment decision and subsequent realization of financial benefits.

In Figure 9, I highlight the basis on which you should be making your investment decisions and building performance measures using the life cycle approach.

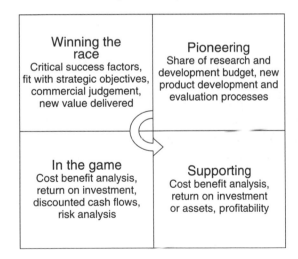

Figure 9: The IT life cycle – investment criteria

Before I leave this topic, I think it is worth highlighting that you should be considering whether your IT function resources are appropriately allocated to projects across these four dimensions.

If for example, the bulk of your resources and IT investment is going into projects in the Support zone, it is very unlikely that you will be having much impact in terms of Enabling or Leading.

Therefore at a strategic level you should be considering where your resources are currently being invested and where you would like them to be invested to achieve the strategic impact which you desire. Indeed you may well establish a performance measure regarding the allocation of resources into each of these boxes. (See Chapters 7 and 8 for more detailed approaches.)

In closing

Successful performance measures are tightly aligned to your strategy, and will drive not only the right focus for your team, but also the right behaviours. However, they also motivate people to perform at consistently high levels and provide a focus on action and delivery.

This is hard to achieve if you are only dealing with financial measures. However, in IT our focus is more likely to be on non-financial measures where the challenges of setting effective targets are greater.

The approaches available to us are varied, but fundamentally come down to providing clarity of direction, enabling you to monitor the progress you are making and linking your staff to your strategy so that they understand what they have to deliver.

At this stage of the book, we understand the business strategy, can visualize IT's role in its delivery, can measure our success and have identified the key components of our strategy. Before we move into delivery, we need to be more specific about the detail of the strategy – are we a Follower, Enabler or Leader, and what do each mean?

TOUCHING

Looking

In the same way as I approached the Looking section in Chapter 5, I am going to provide you with some examples of approaches that you could use to measure the delivery of your strategy. You will not require all of these, and should use the ideas shown below to stimulate your thinking and to provide you with ideas on the approaches that you could use. It is important, as I have suggested in the Touching section, to develop your own measures in a structured way so that they align with your strategy.

Firstly, let me remind you of the structure I proposed for the development of performance measures using a themed strategy map.

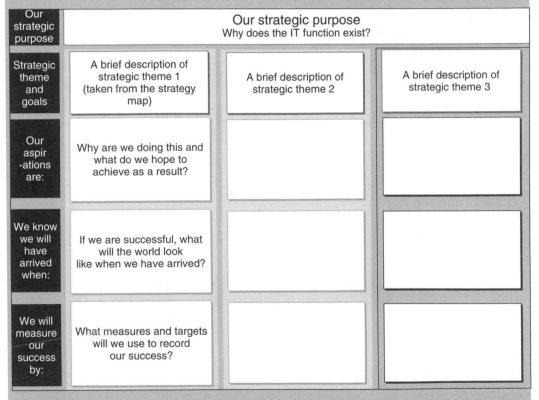

Figure 10: Creating measures for a themed IT strategy map

We can then refer to the example I used in Chapter 5 of a themed strategy map.

LOOKING

Our strategic purpose	Our strategic purpose Proactively providing the IT systems and support that accelerates the delivery of the business strategy		
Strategic theme and goals	Improve the efficiency and effectiveness	Responding to the business needs	Predicting business needs
Technol-ogy strategy	Going back to basics – getting the core systems stable, maximizing standardization and simplification, finding reliable partners	Built on internet-based infrastructure to provide online and real-time systems	Utilising portals to link the business with customers, partners and suppliers to provide flexibility and responsiveness
How we will operate	Establishing performance and governance systems to ensure we are focusing efforts on the right things for maximum impact	Empowered and flexible teams which are focused on and aligned behind business units	Becoming much more commercial, agile and strategically oriented
The skills we need	Implementing the necessary project management skills, process control and governance systems	The management, communication and relationship skills to operate within the matrix environment	The ability to absorb emerging technologies and environmental changes in order to provide solutions before they are asked for
The culture we will develop	Not being blamed for everything – feeling good about ourselves	An enthusiastic team that listens to its customers and has a can-do attitude	An entrepreneurial team that can turn thinking into action, and which enjoys challenging and innovating

Figure 11: A themed IT strategy map for an IT function that needs to get the basics right first

Figure 12 shows the results of this approach when applied to the strategy shown in Figure 11.

However, these only represent a few of the measures you could have used, and as I said in the opening of this section, I wish to provide you with a menu to draw on. Therefore, below I have listed a wide range of measures, under the core themes of the book, namely; Following, Enabling and Leading.

Measuring Following

IT spend versus business turnover %

IT Spend versus end user/ workstation numbers

IT budgets and outsource costs within budget

Our strategic purpose	Our strategic purpose Proactively providing the IT systems and support that accelerates the delivery of the business strategy		
Strategic theme and goals	Improve the efficiency and effectiveness	Responding to the business needs	Predicting business needs
Our aspirations are:	Operating a system which is reliable and easy to use by the business and our staff. Not subject to continual requests for cost benchmarking	We have a reputation in the business for delivery and understanding their needs	To be able to see changes in the business environment and lead the debate in the business over strategic options
We know we will have arrived when:	Systems available when required A minimum number of service interruptions Delivering our service promise	Our staff are able to respond to changing business needs as they occur The business closes the mini IT functions that they keep creating	We are spending less time on maintenance and more time bringing new concepts, services and products to market
We will measure our success by:	System availability percentage System reliability Service delivery versus SLA targets	Business survey satisfaction ratings Project closure meeting performance reviews Count of outlying IT units	Percentage of IT resource invested in maintenance and legacy systems Cost of IT versus benefits delivered from strategic projects

Figure 12: Creating measures for an IT function that needs to get the basics right first

Reliability of selected key processes

- Up time %

- Fault volumes

- % availability related to agreed business need

System reliability

- Classified into major and minor impact

- Customer facing vs. back office systems

LOOKING

Incident resolution

– % of incidents resolved within performance thresholds

Accessibility to support services

– 24/7 cover %

Performance agreements

– Number of SLAs implemented

– % performance against SLA targets

– 3rd party management agreements implemented

Service delivery

– % services covered by SLA

– % SLA targets met

Project delivery

– % project milestones met

– % projects completed within budget

– Volumes of projects outstanding

Staff

– Numbers per user/Support staff per user

– Salary costs vs. role

– Numbers per 1000 users

- End user support staff per 1000 users

- Salary costs – Average IT salary

Breakdown of staff allocation by role

- IT Managers

- Development

- Operations

- End user support staff

Staff utilization

- Staff % working on legacy system issues

Risk and people

- Number of competent people per key service

- % staff turnover

Efficient use of the architecture

- Number of items of hardware

- Number of service/applications

Spend breakdown %

- Development

- End user

- Operations – Software, Hardware, Staff

LOOKING

Measuring Enabling

Business perception of the relationship

- Reputation for competence

- Trust in IT by key partners

- Annual survey to key/all customers: return rate; satisfaction rate, reputation for delivery

- Project closure meetings: repeat issues

- Incident handling questions (sample of calls handled/visits made): satisfaction rating; repeat issues

- Count of number of departments with separate IT capability

Managing business perception

- Hours of contact with the targeted players

- Number of operating Relationship Managers in the field

- Stage of involvement in projects

- IT doing market testing for the business

- Ability to adapt to changing needs

- Operating at same pace as business

Business awareness

- IT staff understanding of business issues – measured through a testing program

- Number of business unit and head office department visits per year and feedback reports produced

Service delivery

- Speed of fault resolution

- Availability

- Phone

- Meetings

Selected key project delivery

- Time

- Cost

- Value

Change plan

- Progress against plan

MI Provision

- Availability to business

- Speed of report delivery

- Timeliness/reliability

- Reducing number of stand alone systems

Improved infrastructure performance

- IT infrastructure costs

- Number of data centres

LOOKING

– Average cost of data centres

Employee of the year candidates

Measuring Leading

IT providing solutions and options

– Volume adopted

Reputation for understanding business issues

– Feedback and satisfaction scores

New system performance

– Staff % take up

– Supplier engagement and performance

– Numbers accessing and using the system

– Speed of take up

– Sales value generated

– Profit generation

– Return on investment

– Performance against original investment criteria

Delivery of selected innovative/strategic projects

– IT effort as a % of total project effort

– Split between new build and rework of current systems

- Cost of IT vs. projected benefits

- Delivery to time

- Delivery to cost

Accelerating time to market

- Business project – overall time to market

- Within IT – % of days spent on new work or amendments

Enabling internet access

- Leads: % handled remotely

- Customers: hits on website

- Staff: % using remote access

- Partners: numbers accessing remotely

Improved infrastructure performance

- Number of data centres

- Average cost of data centres

LOOKING

Doing

What strategic results are we seeking to deliver?

As a result of your interactions with the business and the debate and discussions within your management team, you have begun to articulate your strategy for being a powerful and effective IT function.

The need now is to develop measures that support your strategic goals and drive the right behaviours in your people. It is no good creating measures which, for example, focus your people on cost control to the detriment of the delivery of responsiveness to the customer. I realize that there is always a balance to be struck, but often the need for a balance isn't even recognized.

So you need a range of measures that support the financial goals, but also the customer service aspirations of your strategy, as well your desire to build enhanced skills and capabilities, improved reliability, or the effective use of information, etc.

The Looking section of this chapter provided a number of examples of ways in which you can structure your measures, but equally examples of measures themselves. There is a danger that you use these in a sporadic way, selecting items because they appear to have a relevance to some of your strategic thrusts. Such an approach is insufficient and is likely to lead you to selecting too many measures that do not focus your team, nor reinforce the clarity of your strategy.

So how do you create measures that reflect your aspirations and which drive the right behaviour in your team?

Measuring success

Taking each of your main strategic themes for your strategy, you need to apply the following questions to them to arrive at appropriate measures:

☑ Why are we doing this?

- Start by asking yourself, `why are we pursuing this strategic theme, what are we hoping to achieve?'

- This is the critical question. Understanding why will frame the answer to all the other questions in this sequence.

- For example, if you were pursuing a strategic theme of delivering an increasingly adaptable service, you may want to do this because it 'increased your responsiveness and improved your reputation'.

☑ What levers can we pull to make this happen?

- It should now be possible for you to identify what you can do to bring this success about. This question is very much a check of the aspects you have built into your strategy. The answers you give here should already be in your strategy map, and if they are not then you need to explore why.

- For example, you may have decided that changing people's behaviour, and implementing a Service Oriented Architecture environment are the key levers to achieving the adaptability discussed in the example above.

☑ How will we know when we have arrived/what will success look like?

- Now you need to describe what success will look like. In other words, how will you know when you have achieved your goals – what will people be doing, how will people be behaving, what will have been delivered, how will the business have benefited, what will people be saying about you?

- At this stage you are not looking to create measures, simply to describe the tangible realization of your aspirations.

- Drawing on the same example again, success can be described as being recognized for being able to respond quicker than the business expects and positive feedback filtering through to the boardroom from the business.

☑ Therefore, what measures could we establish to measure this success?

- Having articulated the picture of success, you are now in a position to identify measures which will let you know that you have arrived.

DOING

- It may be that these measures will look very similar to what you have described in your picture of success. If there is a direct correlation between the two then you are very lucky.

- However for most businesses you will not be able to exactly replicate your description of success by way of performance measures; you will need to use surrogates.

- This will be because to create measures that exactly replicate your description will be either too expensive, too complex, or simply you just will not be able to gather the information you require.

- In conclusion of the example I have used throughout, perhaps the measures you would use would relate to 'response times' and 'feedback results from user surveys'.

☑ You now need to repeat this activity to each of the key themes relating to your strategy.

☑ Having done this you will need to look at all the measure areas that you have identified and put them through the following filter:

- Do they provide focus?

  – Measures need to be focused on your strategic objectives

  – Measures must create alignment with strategy to channel daily activities

  – Measures need to be meaningful to individuals throughout the organization

  – Measures need to be consistent throughout the organization

  – Measures need to provide a balance between financial and non-financial aspects of performance.

- Do they create clarity?

  – Measures need to provide accurate and credible results

  – They need to be clear and simple, supported by definitions and calculations that are understandable

- They need to be observable and countable

- More than six measures to each person can serve to create confusion

- Measures should not overlap.

• Will they drive action?

- Measures should give results that are actionable

- Measures need to be available on a timely basis so that they provide the opportunity for action to be taken

- Measures should help people to predict future outcomes

- Measures need to identify where improvement is needed

- There needs to be a balance between the cost and benefits of gathering and using the information.

As a result you should have a set of measures which align with the strategy, will drive up the performance of IT and will force people to take action based upon the information that the measures reveal about your performance.

You are now ready to deliver an aligned strategy to the business.

DOING

Section 3

Following, Enabling and Leading—what does this mean in practice?

7 Following

- Some general principles

- The specifics

- Other aspects

We understand the business and the strategy and we have a pretty good idea of what that will mean in terms of what we have to deliver. But how will the IT function operate, what does it need to be good at in order to be efficient, reliable and cost effective? Indeed, what does it meant to be a Follower?

Touching

So, what does it mean to be Following, Enabling and Leading? In this and the next two chapters I will explore and explain what you will be offering to the business in each of these areas of performance. I will also identify what you need to be doing and what you need to be skilled at to deliver consistently.

Naturally, the barriers between the three areas are blurred but each chapter will reflect the main thrust of the relevant approach to your role in the business:

Following

– Delivering consistently and reliably, managing the costs effectiveness and efficiency of IT systems.

Enabling

– Maximizing the performance of the business and delivering the business strategy.

Leading

– Understanding and introducing emerging technologies and approaches to the business in order to present the business with new strategic opportunities and direction.

As I explained in an earlier chapter, it is your choice whether you pursue a strategy of being an IT function that is either Following, Enabling, or Leading, but your options are influenced by your starting point (i.e. where are you now) and what is appropriate for your business. You do not arrive at any of these levels of performance by accident. But neither is it excusable for you to fail to perform at the minimum standard of being a Follower.

Unfortunately, many IT functions are failing to perform at even this basic level with consequent damage to their reputation, and lowering of the reputation of IT across the business community.

It is important to make it clear that Following can be a justifiable level in its own right and may well be appropriate in the circumstances of your business and trading environment. Having said this, I believe that in the vast majority of cases, just being a Follower is insufficient and will not deliver the value that is demanded by the business environment today, and neither does it fulfil the potential that a high value IT function can and should deliver.

So, what does it mean to be Following?

Following — some general principles

In your mind's eye, you need to envisage the pictures you have seen of highly automated and efficient car factories, and the operation of a Formula One or NASCAR pit lane and workshop.

In this sense, you should be able to picture efficiency, tightly controlled and managed processes, cleanliness, clearly identifiable roles and procedures, clear objectives, performance measuring and monitoring and on time delivery.

I ask you to picture car factories *and* the pit lane because they are very different in the way they operate, but it is likely that your IT function will need to encompass the operational procedures and approaches represented by both; one is about high-volume and low variety, and the other low-volume and high variety. For example, your helpdesk will be about the former, where staff will have to cope with high volumes, but where the range of issues covered will be quite repeatable and within a relatively narrow range. In contrast, your project office will deal with much lower volume of activities but will need to be able to handle much broader levels of variety of topics and issues.

In the same vein, it is easy to see some other key differences between the two types of operation:

The helpdesk – utilizes standardized procedures and processes, algorithms, dedicated software systems, requires less highly skilled staff, is about instant delivery to standard measures of performance, and demands the continuous availability of staff to answer phones.

The project office – highly skilled staff that are able to operate flexibly in response to a wide variety of demands, utilizing a mix of approaches, tools and thinking in order to find specific solutions to specific issues. In other words, this is professional service and project management rather than mass production.

I make this distinction in the opening section of this chapter because I need to make explicit the range of issues and services that you need to offer from within your IT function. In some ways, it is easier to operate a car factory, *or* a Grand Prix garage because you are focused on only one of these dimensions of operations management. But in the standard IT function, you have to be able to manage both, and most probably a mix of operations somewhere in between.

TOUCHING

However, regardless of the type of operation, you need to deliver on five core dimensions of performance:

Quality

– This is about conformance to the specification, whatever shape it may take, accuracy, speed, reliability, error rates, appearance, durability, customer perception, availability, timeliness, failure rates, etc.

Speed

– How quickly you can do things.

Dependability

– How reliable you are and your ability to consistently deliver on time.

Flexibility

– The degree to which you can adapt your service in terms of volume, project type and range, and speed.

Cost

– Managing the cost base of IT so that it can deliver within budget, and increasingly efficiently, and consistently.

Each of these dimensions are linked. For example:

– Higher quality increases speed and dependability at the same time as reducing costs.

– Forcing an increase in speed will pressure you to ensure that you are more dependable; greater dependability will improve organizational stability and again reduce costs.

– High levels of flexibility will enable you to cope with a crisis, make changes more quickly and improve response times. When combined, these attributes will enable you to reduce your costs of operating.

Equally they are linked in terms of the impact that they have on the business units with whom you work:

- Higher quality means higher performance and therefore higher levels of customer perception

- Faster delivery will lead to higher levels of customer satisfaction

- Dependability will improve your reputation

- Improved flexibility will mean that you can respond more quickly to the wide variety of demands made of you.

Hence, the point is that you need to be sufficiently skilled at operations management to be able to:

- Distinguish between the different types of operation for which you are responsible.

- Know how to manage them appropriately, deploying tools, systems and management styles that fit the circumstances.

Following – some specifics

Having explored the general principles of Following, what are the specific IT issues that you need to focus on? What do you need to be offering to the business to deliver a high level of performance in a way which delivers value to the business? And let's not forget that Following, when done well, can deliver massive amounts of value to the business through cost savings and by enabling the business itself to become faster, more flexible and more dependable.

In other words, what do you need to be doing that will make a difference?

An operational focus

Drawing from my car manufacturing analogy earlier in this chapter, you can certainly start by applying some of the core principles of lean and just-in-time manufacturing processes. This doesn't mean that you need to become a lean manufacturing facility (although in some circumstances this may be appropriate), but it does mean that there are applications which can be and should be applied to the IT function.

Lean and just-in-time manufacturing approaches seek to increase throughput efficiency, lower labour costs, reduce production times, minimize waste, and generally increase the speed of supply. All things that IT functions aspire to achieve. The underlying techniques encompass:

- Very effective planning and control mechanisms operating around principles of operational simplicity

- A focus on speed, quality and reliability

- Continuous problem solving and system development

- Preventative maintenance

- People involvement and autonomy

- Visibility of performance.

In turn, success in these areas demands a shift in the culture of the function to a situation where:

- Everyone has adopted a quality focus which is built upon meeting your customers (in your case the business units) requirements

- Team working dominates and is used to remove physical, procedural and systems based barriers to successful delivery

- Managers act as facilitators creating an environment in which people are enabled to perform

- Managers provide the resources and long-term support necessary to sustain a quality culture

- Staff are empowered to take ownership for processes and quality performance

- There is attention to detail and shared responsibility for the quality of what is produced

- Performance measures are visible and focus both on outputs as well as process and system improvement, costs, learning, the costs of failure, availability and reliability

- What you mean by 'quality' is clearly defined (covering areas such as reliability, durability, customer contact, recovery, and appearance)

- Backup systems and recovery processes are in place and tested

- Processes and systems are documented and controlled

- Processes and systems are subject to continuous improvement in order to seek higher levels of performance.

How might these philosophies and principles translate themselves into practice in an IT function?

- Simplification by building an IT organization where there is a common language, and well understood set of principles and architecture based on a common set of databases

- Fewer applications and data centres which are more integrated than now

- Applications that are more standardized and more easily modified to meet changing business needs

- Standardized desktops and help desks make support simpler and enable the IT function to respond more quickly to changing business needs and the demand for scalability

- A focus on workflow management and process systematization results in the ability to automate a wide range of processes resulting in improved productivity, speed and dependability of back-office processes

- Proven faith in existing systems facilitates more effective and faster integration of merger and acquisition targets

- Customer data is centralized and more readily available to the whole organization

- Updating and refreshing databases to ensure people are using the best information available and avoid collecting the same information again

- IT investment is focused on projects and activities that deliver higher value to the business

TOUCHING

– Tight contract control and monitoring of performance for hardware and services purchasing, and vendor and outsourcing relationships.

All these factors combine to reduce the overall cost of running the IT function, its applications, and its hardware and software.

However, to get these things in place, you are going to need to build the capabilities and processes that enable you to achieve these results. In this regard your focus needs to be on:

– developing the necessary skills and capabilities,

– improving productivity, and

– deploying technology and architecture.

Developing the necessary skills and capabilities

– You need to ensure that you have the skills and practices in your senior team that enables them to be effective performance managers and lead the implementation of lean manufacturing and process improvement. If they cannot do these things, it is very unlikely that you will realize the benefits of your investments.

– Linked to this is the need to have staff who have the know-how which enables them to improve the efficiency of operations.

– And those staff will need to have:

  – The necessary technical skills to cope with the increasing complexity of IT operations, infrastructure and architecture, and

  – The analytical skills necessary to turn the information in your databases into useful knowledge for the decision-making.

Improving productivity

– Having the knowledge which enables you to pull the operational levers which substantially impact on productivity:

  – Levers which reduce labour costs

- Levers which improve labour or asset utilization, or

- Levers which improve profits by helping the business to sell higher value products and services

- Able to identify and implement systems which permit customer issues to be fixed quickly by staff at the front line

- Understanding where and how process automation can be applied, and how workflow and authorization processes can be integrated

- Managing the business processes across functions and suppliers

- Creating an IT function that is skilled at employing technology to support growth, reduce costs and simplify systems

- Establishing service level agreements for the key processes. You do not need to spend time creating SLA's for the all processes, but focus on:

  - The critical processes and systems first,

  - Those which enhance your credibility in the business, and

  - Those which force people to improve performance in the IT function.

Deploying technology and architecture

- You will need to instigate the policies that govern the use of technology and the standards which apply to the architecture and processes

- Drive simplicity and flexibility throughout the function by the use of service oriented architecture, middleware, and centrally set standards (which are enforced)

- Utilize proven packaged software rather than indulge in customization – this challenges the 'build' approach to development and leans towards 'buy'

- Utilize `modular' applications wherever possible

- Invest in continuous maintenance and upgrading rather than relying on boom and bust investment approaches

- Implement standard infrastructure applications to deliver finance and human resource functions at a lower cost and with increased reliability

- Centralize key functions such as help desks, data centre and network management.

Following – other aspects

There are some other specific disciplines that you need to set in place if you are going become an effective and efficient Follower.

Investment decisions

Somehow, IT funding decisions have become like shopping lists; forever getting longer. In many companies IT investment decisions are taken without proper consideration of:

- The benefits that will accrue

- The implications for the IT function in terms of its ability to deliver, and

- The implications for the business in terms of its ability to absorb the consequent changes.

In an environment where directors and business units continually add large and small scale projects to the task list, IT is bound to fail because there is only a limited resource available. Therefore decisions have to be taken and priorities identified. And if you are going to become an effective Follower, it is your responsibility to lead the way and establish appropriate disciplines for the process of determining where funds and resources are invested.

Therefore, IT funding decisions must be made like other business cases; on the basis and value. This will demand:

- The preparation of much more thorough business cases,

- The ability in the boardroom to make judgements on IT issues and investments, and

- An increased focus on decisions based on the creation of value and achieving competitive advantage.

This demands that you establish the processes which force the board to make the difficult choices between competing projects:

- Establish a decision-making system and criteria.

- Get the directors using it and make it a habit. This must include both executive and non-executive directors. Often the latter fail to understand what is being spent on IT and why

- Ensure the directors make their decisions against the criteria you have agreed. It is clear that many directors consider IT investment appraisal unimportant. Not only do you have to get the new system operating, you also have to get it believed in

- Focus your IT resources on the projects which have been chosen

- Perform baseline measurements at the beginning of the project

- Design the project approach to influence the performance measures that the board has chosen

- Audit completed projects and assess performance in terms of cost, business value, and the development and implementation processes

- Understand the reasons for any shortfalls and identify what actions are necessary as a result

- Review the output of the audit process with your fellow directors against the agreed criteria

- Reassess the decision-making criteria.

In terms of establishing the criteria, they should incorporate both financial and non-financial targets. Chapter 6 provides more detail on determining a range of measures, but if IT is going to have the impact it desires at board level you will not be able to shy away from financial measures such as:

- Return on investment

- Payback

- Net present value

- Cost benefit analysis

- Delivery of identified critical success factors.

Additionally, the criteria should include an understanding of the implications of the resultant change on the organization and its ability to cope with the demands that will be placed upon it, e.g. training time, new behaviours and practices.

Establishing the principles of making investment decisions and managing and monitoring their outcomes are a core discipline which benefits IT in a number of ways:

- Firstly, it forces the board to be much more selective in its choice of projects, thus encouraging greater strategic awareness.

- It demands that board members take responsibility for supporting and arguing the case for the competing projects that they support. In this way, IT do not have to try to juggle priorities using limited information; the board makes its decision collectively on your behalf.

- The discipline forces the IT function to establish much more effective project management approaches.

You will find that adopting an approach such as this will cause you to focus on the delivery of short-term business results. Good.

- Apparent short-termism such as this may feel uncomfortable at first but will counteract the tendency to allow projects to drift and will also add to the credibility of IT within the business.

- You will find that you will exercise tighter management of your projects and delivery against milestones and deliverables.

– You may find that you will begin to develop and implement new systems in an incremental manner rather than adopting the big bang approach.

Ongoing IT costs and performance

The previous section tended to focus more on one-off costs and major projects. However, there remains the significant issue of the ongoing costs of running the IT function, which as you will know cause anguish amongst your fellow directors.

As mentioned above, Chapter 6 provides much greater detail on the development of appropriate performance measures. Given the focus here on efficiency and cost, it is appropriate to highlight some of those measures that could be used in this area in particular, including:

– Overall performance

  – IT spend as a percentage of turnover

  – IT spend per user

  – Number of applications

  – Average maintenance cost per application

  – Number of data centres

  – Average spend per data centre

  – Organizational productivity improvements

  – Organizational service performance (e.g. average call handling time, customer satisfaction, first call resolution, service quality, agent utilization, efficiency, activity levels).

– Staff costs

  – Number of IT staff per user

  – Number of support staff per user

  – Average salary costs.

TOUCHING

– System dependability

- Percentage uptime

- Percentages of services covered by service level agreements

- Performance against service level agreements

- Percentage of project milestones met

- Percentage of projects completed within budget.

In pursuit of becoming an effective Follower you may decide to make transparent the costs of running the core systems so that business managers can understand the implications of their decisions and use they make of systems in their day-to-day operations. This will mean that you have the opportunity to implement some form of transfer-charging of these costs (if you wish):

– On the one hand, transfer charging can be incredibly time-consuming and complex, but on the other, it can promote accountability and maximize visibility.

– My simple rule of thumb is that if you don't believe that people will change their patterns of spending on IT as a result of this increased visibility, don't bother.

You may consider benchmarking as an approach to establishing a more demanding environment. I have to admit that my preference is not for benchmarking, but for a year-on-year focus on improvement in performance. However, I recognize that in the early days your credibility may not be strong enough to enable you to withstand the pressure for some form of benchmarking activity. But resist if you can, because benchmarking could take a substantial amount of your resources at a time when you need to focus on delivery.

Project management

Much of the above demands strong project management skills and clearly this is a capability that needs establishing throughout the IT function.

IT projects are complex (there is uncertainty over cost, timescales and performance criteria. Alongside is the need to serve many masters, including; individual users, departments and teams, global business units, other functions, subsidiary companies, regulatory authorities, suppliers and the organization as a whole).

Alongside, there are a number of additional risks that serve to exacerbate the dangers:

- Lack of support from top management

- Poor fit with organizational needs and a failure to specify and agree objectives

- Failure to use the right project approach

- Poor project management skills and disciplines

- Poor communication

- A failure to involve users

- Poor project definition and inadequate resources

- Numerous changes to the project and system requirements

- New technologies which often present uncertainty over performance

- A failure to assess or understand the impact on people and their willingness to adopt the new systems and technology.

Given that these projects are often used by the business as windows on the performance of IT, it is imperative that you take steps to minimize the risks through strong project management approaches utilizing skilled project managers and project staff, and exercising robust project management disciplines.

Governance

IT governance is a topic demanding increased attention and most of you will be familiar with its principles. Equally you will realize how the focus of this chapter aligns tightly with concepts contained within most governance discussions. Therefore, I do not propose to describe the components of an IT governance system, and simply make the point that effective Following complements a governance 'system', and demands practices and approaches that become a way of thinking, acting and behaving.

Risk management

The nature of the IT, its business-wide pervasiveness, its use of new technologies, and the need for organizational-wide change programs means that IT is exposed to a wide range of risks, including:

- Technology risk: The dangers of choosing the wrong technology.

- Security risks: The dangers of breaching internal data protection rules or external legal requirements, as well as unwanted access to company systems.

- Business risks: The loss of proprietary information or the failure of systems that damage the company's competitive position, brand or financial performance.

Effective Followers need to be able to make these risks transparent in the organization and find ways to mitigate, accept or transfer them to others.

Outsourced and supplier relationships

This is no place to go into detail on establishing outsourced and vendor contracts; there are many people much better placed than I to comment. However in terms of becoming an effective Follower there are some issues that you need to bear in mind. In terms of outsourcing:

Strategic and capability issues

- What should you be outsourcing? Cutting costs may be attractive, but if this undermines your company's competitive abilities or your core capabilities, the medium and long-term costs will be much greater than the short-term savings that you may achieve

- Is your management up to the task of acting in the interface between the business and the outsourced provider?

- How important are the interactions between IT staff and those within the business? Simple operations that demand minimal interaction between people can be more readily outsourced, but more complex relationships demanding the solution of individual customer needs and the use of judgement are rarely suitable.

The nature of providers

- Are potential providers offering more than simply replicating what you do already? Can they deliver value in the areas of improvement of internal processes and year-on-year cost savings?

- Can outsourced providers be creative and responsive to the changing needs of your business?

- Do providers have the necessary knowledge of your business and industry and how it works?

- Managing change is a massive component of these arrangements, and what skills do the potential providers have to aid and ease the transition

Preparing for transition

- Undertake a detailed business case analysis to include current costs, systems transfer costs, and specify the potential benefits

- Ensure that you have systems in place to manage the change, the inherent risks and the delivery of the promised benefits

- Be wary of a big bang approach. Instead test and establish the model and the relationships that go alongside. Once happy, incremental roll-out can continue

- Identify the criteria and performance measures for the outsourced arrangements and establish metrics to measure service levels

- Communicate to everyone, and then communicate again.

In terms of vendor relationships

If you are going to succeed in the areas of being an effective Follower, you will need to put in place the relationships with your suppliers that will support and complement the approaches that you will be implementing within the IT function. This demands that:

- You don't just focus on cost as the key aspect of the relationship. Often an approach such as this destroys value or results in inconsistent and under resourced performance delivery by suppliers.

- Instead, focus on a smaller number of suppliers and get them to better understand your business and needs. In return, expect and demand that vendors respond by:

  - Bringing new knowledge and understanding to the issues that you face

  - Coping with the demands placed on you by the business.

- Ensure that major suppliers engage with key people at senior levels within the business so that they can understand evolving and developing business needs.

- When preparing contracts, ensure that you consider and cover issues such as pricing, information property rights, service delivery, business continuity, governance, dispute resolution and exit.

- Ensure that there is clarity regarding the respective roles of your staff and third party providers.

- Provide regular feedback to suppliers based on their performance against the agreed service levels and use these meetings to maintain an open dialogue to share information in both directions.

In closing

Being effective as a Follower demands discipline and focus, planning and control, and a sizeable shift in the mindset of your staff so that energy is driven towards quality, speed, dependability and flexibility so that you can deliver more reliably, faster and at a lower cost.

As anyone in the manufacturing sector will tell you, the shift demanded is substantial, and will not be realized overnight. However, the gains to be enjoyed in reputation and performance are substantial, particularly in an environment such as IT where such disciplines have not been previously considered, let alone applied.

Also, the disciplines are necessary because unless you can establish the reliability and hence reputation, it is unlikely that you will be able to make the transition to becoming an Enabler. And even if you try, it is unlikely that the business will let you do so, because you will not have the necessary credibility which offers the freedom to adopt the higher level role.

Looking

The challenge of Following and the demands it places on organizations to become more reliable, productive and cost-effective can be seen in a host of organizations.

The National Health Service

The NHS in the UK is undertaking an ambitious program to create electronic records for all its patients that will enable information to be available "whenever and wherever it is needed".

As a part of this £20 billion program, technology is being used to simplify work processes and systems:

• Choose and book – will allow 13 million outpatient appointments to be booked electronically

• Electronic prescribing – will mean that the 330 million prescriptions that are written each year can be transmitted from doctors direct to pharmacies

• Digital x-rays and scans – images will be exchanged electronically rather than physically

• Broadband – means that patient demographics can be accessed electronically from more than 9000 locations and that general practitioners can be paid directly and measure the quality of their care.

Continental

The German tire and braking system manufacturer Continental was a basket case some four years ago, sadly awaiting a takeover bid. Today though, it is performing at record profitability and expects continued substantial growth in earnings.

Continental has achieved this through the focused pursuit of three simple ideas; quality, low-cost production and innovation. They describe these elements as the basics that have to be continually improved just to play in the market.

In terms of quality, Continental operates in a marketplace where safety demands that not even one mistake is acceptable.

Low-cost production is a challenge to a company located in a country where wage differentials may mean that factories operate at a 10–15% price disadvantage. To compensate, Continental:

– has moved as much of the production as possible to low-cost countries,

– have won the agreement of German employees to a longer working week, and

– uses innovation and technology to reduce the volume of labour costs in the production processes.

Innovation is applied to product development processes where the company recognizes that skills and knowledge that they uniquely possessed today will be known by all their competitors in five years time.

Ahold

Ahold is a Dutch retail group that three years ago almost failed due to a €1 billion accounting scandal. However, when the new chief executive Anders Moberg was appointed in 2003 he was more concerned by the chaos in operations management. So Mr. Moberg set about the rebuilding the basics of the company which has sales of €52 billion and is about to complete a €650 million savings program.

Essentially, this was about re-engineering the value chain by changing processes, components and activities to lower the cost of good sold.

Wal-Mart

Wal-Mart is targeting even further reductions in levels of the stock it holds in its stores in order to reduce 'clutter', give a better return on capital, and to reduce the need to cut prices on old merchandise. It is estimated that the project could reduce annual inventory by approximately 18%, which would generate a $6 billion reduction in working capital.

They seek to achieve this through increasing the velocity by which goods move through its stores and undertaking a "return to basics by getting more disciplined". Inventory reduction will be linked to managers' incentives, and will be aided by the operation of a new distribution system that will speed the delivery to stores of 5000 high turnover items and the use RFID radio-frequency tagging.

All this In a company that was already regarded as one of the most efficient logistical operations in American retailing.

Toyota

The second largest car manufacturer in the world has recently announced that its UK factory has matched Japanese levels of productivity for the first time. At the same time, continuing and growing profitability at the factory contrast with the declining fortunes of other UK car manufacturers.

Their success is attributed to the ongoing and continuous focus on manufacturing techniques and processes. However, the UK plant still struggles with higher wages than the company's other European factories, and the cost of shipping components across the Channel adds $20 to each car. Accordingly, and whilst productivity levels may now match Japanese performance, focus will shift to other costs including logistics and component quality.

Stroud and Swindon

The Stroud and Swindon is a UK mortgage company. Over recent years it has focused on delivering operational efficiency in its core mortgage product range. Success has been driven out of establishing an optimal balance between the three components of technology, process and people.

From a low technology base some 18 years ago, they have moved to a point where technology facilitates:

- Straight through processing

- Automated links to third-party systems

– Front, middle and back-office integration

– Marketing database integration

– Telephone integration.

They have found that changes in regulation have made processes more complex to manage, despite their endeavours to use technology to simplify and speed processes.

As a result, they had described the management dilemma as being one where they have to seek and construct simplicity within a complex framework. At the same time have to make optimal use of internal resources, deliver the results customers want, and deliver a good customer experience. And they have to do all this profitably.

The alternative Ryder Cup

Whilst Europe may be able to beat America in the biannual Ryder Cup golf competition, it has been no match for America in terms of productivity growth over the last decade.

Research by the Centre for Economic Performance at the London School of Economics has shown that the massive difference in output (up to 40%) between US owned plants in Britain and their British contemporaries, can be attributed to three main factors:

– More aggressive human resource management in terms of the quicker promotion of top performers and the quicker removal of underperformers.

– The greater use of technology.

– The ability of US companies to derive higher return from their investments in IT by devolving responsibility to managing IT to local plants rather than by centralizing.

The message is clear, productivity can be improved both by the use of technology and the management practices that support it.

Doing

'Following' demands an ability to deliver consistently and reliably, while managing the costs and the efficiency and effectiveness of your IT systems. To succeed, you need to apply a number of principles and disciplines to the operation of your IT function, many of which build upon the concepts of lean and just-in-time manufacturing. It may not be appropriate to apply a full lean manufacturing approach, but the core lessons will be very applicable to creating an IT function that becomes an effective Follower.

☑ Team selection

- Select a team representing a mix of departments within the IT function. Draw on all levels in the hierarchy and a wide range of experience.

- If you have anybody who has previously worked in a lean environment, try to get them involved.

☑ Introduction to lean manufacturing

- Initially, the idea of lean manufacturing will be very unfamiliar to people working in the IT function and it is likely that they may not have experienced the disciplines that are involved.

- Therefore, some exposure is necessary as your first step. This will demand visiting manufacturers and service companies that have adopted lean manufacturing approaches to see how it works in practice. The experience will not only provide visible stimulation, but also the opportunity to understand the cultural changes that are necessary to support the practical steps involved.

☑ Team building and training in principles of implementing lean manufacturing

- These visits can be complemented by 'mock-up' activities which can be facilitated by specialist consultants to help the team to start to explore the underlying principles, and the possible benefits and issues.

☑ Team-based project planning

- With the benefit of an understanding of the principles involved, the team can start to plan its approach towards applying the approaches within the IT function.

- As noted above, this may or may not involve the full application of lean management principles, and therefore the scope and depth of the project needs to be carefully identified at this stage so that focus is given to the steps necessary to deliver the returns required.

- In the first instance, it would be best to apply these types of approaches to a single area of operation which experiences high volumes and a relatively narrow range of activities.

- Once the principles are understood and the value of their application appreciated, roll-out can be continued in other parts of the function.

☑ Process mapping of all key processes

- The team needs to gather base information on current performance factors such as the lead times for key processes and the resources used on those processes.

- Gathering this information will enable the team to start to identify value adding and non-value-adding activities.

- Plan a future state and generate an action list that will deliver results, and eliminate waste in the system. Other approaches that could be adopted in order to identify system improvements will include Statistical Process Control (SPC), de-bottlenecking.

☑ Implementation

- Elimination of the identified non-value-adding activities.

- Workplace organization to reduce waste and cost by implementing visual controls to organize the workplace, sending clear/simple signals to employees, and increasing work flow, quality and safety.

- Visual reporting of performance.

- Preventive maintenance to maintain equipment and systems at peak productivity.

- Increase equipment effectiveness and avoid production interruptions.

- Application of capacity management principles and the deployment of self-managed teams.

But, the selective application of lean management will not be sufficient on its own. You need to be deploying complementary approaches to the management of the function.

☑ Developing the necessary skills and capabilities

- Improving the performance management skills of your managers.

- Establishing the controls and management processes necessary for increasingly complex IT operations.

- Developing the necessary skills in your staff to enable them to operate in a high quality environment.

☑ Improving productivity

- Creating a mindset which seeks out and applies simple ways of doing things.

- Facilitating teams to solve problems first time for the customer.

- Implementing service level agreements for the key processes and activities.

☑ Deploying technology and architecture

- Establishing and implementing common standards and policies.

- Implementing infrastructure applications that are shared across the business.

- Building a highly robust and flexible infrastructure.

☑ Making investment decisions

- Implementing board level criteria and processes for making, monitoring and reviewing investment decisions.

- Focusing energies on the delivery of short-term business results.

☑ Managing ongoing costs

- Identify key performance measurement areas.

- Establish a culture focused on year-on-year improvement in each of these areas.

☑ Project management

- Develop the project management skills of your managers and staff.

- Implement strong project management disciplines.

☑ Managing third party relationships

- Decide what you should be doing in-house, and what should be done by third parties.

- Select providers who can add value to your business.

- Tightly control contracting arrangements.

- Open up communication and feedback channels.

- Establish and monitor performance levels.

8 Enabling

- A context

- What does it mean?

- Making it happen

The concept of Enabling is central to this book and many of the principles are reinforced elsewhere. But what does it mean in terms of structure, management systems and technology or the application of knowledge? What capabilities will you need and how can you establish the agility and flexibility that will enable you to cope in disruptive environments?

Touching

Enabling – a context

A recent global survey of CIO's revealed that they expected spending on IT to increase and that their capital spending will be focused on:

– Upgrading hardware

– Optimizing systems

– Improving security and reliability.

Other surveys reveal that it is not unusual for CIOs to handle in excess of 100 projects a year with values in excess of $1 million each, and several thousand smaller requests for system fixes and minor improvements.

Depending on whose reports you read, between 80% and 90% of the typical IT budget is spent on running the existing IT operations. And yet, surveys of CEOs reveal other priorities.

When asked which single factor contributes the most to the pace of change in the world today, they tell us (*McKinsey Quarterly Global Survey of Business Executives*):

– Innovation in products, services and business models

– Access to information

– Rate of change in technology

And when asked what makes the world more competitive, they say:

– The improving capability of competitors in the areas of knowledge and talent

What will have the most impact on the profitability of your company?

– Greater ease of obtaining information and developing knowledge

Other surveys (CIO Connect/SAS Census) reveal that CIOs believe the biggest business challenges are:

– Substantial internal reorganization

– Ensuring customer loyalty

– Coping with downward pressure on prices

In the same survey, CIOs believe that organizations gain the most value from IT by way of:

– Improved business processes

– Providing key financial and management information to those who need it.

Enabling – what does it mean?

So, if this is what CEOs describe as the pressure points and CIOs can so clearly articulate the need to undertake projects that add substantial value to the performance of the business, why do we spend so much of our time and our limited funding on legacy systems, upgrading hardware and improving security and reliability?

Regrettably we do, and this is the starting point from which we have to build; too much time and too much money is being spent on legacy systems and system maintenance.

This presents a massive challenge; not only to make the shift, but also to develop the skills and ways of operating that enable that shift to be sustained in fluid and dynamic environments.

What this means is that not only have we got to deliver the challenges discussed in Chapter 7 (Following), but we have to be able to do them quicker and for a lower cost. In other words how do we find the time and capability to be more strategic?

In Chapter 6 I introduced the following lifecycle model.

As you will recall, I proposed that products, IT projects and systems, progress through a cycle from being Pioneering through to being Support Mechanisms that improve productivity as shown in Figure 1 overleaf.

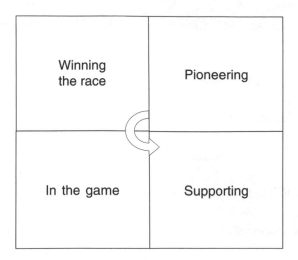

Figure 1: The IT lifecycle

The challenge for us in respect of this chapter is to question whether our energies are suitably directed into each of these four zones. If, for example, 80% of your time is spent on being 'In the Game' and 'Supporting', you have to ask yourself whether this is appropriate and consider how you will reduce this so that more time is available to be invested in 'Winning the Race' and 'Pioneering'.

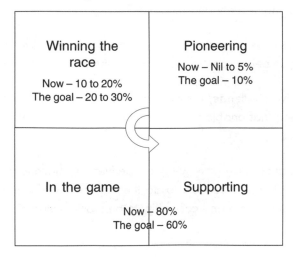

Figure 2: The IT lifecycle – allocating resources

Indeed, if we are going to Enable (maximizing the performance of the business and delivering the business strategy), then the challenge has to be to create an IT function where no more than 60% of our time is spent on legacy and maintenance (Following), and something like 20 to 30% is spent on Enabling, with the balance invested in Leading.

We therefore have to ask ourselves what are you going to do about it, and how are you going to bring about the shift?

For you

This is about the focus you bring to your own personal role. It is about:

- Dropping many of your operationally related activities

- Spending more time working with business unit leaders

- Concentrating on finding the technologies that will allow your business to achieve its goals faster than could otherwise be achieved

- Spending more time on effective strategic planning and strategic implementation.

For your team

At the level of it for your IT team this means that you take staff away from the legacy and maintenance roles and refocus them in the business analyst and relationship management roles (see Chapter 11). Without doubt, this will present a challenge to the skills and resourcefulness of your management team as they too will need to refocus their energies and activities and run the function in a different way.

For business leaders

Equally though it is about changing the role of business leaders so that they take fuller responsibility and accountability for the delivery of value creating IT projects.

In Chapter 7, I introduced some ideas around establishing a mechanism for investment appraisal and prioritization for IT projects. This included:

- Establish a decision-making system and criteria and get directors using it.

- Ensure the directors make their decisions against the criteria you have agreed.

- Focus your IT resources on the projects which have been chosen and design the project approach to influence the results targeted by the board.

- Understand the reasons for any shortfalls in performance.

In many ways, this list echoes the tenor of that 'Following' chapter. However, if you are going to be an Enabling function, then your challenge is greater. You need to get business executives to take responsibility for the delivery of the investment decisions that they take. In other words, they lead because they have the responsibility for business performance and the primary role of bringing all the components (including IT systems) together so that they deliver the targeted results.

The results of Enabling

So what does this shift in focus mean to the function as a whole? When you make that move to being an Enabler (from being a Follower) and refocus your function's energies and resources what will be the outcome?

- Fundamentally, you will gain the credibility to influence the direction of the business and the role of IT; you will be in control of your destiny

- You and your fellow business leaders will have a shared view of the value that IT is delivering today and the additional value it can bring in the future.

- You and your fellow business leaders will have a detailed understanding of the costs of running and managing the IT infrastructure and systems. You will also have visibility of how the demand for IT resources impacts on those costs. This awareness is not simply a 'nice to have' but it allows the executive team to make soundly based financial decisions.

- There will be an IT awareness and literacy amongst business executives and senior management which allows them to actively and constructively participate in the investment decision-making and implementation processes.

- Senior executives consistently make business focused IT investment decisions based on detailed understanding and analysis of the strategic and financial benefits that will be delivered.

- Supporting the decision-making is a mechanism and system of business case assessment which is applied throughout the project leading to monitoring of the delivery of the planned benefits.

- Responsibility for delivery of those projects and the planned benefits is shared across the business, and therefore business executives and their staff are deeply involved in implementation.

- IT and senior executives are regularly exploring the potential to use new technology to improve business processes.

- The resources of IT are focused on work that delivers the greatest business value.

- The speed by which new innovations and products are brought to market is substantially increased.

You will gather from this list, that Enabling is not just about the way the IT function operates in isolation. It is also about the IT function building a culture of IT literacy and accountability across the business so that there is a shared recognition of the value that IT can create, and a shared desire to realize that potential.

Enabling – making it happen

How do you bring these changes into being? What are the main things that you need to put in place so that you will become an Enabling function?

Firstly, you can go nowhere unless Following is working well; both to win the credibility that is needed to allow you to embark on Enabling, but also so that there is the opportunity to transfer resources from managing and maintaining legacy systems into 'Winning the Game'. But what else do you need to be doing? Figure 3 provides some headlines to focus on, and the following sections go into more detail.

Structure and roles

Within your IT function you will have to identify whether you need to implement a structure that will support and reinforce your goal of creating more time for Enabling. This may mean centralizing the units which focus on core systems and processes (Following), and putting the relationship managers (or business analysts) and project teams closer to or within business units so that they have the necessary proximity to work with the business implementation teams.

In order to protect them from 'going native' and ending up with a series of decentralized IT functions, the relationship managers should still report directly into the IT function, but with responsibility to business executives.

By keeping them within the IT function, you can:

– Maintain strategic alignment

– Utilize the resources flexibly across the organization, to maintain flexibility and fluidity, both of role and mindset.

– Ensure that there is sharing of knowledge.

– Coordinate and prioritize activities and projects.

– Better predict and manage the future demand for IT resources and skills.

You also need to build business focused relationships across the business; you at board level and your relationship managers everywhere else (see Chapter 11). These relationships will both:

– Focus on understanding the needs of and challenges within the business.

– Provide the conduit through which you can inform and explore with business leaders the implications of emerging technologies, competitor activities and changing patterns of behaviour amongst your customers.

Managing system and technology lifecycles

Earlier, I used the project lifecycle model to question the allocation and utilization of IT's limited resources and to make investment decisions. The same model can be used in other ways.

At the systems level, its application allows you identify the appropriate management and governance approaches. Firstly, you need to identify which of your systems fit in the four stages of the lifecycle.

In this example of a supermarket, you will see how the different systems mature with time. Once upon a time, automated payroll and accounting (now in Supporting) was a Pioneering system. Later they provided the opportunity to Win the Race by helping the owner of such systems to become a cost leader. Now these systems have fallen away to simply being Support systems offering no competitive edge at all. In the same way, systems that help the supermarket Win the Race today (e.g. by way of facilitating cross-border integration) will

Winning the race Delivery of systems critical for future success; e.g. cross border integration on-line sales, in-store technology & service delivery	Pioneering Exploration of emerging technologies; e.g. technology to support environmental strategies and triggering customers' buying behaviour
In the game Operation of core business processes; e.g. logistics, customer databases, management information systems	Supporting Shared services, back office functions; e.g. payroll, accounting, stock control

Figure 3: The IT lifecycle – identifying systems and technology

one day move to becoming commodity systems, simply allowing the business to be In the Game.

Therefore, you need to:

– Allocate all your systems and technology to each of the four zones so that you can see where your current investments are focused.

– This analysis will offer you the opportunity to examine whether this is an appropriate spread and whether you need to make a strategic decision over the future format of your portfolio. This should be undertaken in conjunction with the business executives and be framed in the context of the business strategy.

– As a result, you will have agreement with the business on the future shape of the IT architecture and a joint understanding of the potential value of IT. And as you will see below you will have a vehicle for determining the appropriate management approach for each system.

– You must maintain this model as a live system. As systems and technologies decay in terms of their ability to help you to Pioneer or Win the Race, they must be reallocated to the next stage of the cycle so that they are subject to the appropriate management and resource investment.

TOUCHING

Winning the race Fast implementation, delivery of critical success factors, commercialization, competitive environment scanning, building new capabilities	Pioneering Innovation and creativity, organizational agility, scanning emerging technologies
In the game Ensuring reliability & efficiency, improving performance, BPR, maximizing integration & simplicity, system rationalization, operational excellence	Supporting Productivity, driving down transaction costs, reducing levels of working capital, operational excellence, standardization

Figure 4: The IT lifecycle – identifying management styles

However, to fully benefit from this allocation of your systems and resources, you also need apply different management and governance approaches to each stage of the cycle.

This version of the lifecycle summarizes the key management focus that should be adopted at each stage. Thus, during the stages of:

– Pioneering: Approaches and cultures conducive to stimulating creativity and innovation will be the key features of the management style within IT. Outside of the IT function, the focus will shift to energizing executives to explore technology opportunities. Outside of the organization you will seek relationships with 'pioneering' partners and companies in order to bring and external stimulus to your thinking and planning.

– Winning the Race: Management focus shifts to working closely with business managers, rapid project delivery and focus on realizing commercial and competitive benefits. As a result, change management skills will be in high demand and you are likely to see a higher degree of centrally planned and managed approaches.

– In the Game: Operational efficiency and process management will dominate, complemented by effective performance management. It is likely that you will also focus on the coordination of approaches across functions and business units.

– Supporting: Operational efficiency and process management will again dominate with managers looking to leverage economies of scale and establish common systems across all business units. The creation and management of outsourced contracts will also feature strongly.

However, it will be clear that whilst the IT function can attempt to operate in these different ways in different parts of the function, the CIO certainly cannot do all these roles at once, particularly as each demands different skills. Therefore you have to face reality:

– As a function, what will be your dominant zone and dominant (but not exclusive) managerial approach?

– As a CIO or team manager, what will be your dominant role and approach? How do you need to develop to be able to fulfil the role?

– As a CEO choosing a new CIO, what type of CIO do you need and what management skills and experience will this demand?

In each case the choice will be led by asking what is most appropriate for your business. In turn, this also means that a relationship manager must adopt the role that is most appropriate to the business unit that they are focused on serving.

Complementing this is the need to ensure that the basis of investment decisions similarly reflects the stage of the lifecycle being considered. In the version of the lifecycle shown below, the different approaches to financial decision-making are clearly identified.

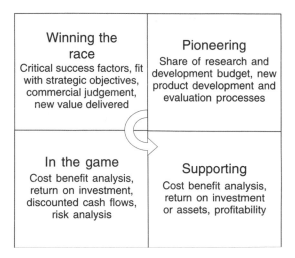

Figure 5: The IT lifecycle – investment criteria

TOUCHING

Primarily, Enabling is about Winning the Race. Therefore, when considering investments in systems and technology that support your aim of Winning the Race, decision-making will be strategically aligned and your assessment will be based on the ability of the investment to deliver results in terms of your strategic critical success factors or the ability of a new system to restructure completely the value delivered by you in the marketplace.

By contrast, in the Supporting stage where productivity is the focus, then an investment will only be worthwhile if the costs can be recouped in a short period of time and hence simple tools such as cost benefit analysis and return on investment are appropriate.

These decision-making principles need to operate within the decision-making *processes* I discussed in Chapters 6 and 7. They should also be extended to cover project planning and delivery, and staff incentives (covering their goals, measures and rewards) for both business and IT staff. As a result, you will benefit from a shared understanding in the business and IT of what is required and a shared desire and motivation to make it happen.

To complement these financial disciplines you need to implement strong reporting and communication processes which keep you and the business informed on your performance against key metrics in relation to both Following and Enabling, as well as project delivery.

As a result of this focus, you will start to 'maximize the performance of the business and deliver the business strategy' – in other words you will be showing signs of becoming and Enabling IT function.

Building the right IT capabilities

In order for the demands of Enabling to be delivered, IT needs to possess the appropriate capabilities. There are five main specific areas in which your function needs to be highly capable:

- Knowledge: Your company will possess untold amounts of data on customers, processes, products and performance, and you need to be able to manage and manipulate this and make it readily available for executives and management for decision-making purposes, when and how they want it.

- Communicating: In today's marketplace and in today's organizations you need to be able to facilitate very effectively the communication links between the company and its customers, and between individuals within the organization. This demands skills in the areas of networks, video and voice as well as EDI, email and Internet.

- Distribution: Your business will reach, sell and distribute to customers through a wide variety of virtual and physical outlets. Supporting these channels is one issue, but the real challenge is integrating them so that they appear seamless from the customer's perspective, and internally they need to provide a single picture of the customer's relationship with the business.

- Literacy: It should also be clear to you that IT literacy across the business will be demanded if you are going to be successful. Hence the IT team must be capable of educating the business in the use and potential of technology, knowledge and systems.

Managing knowledge

It is evident from the above (and indeed from the rest of this book) that the ability to manage knowledge is the core skill of the IT function in the Enabling stage, and therefore the topic is worth a little extra consideration before we press on.

If IT is going to be successful in maximizing the use of knowledge and information within the business, you need to take a lead. This means that you need to provide systems that facilitate its application for improved performance across the business. This demands that when creating knowledge management systems, you ensure that there is clarity over:

- The business objectives for the use of the information and in particular the links to the company strategic goals and critical success factors.

- What information people need and why.

- The decisions that will be taken as a result of the availability and use of the information and the likely actions that will flow from the decisions.

- Who will be using it and where.

- The current nature of users and the changes required in behaviour and activities as a result.

- The location of the data (which may be within multiple databases) and the point of delivery (in other words, where will it be received?).

With the benefit of this analysis, you should be able to present the business with:

- Alternative options both in terms of systems and technology and likely impact on users.

TOUCHING

– Technical feasibility.

– Implementation issues in terms of speed, technology, and people and organizational behaviour.

In many ways, the above is quite a procedural approach to knowledge management and yet success in the Enabling stage is much more than process; it is about the impact IT has on the business so that more is achieved strategically than could ever be realized without their knowledge and skills. This means that IT needs to have the resources to analyse the issues and present solutions that not only provide an immediate technological answer, but also drive sustained improvements in performance and organizational culture. Specifically, in terms of knowledge this will mean that IT will take responsibility for making the organization more effective in the following areas (Marchand *et al.*, 2000):

– Sensing: Ensuring that information is proactively sought about the environment in which the business operates so that the business is better able to anticipate changing environmental conditions and the need for new products and services.

– Collecting: Enabling the organization to collect accurate and complete information without overloading systems and people with too much knowledge.

– Organizing: Shaping and classifying the information so that it is accessible and is in a suitable format for analysis and decision-making.

– Educating: Ensuring that staff within the business have the analytical skills and behaviours necessary to turn information into knowledge on which decisions can be made.

– Transparency: Ensuring that knowledge is shared openly and freely, without political manipulation for personal gain with the result that information is trusted.

Being agile and flexible

A common theme throughout this book has been the need for the organization and the IT function to have the ability to operate in an uncertain environment where planning cycles are shorter, the likelihood of disruptive technologies and business models have increased, and consumer behaviour is much less predictable.

As a result, the need for increased agility has multiplied, and IT has a key role in enabling the business to respond at speed. As ever, if IT is going to have the necessary impact, this role stretches from managing technology through to organizational behaviour.

Regrettably, the starting point in many businesses is that your technology and business pro cesses will be hardwired, particularly in respect of enterprise wide ERP systems which make it difficult to introduce new products or services at the speed necessary to compete.

In their book 'The Only Sustainable Edge: Why Business Strategy Depends on Productive Friction and Dynamic Specialization', John Hagel and John Seely Brown (2005) described the concept of "loose coupling" which results in organizations being able to innovate and improvise much more quickly both within and across enterprises.

They particularly focus on:

– The use of the Service Oriented Architecture (SOA) to overcome the constraints of ERP.

– The concept of the modularity, where activities are grouped into separate modules which can be operated independently or easily combined with other modules to find new solutions.

– Global process networks that can mobilize and integrate large numbers of highly special-ized partners: e.g. the Cisco model. This not only demands the use of modules, but also standardized capabilities, performance requirements, vocabulary and interfaces so that the modules can be bolted together quickly and easily.

– The need for trust, and the formation of long-term relationships amongst players in the network; both in the organization itself and amongst partners.

However, the need for agility also demands that the management team and the organiz-ation employs responsive and flexible people, who operate within an entrepreneurial culture that permits them to identify the challenges, find solutions quickly and deliver the necessary change in the business.

Therefore, to succeed in creating an organization and IT system that is suitably agile, you also have to focus on developing the skills and culture so that you become more resourceful, proactive and opportunistic.

TOUCHING

In closing

To me, Enabling is at the heart of this book and is principally about three points:

– Putting in place the technology and systems that facilitate success.

– Managing behaviours, mindsets and skills within the business so that executives and managers can take advantage of the technology and information that is available to them.

– In turn, this means that IT leaders have to be highly skilled at managing changes in hardware, systems and processes, and also changes in behaviours and mindsets.

Frankly, too few IT leaders possess these capabilities at a high enough level. Do you?

TOUCHING

Looking

If you become an IT function that is Enabling, what will be the benefits for your organization? In the next few pages, I would like to look at some examples of companies that are using IT to enable them to deliver their business strategies.

Maximizing business performance

BAA Plc

BAA, the company that runs seven of the UK's airports worked with the C&C Technology (www.cctechnology.co.uk) to develop its desktop infrastructure for 10,000 users in 12 locations to improve individual performance, mitigate security risks and facilitate increased levels of flexible working by staff.

As ever, the program combined components of Following as well as Enabling. The massive reduction in the number of applications in the company (from 3000 to 400), simplified and reduced the cost of managing and maintaining the IT systems (Following), but more importantly, the focus on Enabling meant that:

– Information is shared more freely, yet within a more secure environment.

– The needs of users for remote working and flexible working practices can be supported.

– New applications and technologies can be exploited and implemented with minimum disruption to the business.

Successful implementation was assisted by way of a substantial program of communications with business users before, during and after the project, which not only gave the project team the necessary proximity to users' needs, but also encouraged and developed staff IT literacy and skills.

A capability steering group now focuses on utilizing the new infrastructure to leverage improvement in business processes, customer service and staff performance.

LOOKING

Philips

The Dutch electronics business Philips is a diverse company incorporating a range of businesses encompassing lighting, small electrical appliances, medical equipment, semiconductors and consumer electronics. The approach the company has taken to the supply chain echoes the challenges we face in IT. They have sought a structure that keeps them close to the business, improves the speed of delivery, yet which allows them to take advantage of shared knowledge, deliver economies of scale and prioritize strategic imperatives.

In the case of Philips, this challenge is being faced in the purchasing function and the company's first Chief Procurement Officer, Barbara Kux, has adopted an approach which balances these often conflicting issues.

There is a Central Purchasing Officer in each of the five business units who has responsibility for purchasing in that business unit and also for enterprise-wide procurement of a specific range of components. For example, the Central Purchasing Officer in consumer electronics buys all the group's plastics. Alongside, the Central Purchasing Officers have staff located around the business who work closely with line managers to gather information on future demand and requirements. This information is fed back to the appropriate Central Purchasing Officer, who undertakes negotiations with suppliers on behalf of the group.

This approach has reduced the number of suppliers to Philips from about 50,000 to 30,000, group wide purchases now represent over 50% of the total spend (from 6%) and procurement and savings are running between 12% and 16%.

Further work is being undertaken with 30 key suppliers who will become partners to the business; being involved earlier in innovation, identifying value-added services and finding new solutions.

The similarities of this approach to the challenges that we face in IT provide us with clear examples of the ways in which we can operate in the future in order to Enable business success.

AES

AES recently won the UK's Institute of Mechanical Engineers Award for Manufacturing Excellence, and like Philips it provides us with a clear picture of how we can run IT in the future.

AES, like many manufacturers around the developed world, has to compete with the threat of low-cost Chinese production. It could do this (possibly, but not probably) by seeking to compete on cost and therefore relying on a 'Follower' approach, whereby efficiency, reliability and cost reduction dominate.

In reality, they are not likely to succeed and neither are other manufacturers operating in the high cost regions of Europe, North America and Japan.

Instead, AES has decided to invest in the 'service' element of their product offering, which according to its chairman Chris Rea, often accounts for up to a quarter of the price of a product, and which now involves nearly half of the company's staff.

AES manufactures engineering seals which are mechanical devices used on rotating machines to stop fluids leaking. They manufacture in the UK and sell globally. AES and companies like them use a number of core approaches by which to defend themselves from low-cost producers:

– Consulting services – working with the buyer to specify and design the precise product that the customer needs.

– Maintenance support – maintaining the product once is it is installed and operating.

– Deploying technology – using technology in new ways to speed the design and delivery of new products.

In the case of AES and companies like them, information and specialist skills could easily play second fiddle to the product, and yet they are completely complementary. In IT, information and specialist skills could play second fiddle to technology, and often does. If you are going to Enable, then your use of information and the development of specialist skills need to be developed to match those of manufacturers like AES.

Indeed, AES have to apply their relationship role with customers who reside outside of the organization; at least your customers are within the organization which should in some ways simplify the task in front of you. The question is whether you are willing to perform at a level that matches the world's leading manufacturers?

Government and public sector technology investment

Whilst Philips and AES provide us with strong role models of how we can operate, a recent report by Alexandra Jones and Laura Williams on behalf of The Work Foundation

(*Public Services and ICT. Why ICT? The role of ICT in Public Services*) reveals a propensity among public-sector IT project managers to be too ambitious by trying to solve too many problems at once and being dazzled by the potential of technology. The authors make clear that the public sector "should not be about cutting edge innovation. If someone gets their pension or benefits late due to computer failure, it matters in a way that simply doesn't when private sector ICT projects fail. The private sector can afford luxuries of innovating: in the public sector, ICT needs to work. "

The report highlights that too often managers overcomplicate matters and reinvent the wheel. They also suffer from scope creep and too little advice is taken from staff that will use the system. Alongside projects struggle to make the necessary people and process changes to make them effective.

Whilst the report focuses on the public sector, the lessons for all of us in IT are clear.

IBM

In June 2006 Samuel Palmisano (2006) the Chairman and Chief Executive of IBM wrote an article in the *Financial Times* reflecting on the nature of the multinational or global corporation.

His contention was that thinking about an organization as "multinational" is wrong and that it is now necessary to consider organizations of this type as "the globally integrated enterprise".

He describes the new organization as one which "fashions its strategy, management and operations to integrate production – and deliver value to clients – worldwide. That has been made possible by shared technologies and business standards, built on top of the global information technology and communications infrastructure. Because new technology and business models are allowing companies to treat their functions and operations as component pieces, companies can pull those pieces apart and put them back together in new combinations, based on judgments about which operations the company wants to excel at and which are best suited to its partners."

"Rather, they are about actively managing different operations, expertise and capabilities to open the enterprise up in multiple ways, allowing it to connect more intimately with partners, suppliers and customers and, most importantly, enabling it to engage in multifaceted, collaborative innovation".

"But shifting to the model of globally integrated enterprises also presents big challenges to the leaders in every sector of society. Let me mention two.

First, skills… the single most important arena will be securing the supply of high value skills. As a minimum, nations and companies must invest in educational and training programs, if they hope to keep up.

The second, trust… a company's standards of governance, transparency, privacy, security and quality need to be maintained even when products and operations are handled by a dozen organizations in as many countries. This will mean significant changes in organizational culture."

Need I say more?

Integrating physical and virtual worlds

Burger King

Burger King, the second biggest hamburger chain in America has started a marketing campaign on MySpace.com. Whilst Burger King's decision and investment is one of the largest to date in the social network community, it follows earlier steps by companies such as Pepsi and Toyota, all of whom need ways to reach younger consumers who are proving harder to reach because they watch less television.

In some ways, this is simply a marketing and promotional activity and you may wonder why I bother mentioning it in a book on IT. Quite simply, because it reflects the need for organizations to understand both the technologies that underpin emerging web-based channels, but also to be close to the behaviour of users so that opportunities can be grasped at a speed necessary to keep up with the market place. In this regard, IT has a role to both keep the business informed on the technology developments, but also help to facilitate the culture that can cope with the pace of change that is inherent in modern markets.

For example, MySpace.com is being challenged hard by YouTube.Com and BeBo.com. Very shortly after the announcement of the Burger King deal, there was already talking amongst young consumers that MySpace.com was no longer 'the cool place to be', driving a shift in allegiances to the other players in the market place.

How will this impact upon the investment made by Burger King and the returns it achieves? Can they keep up? More importantly, can your business keep up?

Marks & Spencer

Currently, Marks & Spencer the UK retailer, has Internet sales which represent a tiny proportion of Marks & Spencer's total turnover. In an attempt to turn the online channel into a strong contributor, Marks & Spencer's is planning to set up Internet points in-store so that customers can place an order for the item that they want and it will be delivered to them.

There is nothing particularly unusual or innovative in what Marks & Spencer are doing. It does, however, reflect the growing trend for multi-channel retailing:

Argos

Customers of Argos, the UK catalogue retailer, can identify a product in their catalogue, order it online and then pop down to their local store to collect it. 25% growth in Argos Direct in three months and the fact that two thirds of people who book goods on the Internet want to pick them up in store, tell Argos that this is a substantial area of growth and that the multi-channel approach fits very neatly with their customers' needs.

Tesco's

Tesco's is already the UK's largest food retailer, is about to be the UK's largest non-food retailer, and is the UK's fourth biggest online retailer. Online sales feature as a strong element of its aggressive growth plans, but they always complement their physical store activities and in this way the divide between offline and online worlds are beginning to blur.

– Tesco's is planning to start selling large non-food items such as electrical goods, fridges and sofas online as a part of its determined push into non-food goods. This will be complemented by the launch of a non-food catalogue.

– The Tesco.com store in Croydon, South London only processes online food orders.

– It is likely that Tesco's clothing range will be soon available online after a trial in 2006 of its 'Back-to-School' clothing range.

– Tesco.com delivered almost £1 billion of grocery sales in 2005 to go alongside the £20 billion of grocery sales through its stores.

LOOKING

The common issue in all of these examples is neither about the Internet, nor the differences or overlaps between online and offline. Centrally, the common issue is about the ability of your IT function to enable your business to have more impact, more quickly.

LOOKING

Doing

The big issues detailed in this chapter demand that you:

☑ Shift the focus and activities of the IT function away from maintenance and legacy systems into 'Winning the Race'.

☑ Review the structure and roles of the IT team.

☑ Actively manage the lifecycle of technology and systems.

☑ Build the organizational capabilities of knowledge management, communication, distribution and IT literacy.

☑ Become agile and flexible.

☑ Drive behavioural as well as system and technology change.

However, because this chapter is so central to everything we discussed, I believe it appropriate to stop at this juncture and assess how you are currently doing as an IT function

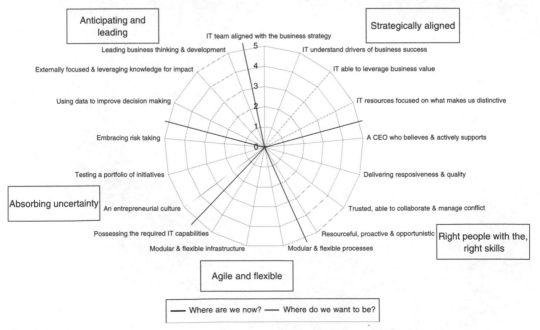

Figure 6: Your strategy – do you have what it takes to deliver?

in creating an organization that can indeed deliver its strategy and substantially uplift the performance of the business.

To undertake this self-assessment, I ask you to complete the radial graph in Figure 6. On each axis, low scores represent poor performance or weak capabilities, whilst high score means the opposite. Please do not forget to join the dots as the performance picture really only becomes visible when you do this, as shown is Figure 7.

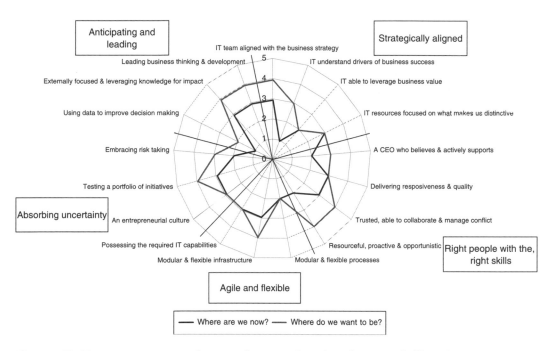

Figure 7: Your strategy – do you have what it takes to deliver? An example

Ideally, you will undertake this activity with colleagues both within IT and the business. This will aid your understanding of how well IT and the business are interfacing and how effectively IT is developing the organizational capability to deliver its strategy.

In terms of each of the sections of the graph, you should bear in mind:

☑ Strategically aligned: Here I am looking for you to assess the degree to which the IT team is aligned with the business strategy both in terms of understanding and in the application of its resources.

☑ Management: right people, right skills: How capable are the IT management team at delivering an IT function and business which can perform?

☑ Agile and flexible: Is the necessary flexibility built into the organization which enables it to respond at speed to a fast paced, changeable environment?

☑ Absorbing uncertainty: Does the IT function and the business at large, possess a culture and mindset that enables it to embrace the anticipated disruptions that are a feature of modern corporate life?

☑ Anticipating and leading: Is the IT function sufficiently aware of the world around it, and can it help the business to use that knowledge to shape management and executive thinking?

In these discussions, you should both assess where you are now and where you need to be in order to achieve the levels of performance demanded by the organization. These two perspectives will identify key gaps in capability. The biggest gaps should be those which should receive the focus of your attention in the coming weeks and months.

DOING

9 Leading

- Leveraging emerging technologies

- Leading the debate

The potential for IT to lead is enormous and yet it is rarely grasped. Why is that? In part it is because the role is poorly understood, and equally, it is because the challenge of becoming a strong Follower and Enabler is so demanding that IT functions rarely succeed to break through to this ultimate layer. So, what does Leading mean and what do you have to be doing to realize the potential benefits for your company?

Touching

This chapter considers two elements of your role in terms of Leading. Firstly, your responsibility to enable the company to take advantage of emerging technologies, and secondly, your role in leading the strategic debate at the board table as IT becomes increasingly viewed as a value creating partner.

In respect of the former, I will not be using this chapter as an essay on the innovation process, nor an attempt to describe the culture that you need to create in which creativity can prosper. Whilst important, focus on these elements would detract from identifying the key responsibilities of the IT in respect of the leveraging the potential of new technology.

Leveraging emerging technologies

Faith in IT?

Over recent years, IT has been the central source of new business models, processes, products and services that have brought enormous success to the businesses they serve. One only needs to think of Dell's supply chain management, Amazon's online trading, Google, the iPod and the Xbox to realize the impact and reach achieved by IT.

If the 50,000 people interviewed in 68 countries for the Big Debate at this year's World Economic Forum are to be believed, then 'advances in technology' will continue to be the most important global challenge to which businesses must adapt. (WEF Gallop International Association. Voice of the People 2005) If this is the case, then IT functions have a key role in helping their companies to be alert to, absorb and leverage the changes and opportunities that will result.

If the pace of those changes accelerate as anticipated, then IT functions also have a key role in enabling their businesses to respond more quickly. And yet many CIOs and their departments still struggle with the fact that they are perceived as being engineers whose job it is to maintain the system. Why should that be?

In part, it is because IT functions have failed to deliver the basics (Following), and in consequence, have undermined the trust that business needs to have in them before they will listen. Alongside, the fact that IT functions often focus so much of their energy on today's technology and processes rather than future opportunity, means that most people only consider them as being capable of operating in that arena and wouldn't even think about them as valuable partners in the innovation cycle.

The result; executives know that technology is vital to driving and delivering new business opportunities and yet they do not believe that their IT function is either a source of innovation, nor a suitable tool for delivering it.

Capability and desire

This must cause us to stop and consider whether IT actually has any role in leveraging emerging technologies at all? Well that depends on whether your IT function has the capabilities necessary to have any impact. In *Make IT Matter for Business Innovation* by Laurie Orlov (2005) we are provided with the basis of a useful checklist of those capabilities against which you can check the skills of your own function.

Can you be an innovation enabler?			
Asset	Description	Your score	Key gaps
Problem-solving creativity	Identifying technical and organizational patterns and finding solutions		
Business process knowledge	Delivering effective applications that work across all stages of the business process		
Technology awareness	Deep knowledge of existing and emerging technologies and their application to business problems		
Utilizing knowledge	Extracting business opportunities from disparate organizational data		
Infrastructure flexibility	Providing flexible infrastructure which facilitates fast and simple implementation		
Enabling collaboration	Providing technologies that facilitate knowledge sharing and collaboration		

Table 1: Can you be an innovation enabler?

Together with selected business partners you should score yourself on a scale of one to four:

– Identify the key gaps that exist in your capability to become a valuable partner in the innovation process.

You may conclude as a result that you do not currently have the assets necessary to contribute.

– If so, you have to decide whether this is a permanent state of affairs or a situation that can be rectified.

– For most though, this will be about addressing the gaps that exist, rather than pulling out completely.

– Weak scores will not only limit the opportunity for the involvement of your function, but most probably will also limit the opportunities for your business to utilize emerging technology to succeed. That should worry you and your shareholders.

Use this rating assessment to open up the dialogue with the business units.

Identify the resources that you possess and can utilize in the process of innovation in your company.

An alternative consideration is whether your organization should be 'leading the market' or 'following the market'. Your discussions should centre on both the internal and external aspects:

– Internally, you should recognize that first movers often have difficulty getting a return on their high level of investment in pioneering activities. This is particularly the case when the results of endeavours are not particularly disruptive or are easy to copy.

– What is your company's track record in translating innovation into competitive advantage and its appetite for risk? If the appetite is low or a poor track record is evident then it is most probably better to seek to follow, rather than lead.

– Externally, what is the scale of the opportunity that may occur as a result of the innovation? Again, if the scale is limited in relation to the resources of your company, then perhaps the pioneering approach is not for you.

What do we mean by innovation?

Assuming though, that you do possess sufficient capability and the desire to be involved, what do we actually mean by innovation that is driven by the use of technology and information?

In this regard, the challenge is to either:

- Disrupt or change the way tasks and processes perform

- Fundamentally accelerating processes

- Opening up new business opportunities

- Radically lowering costs or increasing income.

You can achieve these goals by using technology and information to deliver:

Product or service innovation

Using databases and applications to move establish markets to new levels of performance, cost or usability. Very often this is about incremental improvements such as the ongoing and incremental development of various versions of Palm Handheld PDAs. Similarly, Apple achieves this through the development of the various incarnations of the iPod either by way of size (iPod Nano) or capacity (20 GB and 40 GB versions). This approach also encompasses the shift by manufacturers away from a focus on products to a proposition which incorporates a complementary service or range of services.

Experiential innovation

Using technology combined with knowledge of customers' emotional behaviour to add additional features to core products which make them more enjoyable or satisfying to the customer. Amazon utilizes database information and supply chain management systems to show us what 'people like you' also bought and to reassure you by telling you that your book has been dispatched.

Marketing innovation

Finding new ways to reach and communicate with customers utilizing technology. Burger King has recently invested in advertising space on MySpace.com in order to reach the community's gathering around the social websites.

Process innovation

Using technology to transform or completely change business processes in established markets to make them more efficient or effective. The call centre based car insurance model (e.g. Direct Line) is an example of this, and so is Dell's approach to the assembly and supply of PCs. Often this approach will demand partnership working and innovation with players throughout the supply chain. For example, the success of the Xbox and Sony PlayStation is reliant upon a continual stream of new games from software development companies such EA Sports.

What do we need to be doing?

Innovation of this nature is not a one-time event. It is a process that must be continually managed and undertaken across the organization.

Okay, but what might this involve? As I said in opening, I do not propose to list here all the approaches that are proposed for innovation, but simply identifying those that are particularly pertinent to the use of technology and information. At the highest level, this will include:

– Collaborating with the business to continually find and explore innovations of every kind which may include business concepts, new customer behaviours and technologies.

– Stimulating new thinking by:

  – Using information about market trends, competitors and customers

  – Learning from specialists and thought leaders in universities, vendors and other industries

  – Utilizing team experience and knowledge and organizational competencies.

– Establishing a process by which we can filter the ideas that we generate so that we can put energies into those which have the maximum chance of success and providing a profitable return for the business.

– Test, fail and move on to the next possibility.

To support and sustain your drive to deliver value from emerging technologies you need to consider the following.

Establish a supportive environment

This is about winning the active support and involvement of the CEO and your fellow members of the executive team so that your program has the energy, support and strategic focus that is necessary both to initiate the program and sustain it.

Alongside, you need to get people in the organization acting and thinking in the right way and recognizing the value that can come from technology and information innovation. This is about hiring the right people, giving them incentives to make things happen, and also creating a culture where performance, co-operation and trust dominate.

To achieve this you need to forge stronger links with leading thinkers, customers and suppliers, and look across at other industries to see what they are doing.

Create a business innovation team

Once you have set the scene, you need to get a group of people in place who can make it happen. You need to give them freedom and encourage them to explore, challenge and question.

They can build upon the links you will have established personally with leading companies, but they also need to forge strong links with key partners within the business and spend a lot of time operating and working in the business to intimately understand their needs and to gain new perspectives.

Create value generating processes

Innovation and creativity may appear to be 'soft' issues, but the delivery of results demands that you put in place the disciplines that are necessary to ensure effective working and a return on your investment.

Therefore, you need to learn from companies like 3M who have rigorous new product development systems that consistently take concepts to successful commercialization in greater volumes than almost anyone else in the market.

The systems shouldn't just address the specifics of the concept being explored; they must also provide the necessary support too:

- Developing capabilities in Rapid Application Development to replace or complement classical Waterfall approaches to accelerate development processes and meet business demands and timescales.

- Utilizing the technology and systems life cycle (see Chapter 8) to manage systems and technology appropriately.

- Getting in place the performance measurement systems which maintain management focus and attention:

  - However, there is no perfect measure. Usually there are a few which when taken together give you a picture of the progress you are making.

  - The aim should be an end result which creates customer value that generates greater profit. So you have to measure the outputs in terms of customer perception of value and price sensitivity, On the other hand, you need to measure the inputs into the innovation process and how well your innovation processes are working. This may include measuring the number of new ideas, the numbers of concepts implemented, and numbers that you result in profitable products or services. In other words you need to measure inputs, processes and outputs.

  - Given that innovation comes from the capability of your people, I also believe it worthwhile to measure the specific skills that they are developing and your ability to retain those people who have the skills you require.

The IT function has a key role to play in enabling the organization to take advantage of emerging technologies and the information it holds about its customers and the market place.

If IT is going to deliver to this potential, then it should be clear that this is not going to happen by accident, but because you set out in the determined way to create an environment, team and processes that will:

- Facilitate the innovation process

- Accelerate the development and implementation of new ideas

- Deliver income generating results.

Leading the debate

The other facet of Leading, relates to your role in the boardroom, and the function's role right across the business. This is about you:

- Leading the debate in the business

– Facilitating discussions

– Enabling people to see new opportunities, and

– Progressing the organization's thinking about strategic and competitive possibilities.

If successful, the company will be able to see further into the future, make faster progress than it would otherwise, and IT will be recognized as a key catalyst of that success.

I would love to suggest here that there is a silver bullet which will gain you this degree of success and recognition. Unfortunately, this is not the case. Success comes from:

– The purposeful application of the concepts explored throughout this book

– Being an efficient and reliable Follower, and a highly effective Enabler

– Having a track record of service and project delivery

– Having costs in IT under control giving the business transparency on where and how their money is spent

– Leveraging the potential from emerging technologies in order to introduce new income generating products, services or processes.

In other words, it comes from performing. If you perform and you deliver, people sit up and take notice and yes, in the short term you can rely on force of personality. Being a CIO who is charismatic, energetic and inspiring will help you in the short term, but however strong your personality, your fellow directors and business executives will soon undermine your desire to Lead in the organization if you cannot deliver the results that you promised and which are expected.

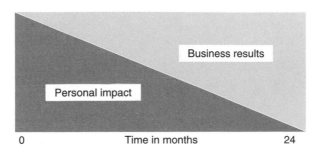

TOUCHING

Another way of looking at this is that you only have limited time until you start to deliver results.

In closing

There is a real need for IT functions to help the business to see the future and grasp the opportunities and benefits available. Equally, there is value to the IT function of winning credibility and enjoying the freedom that results from leading the key debates about the future direction and performance of the organization.

These benefits will not be realized unless credibility is built as a result of consistent delivery and unless 'nice ideas and concepts' are commercialized with tangible benefits being delivered to the business by way of improved growth and profits.

Being a Leader within your business is a very attractive proposition, but do not underestimate the challenges of getting there and staying there.

TOUCHING

Looking

First mover or follower?

During this chapter we have considered whether it is best to be a first mover or follower and whilst you would naturally think about the iPod as a leader in its field, some of the more interesting aspects of the commercial world relate to the developments that have followed its launch.

Most of us are not an Apple, nor do we have their culture of innovation and design. Most of us work in fairly mundane companies doing fairly standard things, trying to maximize our performance in a highly competitive world, and it is difficult.

So rather than spend our time looking at first movers, how have companies (much like ours) created new opportunities for their companies by following leading innovators such as Apple?

Audio books

Two companies, Spoken Network and Audible, have enjoyed enormous success on the back of iPods and MP3 players. As you may recall, audio books were first introduced in tape cassette versions and then on CDs for people to listen to whilst traveling in their cars and on trains and planes. The bulk of sales were made in service stations alongside motorways and highways. Principally they were bought by people in the 45–60 year old range and the market was pretty stagnant.

However, by the end of 2005 there were 7.3 million MP3 players in the UK alone and as a result, the sale of audio books doubled during 2005.

Not only that, but buyers have shifted to the 'thirty-something' iPod generation who have never previously bought an audio book in either CD or tape format. Buyers also seem to buy more on impulse than they did previously.

Alongside, the publishers benefit because the cost of turning a book into a digital audio file to download is minimal, especially in comparison to the traditional CD and tape format because packaging and distribution costs do not exist. This means that books that may not have been published previously now become available for commercialization.

In this regard, innovation has taken advantage of technology in a wide variety of ways; recognizing shifting behaviours, opening up new market segments, creating the opportunity to renew a range of product introductions, reducing the cost of business processes, changing the distribution model.

Video downloads

Ann Sweeney is the president of Disney-ABC Television Group and is credited with leveraging the opportunities presented by video iPods to create new income streams for the group which is enjoying a substantial revival particularly on the back of the hit show's *Desperate Housewives* and *Lost*.

Following an initial meeting with Apple, Disney concluded a deal within three days to supply these two programs as iPod downloads. Interestingly, it seems that the availability of these programs on iPod supported rather than cannibalized audiences on television, where viewing figures grew.

Speed is also a feature of Disney's ESPN network, who managed to re-edit coverage of the Rose Bowl football game into a 15 minute package and download via iTunes the very next day.

In both cases, marketing may have led the strategic push and discussions, but nothing could have happened without the close proximity, capabilities and agility of an effective and Leading IT function.

Process innovation

Nordea

Nordea is a financial services group operating in the Nordic and Baltic region offering online banking and insurance as well as information to investors.

However, it is in the area of its online banking service and e-business that it has been able to make substantial progress in introducing process innovation to drive down costs.

It is estimated that on average it costs €30 for a bank to handle an invoice for payment and large corporate customers may pay up to €60 each incoming payment. In the Nordic countries alone, one billion business-to-business invoices are issued annually.

Nordea created an e-invoicing model and complementary infrastructure that also allows the exchange of comprehensive documents and comprehensive interaction between customers. The service makes a substantial leap by removing Nordea from the payment chain by allowing end-to-end, straight through processing between customers. It is estimated that the cost saving is at least 50%.

Nordea believe that within three years all their corporate customers will be operating e-billing. On the surface their own exclusion from the payment cycle may seem counter productive, but the availability and cost savings that can be passed on to their customers is winning them valuable market share.

Product and service innovation

Samsung

The Korean mobile phone and electrical products manufacturer spends 9.2% of its revenues (over $5 billion) on research and development with particular focus on miniaturization. However, it also seeks to accelerate supply chain and decision-making processes, something that cannot be done without the highest quality staff and input from the IT function.

Combined, these three aspects have enabled Samsung to make the move from being a producer of 'me too' electronic commodities to making and distributing sophisticated, cutting-edge technology with a reputation for being some of the coolest products in the market.

In terms of the networks they use to help to stimulate new thinking and ideas, they benchmark themselves against IBM, AT&T and Lucent.

Norwich and Peterborough Building Society

Norwich and Peterborough is a UK mortgage lender which generates most of its income from selling mortgages and 55% of its new lending is sold by independent brokers.

A change in regulations meant that the society had to ensure that these independent brokers were complying with the new rules. Alongside the society believed that there had to be competitive advantage from having a fully featured online trading solution that offered their loans direct to customers and brokers.

LOOKING

Research with brokers, customers and the business identified three big drivers; time (it had to be completed and operational by a certain day that could not be moved) user experience, and efficient processes that resulted in no cost increase either to the business or its broker customers.

The project has proven to be a massive success, not only was it completed within a year, but broker uptake has been incredibly high without the need for any financial incentives to encourage them into the site and system.

Experiential innovation

Green Hills Supermarket, Syracuse, New York

Green Hills may look like many other independent grocery stores. However it is using leading-edge biometric marketing and payment systems under the 'Smart Shop' brand. Customers swipe their fingertip and type in a pin number to print out a list of 20 targeted offers which are selected to reflect past preferences and buying behaviour.

This concept is still at test stage, but early indications are that this approach could completely change supermarket loyalty programs. Green Hills has been operating loyalty card programs for nearly 15 years, but this biometric approach takes the concept a stage further. Not only does it include sales promotional activity, but also a payment system. More importantly individual targeting of promotions are based on individual customer information rather than demographic groupings as used by most other loyalty systems.

Whilst the debate will rage over whether or not customers are willing to submit themselves to this degree of sophistication and openness, the reality is that customers are using it and Green Hills are already seeing substantial sales improvement that is specifically related to the recommendations made to customers by the system.

Marketing innovation

Carphone Warehouse

The Carphone Warehouse Group has the aspiration to be the biggest and best mobile retailer in the world. Founded in 1989 it now has 1700 stores across 10 countries and employs 14,000 people. In 2006 it will sell over 10 million handsets and manages over one million mobile customers.

The IT function under the guidance of Jeff Wollen has done much to prepare it to anticipate and lead to change. Organizationally, it has implemented a business relationship model and has placed credible, mature and well-established individuals into the relationship management roles.

On the process front, it has broken out the supply side (standard delivery of supporting infrastructure) from the demand side (projects), and has established a 'skunk works' team to identify the opportunities for technology exploitation. The focus is particularly on exploiting economies of scale and the skills within the business.

In terms of systems and development, they have made a major shift towards 'buy' and away from build, and towards service oriented architecture. Alongside projects are increasingly managed on a Rapid Application Development approach rather than the previously dominant Waterfall method.

It was against this background that their Chief Executive, Charles Dunstone came up with the idea during Christmas 2005 of offering 'Free Broadband Forever' as a marketing innovation. Whilst marketing and business growth were the key drivers, the implications for IT were massive, particularly as first mover advantage was considered to be critical, demanding that the supporting systems needed to be in place within three and a half months.

IT was clearly critical to success and they managed to deliver within these demanding timescales by establishing an effective team working jointly with business colleagues to accelerate the whole development-to-test-to-production process. However, the ability to succeed in the way they did was not built upon these short term teams, but the long term ability that had been established, and reputation and relationships that had been previously created with their business partners

The consequence was not just successful implementation, but also substantial market share with knock-on benefits for the core business. So successful has it been that Orange and Sky have followed their lead.

LOOKING

Doing

Leveraging emerging technologies

What do you need to put in place to move yourself beyond the Enabling and becoming a Leader? From an operational sense here is the recipe to become a Leader within your organization:

Establish a supportive environment:

☑ Obtain CEO active and sustained support, and put the innovation activities in the context of the company strategy

☑ Stimulate discussion of innovation as a part of management daily routines

☑ Establish strong connections across the functions and with other parties such as suppliers, academics and customers

☑ Encourage and enforce cooperation among individuals to build trust and a sense of shared purpose

☑ Create an expectation for individual performance so that staff actively seek success

☑ Hire and retain people who have the talent to succeed in this type of environment

☑ Implement incentives to encourage innovation and sharing

☑ Lead, and be willing to make the hard decisions.

Create a business innovation team:

☑ Construct a group of people who have or can be given business experience and exposure

☑ Provide them with the autonomy to explore new uses for IT systems and information

☑ Given the freedom to link with business units, marketing and product innovation teams and selected external partners

☑ Make IT staff undertake periods of work experience in the business.

Create value generating processes

☑ Establish a new product development process to include testing and commercialization

☑ Develop Rapid Application Development capabilities

☑ Implement the technology and systems life cycle approach (see Chapter 8)

☑ Ensure that sufficient time is allocated in resource planning for innovation activities

☑ Establish a portal to collect, share and screen ideas, and generate public debate

☑ Establish appropriate measurement systems.

Leading the debate

I am sorry if you expected a list of tasks here. The truth is that you need to draw on everything that we have discussed, and will discuss, in this book if you are going to lead the debate. The best I can do for you is:

☑ Do Following brilliantly

☑ Execute Enabling with precision

☑ Convert emerging technologies into income.

And you will have the chance to Lead.

Section 4

Delivering with impact

So what is it?

There is an enormous range of issues to be considered in terms of delivery by the IT function, and in a book such as this I can only highlight and identify some key areas for you to focus on.

In giving you this focus, I have in mind the issues that arise from the following graph:

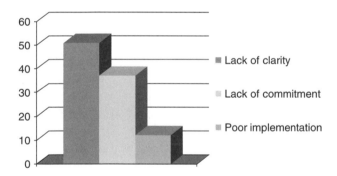

Figure1: What stops strategic change programs delivering (Adapted from Darragh and Campbell, 2001)

This gives us a clear picture of why strategic change programs fail:

– Critically, they fail over 50% of the time because there is a lack of clarity across the team on what has to be delivered and achieved.

– A third of failures arise from of a lack of commitment on the part of management. Here managers fail to put their energies into bringing the strategy alive and making sure it delivers the impact it should.

– And strategic initiatives fail because they are poorly executed and implemented.

Bear these numbers in mind. IT managers tend to focus on 'implementation' because they like the comfort of systems and processes. But you need to focus your energies on the people side of delivery to ensure clarity and commitment.

This fourth and last section will show you how you can turn your understanding of the business and your newly formed strategy into reality on the ground. To do so, I will consider:

– The leadership role.

– Managing the IT brand.

– Managing change.

– Changing the culture.

10 Leadership & management in IT

- The context

- Your objectives

- Your role

- The skills and behaviours you need

- Developing the IT manager

The leader and manager is critical in providing the impetus and energy that initiates the change necessary to deliver your strategy. The leader in IT has to reach right across the organization to create the context in which the IT function can perform, and the business can enjoy success. What is the role of the IT leader and what must they deliver?

Touching

In this chapter I want to look at the practical application of leadership in an IT environment. In that sense, I fully recognize and acknowledge that there are a host of theories and leadership models on which one could draw and which could be explored in the chapter such as this. However, my desire is to identify the main things that IT managers should be doing to have the necessary impact and to deliver the IT strategy for the benefit of the business. Therefore, this will not be an exhaustive summary of all management models, but will be more than sufficient to enable you to perform and deliver.

To achieve this I am going to structure the chapter in five component elements:

– The context of leadership in IT

– Your objectives

– Your main roles in activities

– The skills and behaviours that you need, and

– The development of leaders in an IT environment.

The context of leadership in IT

Who?

Leadership in an IT environment is demanding because there is a need to manage and consider three principal constituent parts; the IT team as a group, the individuals within that team (and the IT manager's direct reports in particular) and additionally, the organization as a whole.

The CIO unusually, but not uniquely, has this last dimension in their role which demands that they have to lead the organization as well as their own team. I particularly use the word 'leadership' in this respect to emphasize the impetus, guidance, and the drive that it is necessary for the CIO and IT manager to provide so that the IT strategy is adopted by the business. In contrast, I do not believe that adopting a passive and reactive approach to the implementation of the IT strategy will be sufficient to deliver the results demanded by the business.

Separately, the CIO has the 'in-house' role of leading the IT team in a coordinated way so that the function as a whole has greater impact and utilizes its full capability.

Additionally, there are the individuals within your team that need managing, developing and improving so that they consistently achieve more than they would do otherwise.

In terms of considering the context of management within IT, it is worth recognizing at this stage the nature of the people you are likely to be responsible for. Whilst I do not wish to be stereotypical, I think it is fair to suggest that the people in your team are likely to be more introverted and analytical than you may see in, say, a marketing department. Even if you disagree with me about this, simply raising the issue is important because as a manager you need to consider the type of people whom you are managing and vary your approach accordingly.

Assuming that there is a greater propensity towards analysis and introversion, this is likely to mean that the high-energy, fast paced and overtly results driven approach that may work elsewhere in the business will be less effective here. In contrast, management styles that are more likely to resonate with your target audience will include:

– Presenting cases and issues in a well-prepared way.

– Drawing upon proven approaches.

– Providing the opportunity for proper consideration of the issues and implications.

Of course, life is not as black and white as this, but any manager operating in the IT environment needs to be conscious of the nature, beliefs, desires and experiences of those they are managing and respond appropriately. Equally, you will need to bear in mind that the style you adopt within the IT function may not be appropriate when engaging the rest of the business.

What?

As noted above, leaders in IT have to manage people, but equally because of the nature of the function of IT they also have to manage process and systems. Additionally, the role of IT within the business also demands the skills and a high level of competence in the management of knowledge.

TOUCHING

These demands could easily be seen as contradictory, but whether this is the case or not is immaterial as the IT manager has to cope effectively with them all.

Looked at in another way, the IT function has the roles of operating as a strategy consultancy, systems developer, innovator, information centre, technical specialist, budget controller, commercial manager, trainer, change agent, helpdesk, service provider, board member, project manager, risk manager, procurement department and process/systems manager and controller. And I am sure there are many more. This does not mean that the leader and manager in IT needs to be a specialist in all these aspects, but it does demand that they have the intellectual capacity and breadth of experience to combine these roles whilst delivering an efficient and effective service to the business.

Alongside, you have to manage knowledge. In this respect IT is in a unique position; it can see all the information that is held by the business at the highest level and also down to the granular detail. It can see who is using it (and who is not) and it can see the methods by which this information is accessed and shared. If it is cute enough, IT will be conscious of the changing external environment, the changing opportunities presented by advances in technology and changing customer expectations and patterns of behaviour. I find it difficult to think of any other function within the business which has such visibility of so many key elements that impact on the performance of the organization. You therefore also have a key role to play to ensure that the business maximizes the opportunities that are presented by these diverse and yet interlinked strands.

How?

Like most managers, those in IT have to be both managers and leaders. There are and have been many definitions of each in leadership literature but I do not want to, nor need to, explore or debate the possible definitions at length here. However for this book I wish to make two points; the first is to say that I have found the simple distinction made by Bennis and Nanus (1985) that "managers do things right" (e.g. plans and budgets, problem solving, organizing and controlling, efficiency and effectiveness) and leaders "do the right things" (e.g. choosing and setting direction, aligning people, winning commitment, energizing and motivating) has served me well over the years and is a sufficient distinction in most circumstances (if required).

Secondly, and in conflict with this tidy separation of roles, one has to ask whether this division really matters anyway. We could debate the differing concepts for hours, but the reality for most practicing managers is that they draw on both types simultaneously, flitting from one to the other unknowingly and unconsciously. Thus, and for most practical purposes, they are one and the same, complementary and completely intertwined. Therefore you will find that I use the words management and leadership interchangeably, without implying that one is more appropriate than the other, or that one is superior to the other. Purists will be disappointed by this, but I simply want to reflect the practical reality of the issues facing IT managers (or leaders) and focus on the more important aspect of what they have to deliver, the role they need to fulfil, and the skills and behaviours that they need to deploy to succeed.

Your objectives

Quite simply, I see the objective of IT leaders as twofold. First, to lift substantially the performance of the IT function and in turn performance of the business that it serves. Second, to embed the capabilities and ways of working that serve to sustain that performance over the long-term. For this to be achieved IT managers have to develop systems, culture and the people both within the IT function and the business at large.

This, together with the issues lighted under 'Who?' and 'What?' above mean that IT managers must have the skills to reach and perform across the whole business and it is insufficient for IT managers to believe that a narrow focus on the IT function alone is acceptable; it is not. And I don't care about your level in the IT managerial hierarchy. As an IT manager your responsibilities stretch across the whole business and you had better prepare yourself and skill yourself to perform and deliver right across this colourful canvas.

This has a number of implications if you are going to be successful. It means that there are a number of subsidiary objectives that you need to achieve on the way. The following diagram captures those elements and the focus of your role.

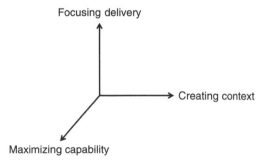

Figure 1: The IT leader – why you exist

Focusing delivery

This means that you have to be successful in focusing everybody's efforts on the delivery of the right things. In other words, those things that have substantial impact on the performance of the IT function and the business.

At board level, this may be about getting the directors to collectively determine the priorities for IT. Often, boards continue to add projects to the IT workload without proper consideration of the implications for existing projects. The discipline is needed to force the executive to choose between competing projects.

At the operational level, it is about putting people's roles in context, inspiring them to deliver the right things and making sure that the task they do on a day-to-day basis supports the strategic objectives that you have set.

Creating context

This demands that you have to establish an environment in which people can perform at the highest levels.

It means that you have to create a culture which provides opportunity, and is stimulating, challenging and creative, and where people trust each other.

It means that you have to establish systems and routines that don't get in the way of the performance of your staff or the business

Maximizing capability

This means that you give everyone within the business the opportunity to leverage and maximize every ounce of potential that they have.

It means creating an environment where people are seriously challenged, but where this challenge is complemented by the support necessary to enable them to achieve peak performance.

It means providing the opportunity for responsibility and autonomy so that people achieve the mastery of skills that they didn't think they could access and enjoy the recognition and rewards that flow as a result.

Your role

As a result, I see three main roles for you as a manager within IT.

Setting direction

You need to provide on an ongoing basis, the path that the team needs to follow. It doesn't matter whether you are the CIO creating the strategy for the function and the business, or

Figure 2: The IT leader – your roles

a team leader in systems development, you need to help and enable people to understand where we are heading and what they have to deliver.

Improving performance

However good you and your team are, you have no choice but to get better. Thus you have a role of improving the performance of your people, your systems and your technology.

Implementing change

Everything you do from providing an executive with a PDA to implementing a new architecture involves change on a number of fronts. It is your role to successfully implement those changes in all their guises.

Each of these demands that you undertake a number of activities; I therefore propose to look at each of these three components of your role in a little more depth.

Setting direction

As I proposed earlier in this chapter, your role here extends from working with the IT team to the whole business. In other words, your role is to work with your fellow directors to develop a strategy for the business, your fellow managers in IT to set the strategy for IT, and your direct reports to provide them with clarity of their role in the delivery of the IT strategy.

This is not just about setting targets for people, it is also about:

– Providing the strategic context in which people have to operate

– Highlighting the main strategic thrusts that they need to pursue

– Making clear the values by which we operate

– Identifying the appropriate behaviours and,

– Setting the goals and targets by which we can assess performance.

All this has to be done in a way that connects people and teams so that they are all pointing in the same direction and supporting each other in the delivery of the overarching goals.

It is also about setting direction in a way which wins their commitment to deliver. In other words it is not about 'telling', but about motivating and energizing people so that they take ownership of the goals that you have set and willingly embark on their delivery. If we consider the different types of people that you will have in your team (and spread across the business as a whole), you will quickly recognize that different people will be motivated in different ways and will see different things as being important. Therefore you need to be able to set direction in ways that resonate with these different audiences and which wins the degree of commitment necessary to accelerate success.

Therefore, what does this mean that you need to be doing?

Setting direction with the executive team

Clearly you need to be focusing on all the issues that we explored in the first five chapters of this book and Chapters 2, 4 and 5 in particular. As a result you should enjoy a shared understanding with your colleagues in the boardroom regarding the market place in which you are operating, the customers you are serving and the strategy that you are seeking to adopt as a business.

Additionally, the result should be that you can explain clearly to the business and your IT function the priorities that should demand peoples attention. In this way, strategy will act as a filter to help people understand what they should and shouldn't be doing.

Equally, you need to be clear about your role in the delivery of the strategy, and the influence and power you wish to exercise across the business.

However, your attempts to increase your influence and impact must not undermine the performance of the executive team and instead should represent a positive force for good.

TOUCHING

The challenge for you as a member of this team is to decide whether you are 'Following, Enabling or Leading'? In other words, is your role as part of the executive team one of reacting and responding to the discussions between your colleagues, or providing impetus from your awareness of the market place, the use of information within the business, and emerging technologies?

You will gather from the nature of this book that I believe that if you are really going to deliver value from IT, you need to at least be in a position of 'Enabling' and most likely 'Leading' strategic discussions and debates in the boardroom. This means that you need to understand how you can support and improve the performance of the executive team. Therefore you should bear in mind that effective boards are to provide the business with a clarity of high quality as a result of their time together.

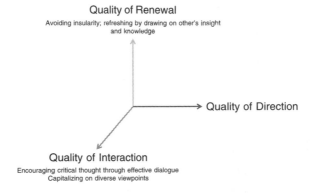

Figure 3: Three dimensions of high performing boards, (Herb *et al.*, 2001)

They achieve this because they have the ability to draw positively on the fresh insight, knowledge and differing perspectives of their team members.

In all these aspects you will need to decide your current role and that which you aspire to achieve:

– If a big shift is required, how are you going to make that move?

– What additional knowledge, or skills, or influencing capabilities do you need to develop or utilize?

– Why are others going to release their grip on power to allow you to increase the influence that you want to exercise?

How will you manage your relationship with the executive team:

– How will you ensure that the executive team understand what it is you are looking to achieve?

– How will you win their support by way of:

  – Providing funding and resources?

  – Their behaviours and actions with their own teams?

(For more ideas on how to approach this aspect, please see the section on Stakeholder Management within Chapter 12.)

Setting direction with the IT team

Having been an integral part of the strategy development process for both the business and IT you should be very capable of providing the necessary context for the whole of the IT function.

As we will see in greater depth in Chapter 12 (change plus), there is a need to put the strategy in context for the team so that they can see why we have chosen the path that we are on, where it is going to take us and how we are going to get there. Also, it is likely that you will need to adopt a number of approaches to the delivery of this story to meet the differing behavioural and learning needs of the wide variety of people that will be within the IT function.

However, you will not effectively set direction for your IT team if you rely on an initial round of briefings to do the job alone. Any strategy involves change and it will be necessary for you to reinforce the principles of the strategy and your progress on a regular basis until the required changes and uplift in performance have been achieved and embedded.

In part, this is about your role of continuing to communicate and reinforce the strategic messages as part of your daily work, e.g.

– Highlighting to people how the achievement of a certain goal, or the evidence of a new behaviour fit with the strategy and help us to make progress.

– Showing the team how you have stopped doing something because it was getting in the way of something else that was much more strategically important.

To do this effectively, you need to be out there with a team, talking to them, seeing what they are doing, reinforcing the behaviours that you want, helping them to change the behaviours that you want dropped.

However, you can't be in all places at once, so you need other vehicles to help to continually reinforce the direction. A lot of this can be achieved by making the aspirations visible to everybody at all times. This may be about approaches such as:

– Making your key performance targets visible by displaying them in key places across the function.

– Using a new reporting pack which is used in team meetings to highlight progress (or otherwise) and to reinforce the direction.

– Using screensavers.

– Large-scale change plans on walls.

To create a set of performance measures that you can use in this way demands that you cascade the IT strategy down to the functional teams and create performance measures to go alongside. Chapter 6 describes the approach that you need to adopt, but the point here is that your leadership role is one of ensuring that this happens and that people are learning, refocusing and changing what they do as a result.

Equally, you need to ensure that the totality of the IT strategy is understood across the function. Also you need to ensure that people are not continuing to do projects that may have been appropriate under previous strategies but which are no longer required. And you need to ensure that where joint working is required, that this is facilitated and supported. If the teams that need to work together to achieve this fall under your control then this should be relatively simple to achieve as a result of your personal involvement and by establishing shared performance measures. However, if it is necessary for systems development to work with marketing, coordination will be more demanding and is likely to need more involvement from you to steer the project through to a successful conclusion.

Similarly, you should be identifying those aspects of programs and projects that would benefit from your additional experience and influence across the business to improve project performance.

TOUCHING

All of these elements demand open communication channels so that messages can flow quickly and cleanly up, down and across the organization. As a result the strategic direction can reach everyone at speed. You can also benefit from feedback on what people think and whether the required integration and coordination of teams is taking place.

Open communication channels do not happen by accident in most organizations. Indeed in most organizations it would appear people go to great lengths to close down those very same communication channels or at least make them totally ineffective.

Because no one else will do it, and because it is so important, it is your role to ensure that you do all you can to maximize the flow of information up, down and across your teams and if possible, the business at large. Indeed, the rest of the business will welcome your ability to set an example and show them how to do it. And given that IT is about the use of knowledge it would be a great pity if we could not achieve success in this area.

This is not to say nor to recommend a massive increase in the number of meetings. This common knee-jerk reaction to the need for 'more communication' invariably results in the opposite, increased frustration and people achieving less. We have to be more sophisticated and find more effective solutions. There is no silver bullet but there are a number of areas that will have impact:

– Clarifying individual objectives and helping them to understand what they need to do and how they need to behave to succeed

– Providing people with as much information as possible about the why, the what and how

– Openly using strategic performance measures to identify progress and to stimulate learning

– Learning from, and sometimes even celebrating mistakes

– Purposefully focusing on and learning from our successes

– Not punishing people for trying new things

– Being open about our own failings and project failures and encouraging others to do likewise

- Increasing responsibility and autonomy, complemented by the development of the skills people need

- Encouraging debates, challenges, and discussions regarding the strategy and its implications so that people can understand what it means to them and the impact they can have

- Moving the team to focus on action, not talking about things

- Motivating staff so that they want to achieve, and want to share their successes with others

- Getting people to take ownership of what they do.

There are many more approaches that could be adopted and this is not meant to be an exhaustive list, but is offered to stimulate you to find solutions that meet the needs of your organization and your people.

Setting direction with the individuals in IT

Much of what has gone before applies both to the IT team as a whole and the individuals within it. However there are other things you can be doing at the individual level to set direction.

Firstly, you need to ensure that the strategy and the related objectives are cascaded down to where they relate to an individual doing something at a desk. This means that you need to be able to take the functional and team strategies and measures and turn them into targets that relate to the individual's job. Examples of how this can be achieved are provided in Chapter 11, where the role of the relationship manager is considered in some depth, including the setting of objectives. This is an extension of the issues explored in Chapter 6, where we looked at performance measures for the function and teams.

However, this cannot just be about targets and hard performance measures for those things that can be counted. You also need to help individuals to understand how the behaviours that they need to adopt to bring about strategic success. For example, in your organization are you looking for people to behave in a way that is acceptable in the dealing room of an investment bank or is the behaviour of a nurse in a hospice more appropriate? Unless you make clear what you expect and why they will not understand the need to change.

To help people change behaviour you need to become skilled at identifying the deeper constraints on people's performance, helping them to see the implications of continuing on their current path, and helping them to identify how they can bring about the changes that are required.

This means that you are able to help people to see the barriers that they are putting up (of which they are often not aware) and showing them how they can move on and progress.

At the individual level even more than the team level, you need to appreciate people's need for recognition and a sense of achievement. Managed well, you can acknowledge successes (without being sycophantic), and at the same time reinforce the strategic themes by pointing out how the results achieved by them enabled the team to progress.

Additionally you can help the individual to set the strategy in the context of their own personal career goals so that they can realize their own potential at the same time as delivering on the functional objectives.

Improving performance

This is very much about your performance management role and the need to continuously improve the performance of your people, systems, culture and technology.

Firstly some performance management principles.

Our aim in any environment is to maximize the performance of our people. This means that we need to challenge them to deliver more, but equally it demands that we offer them the support that they need to enable them to perform at the highest levels. Too much challenge

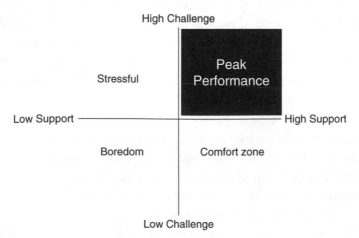

Figure 4: Maximizing the performance of your people

and too little support will lead to stress; whilst too much support and too little challenge will result in people feeling very comfortable.

The principles of performance management are about establishing a cycle of management that helps the individual to understand what they have to deliver, provides them with the necessary support during the reporting period, and utilizes both formal and informal reviews of performance so that lessons can be learnt and an open dialogue created. The end result should be a shared view of how the individual is performing, what they have to achieve and how they are going to develop.

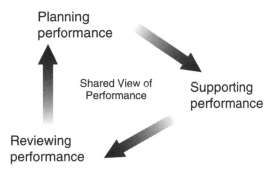

Figure 5: Performance management – the building blocks

If I expand on these three topics you will see that you need to be considering:

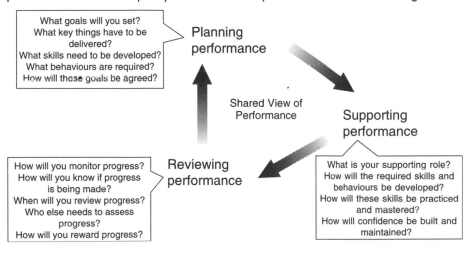

Figure 6: Performance management – building a shared view of performance

Planning performance

This is about being clear with the individual in terms of what they have to deliver, how they need to behave, what they have to do and the skills they need to develop. I have already given this sufficient focus in the section called 'Setting Direction' and will not repeat the details here.

However, I did not cover the aspect of establishing development plans with individuals and teams. As strategy always demands an improvement in performance, this is an important area to focus on. In this regard, you need to ask:

To enjoy success what do you (the team or individual) need to focus development on?

- Within the context of the objectives to be delivered and the activities to be executed, there will inevitably be demands made that stretch existing skills and behaviours.

- Therefore the aim of this question is to explore where they feel stretched, where they feel that the skills and behaviours they have been asked to deploy are beyond their current capability.

- In other words, what is missing that will stop them achieving their objectives?

- Remember, people will not necessarily see the gap and it is up to you to facilitate their understanding of it.

How will the necessary skills be developed?

- What needs to be done to gain the necessary skills and capabilities?

- One of the options you will consider will include formal training. However, there are many other and often more effective ways of acquiring new skills – for example, shadowing, being seconded onto projects, coaching, using online training materials, self-help books and such like.

How will we get good at the new skills and capabilities?

- It is okay to provide the opportunity to learn new skills, but they only become any use when the team or individual is effective at using them. In other words how will they go about practicing their new skills and changing their behaviour?

TOUCHING

– You will need a clear plan of how this is going to be achieved.

What will be achieved as a result?

– You need to be clear what it is that the team and individual will be able to do differently as a result of investing time, focus and money in this developmental need.

– You should be able to make a clear statement of your objectives and how you all measure success. This will then provide you with a reference point to assess progress.

Supporting performance

This stage is not about doing the delivery on behalf of the team or individual. Rather, it means pointing them in the right direction, helping them to achieve, reinforcing the important issues, challenging them regularly, recognizing success, providing development opportunities, ensuring the appropriate training materializes, opening doors, using your influence to remove barriers, arranging secondments and generally providing mentoring or coaching support.

This will also demand that you can identify what it is that motivates people and triggers them to do something. Unfortunately, we do not often sit back and identify what this may be. More likely, we apply motivational techniques that serve to stimulate ourselves in the mistaken belief that what turns us on, will turn somebody else on. Don't kid yourself.

However, and fortunately we can find out what it is that motivates people. We know from long-standing research by Herzberg (1968) that it is not necessarily money that motivates people.

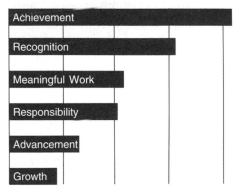

Figure 7: What really motivates us

Herzberg found, and it has been reaffirmed many times since, that people are much more stimulated by a sense of achievement, or recognition, or having the opportunity to do meaningful work, or by being a given additional responsibility. Despite the fact that we have known this for nearly forty years, we continue to think that more pay is the answer.

Alternative methods to understanding what motivates people may include the use of personality profiling. Alternatively, you can simply watch people both inside and outside of the workplace to ascertain what it is that excites them. Of course, you can also just sit down and talk to them and understand how they see things; what motivates them and what frustrates them.

The next step demands that you identify how you are going to trigger the motivators that you have discovered; how are you going to stimulate and motivate them so that they want to apply extra energy to their job? This is not about manipulating people, but working with them so they can operate in a more enjoyable environment.

You can help people to understand how they can trigger those motivators in themselves without assistance from you. In this way they become self reliant, able to spot when they are not feeling good about themselves and able to find triggers that stimulate them and lift their performance.

In reality, therefore, this concept of supporting performance is not just about skills, but also about stimulating the desire in people to improve and build their confidence.

I think it's worth saying here however, that I do not believe that people can operate at 'peak performance' all the time. It simply isn't sustainable. However as a manager you can help people to operate at much higher levels of performance on average, with occasional peaks at levels people never dreamt possible before your involvement.

Reviewing performance

Ideally, review conversations will be undertaken continuously and informally to reflect on successes, failure and the opportunities to learn. They should happen as immediate responses to events and feedback (both good and bad) should not be delayed. This ongoing process should be complemented by more formal interim and year end reviews which should then really just be about summarizing performance during the period in question. In practice, life isn't like that, but this should be the approach that you should be seeking to adopt.

Some of the issues to consider when undertaking performance reviews include:

What is going well?

– Get people to express what they feel has been going well. In other words, identify the areas where they feel they have had some success or are in the process of creating some success. Get them to talk positively about where they feel good about performance, and where they are feeling challenged.

– Your aim at this stage is to provide plenty of positive reinforcement of the good aspects of performance

What is getting in the way?

– This is not simply about underperformance, although this must encompass part of it. it is simply to understand the ways in which people are feeling challenged and why this might be; in what ways are they experiencing difficulty, and why?

– What is the impact to the team and to the business if continued difficulties are experienced?

Where is more support needed?

– This question seeks to draw from the conversations above. Don't just focus on the negative, even though it is very easy. More importantly focus on:

 – Where do they need support so that they can achieve even more?

 – How can that support be provided and by whom? (You should not take all the responsibility for this onto your shoulders; primarily it is an individual's and perhaps the support can come from other members of the team or the individuals themselves.)

– Identify where they can stretch further and achieve more in those areas where they have performed well; how can they build on that success and develop further?

Where should energies be focused now?

– What demands attention and what needs to be done differently to achieve more success?

– What two or three things demand focus that will get them back on track to deliver the planned outcomes or push them ahead to deliver at an even higher level?

— How can more energy be put into those things that are going well?

— What issues need to be addressed to overcome the difficulties and continue to deliver the planned outcomes?

What have we learned?

— Jointly identify the key lessons.

— What can we learn for similar projects in the future?

Agreed assessment

— Reach an agreed view of performance against objectives.

— Other useful questions that can be explored here are:

– Was the performance commensurate with potential?

– Could more have been done? If so, what?

– What additional support could be provided to accelerate success?

All these questions can also be used to explore performance in respect of projects, systems, new technology or change programs.

In many ways these are standard performance management disciplines, which should have been already adopted across your team. However, they become even more important when working with a new strategy which is demanding new skills, behaviours and ways of working from the team.

There are three other areas that you should give focus to in terms of your role as a manager with responsibility for improving performance:

Developing the culture

In what way do you need to adapt your culture so that it meets the needs of your strategic intent? This may involve you addressing issues such as values and behaviours, organizational structure, and controls. I will consider these in great depth in Chapter 13, but the point at this stage is to highlight that as a manager you are responsible for creating a culture which provides the context for high performance.

Developing talent

In the same vein you are responsible for creating the talent that will sustain the function and the business over the long-term. We will look at this again later in the chapter, but the responsibility is yours for identifying and developing successors and tomorrow's managers.

Creating the capability to be innovative and agile

As discussed in chapter 8, the ability to innovate and be agile is increasingly important and your role as a manager is to accelerate improvement in these areas by helping the team to:

– Resolve complex issues

– Find ways to generate new value

– Recognizing and rewarding evidence of flexibility and agility

– Helping the team to absorb uncertainty

– Helping the team to explore how they can start to anticipate marketplace and business changes.

The performance leader

All this demands that the line manager is able to operate as a performance leader and coach, enabling the individuals and teams to be clear about what they have to achieve, how they can go about it, and how they need to develop to succeed. This is likely to be demanding for you and your managers in terms of both behavioural and motivational skills. Therefore, consideration should be given to developing the necessary capabilities amongst your management team so that they can effectively fulfil this important role and motivate and sustain the performance of the people in their charge.

In part, this is about managers recognizing that they need to fulfil this role, but it is also about them developing the skills that enable them to:

– Increase individual and team expectations of themselves

– Maintain individual and team belief by managing doubts and anxieties

– Push the team performance to higher levels through triggering self motivation.

As highlighted in the previous section, a manager in IT has to deploy all these performance improvement capabilities across the constituencies of the business as a whole, the IT team, and the individuals within that team.

Once the capabilities are built, the opportunities to exercise them are many; board meetings, project review meetings, relationship review sessions, benchmarking activities, the assessment of outsourced providers, procurement reviews, implementation of change programs, etc.

The potential value is massive; the challenge is to get into the habit of doing it, practicing it, and getting skilled at it.

Implementing change

Delivering a new strategy demands an ability to implement change.

Once again, you will be doing this at the three levels of the business, with the IT team as a whole and with your staff. Unfortunately, the focus during the implementation of IT strategies is often on the issue of changing the structure and processes of the business and IT function. Whilst not wishing to play down the importance of this aspect of the delivery of your strategy, I have to highlight the need for IT managers to be able to manage change and performance, everywhere.

A common refrain is that "The IT function is too slow, they don't know what's going on in the world outside, IT can't keep up with us", but if you really started to deliver and push new technologies, and new ways of doing things into the business you would suddenly find that the business itself would struggle to keep up. In this respect I am conscious that the current state of your IT department is very often a result of inadequacies in the business itself; IT is simply a symptom of a deeper sickness, but one which can be easily picked on and blamed.

My point is that you have to prepare the business to be ready to assimilate and utilize an IT function that is really delivering value. So as a manager in IT responsible for implementing change, not only must you manage and plan for change in your function, you must do likewise for the business at large.

So important is the concept of managing change, that I have included a separate chapter (Chapter 12) to provide the necessary focus on the issues that you need to consider and the approaches that you can adopt. In consequence, the space allocated to the topic in this chapter is limited in order to avoid duplication and confusion.

However, I think it is worthwhile at this juncture to highlight the roles that you need to be able to adopt as a change manager with responsibility for the delivery of a high value IT function:

Igniting change	Creating the case for the IT strategy, and the resultant change program
Defining	Scoping the breadth, depth, sustainability and returns from the IT strategy and change program
Facilitating and Enabling	Helping others, through effective facilitation to understand the need for change, understand the main changes they need to make and developing the confidence to achieve the change goals
Leading	Influencing and infusing others, through vision and drive, and to go out and make the IT strategy a reality
Learning	Scanning, reflecting and learning to ensure that insights are transferred and used across the IT function
Controlling	Formulating and guiding the implementation of your change plan by establishing appropriate goals, resources, metrics and review mechanisms
Energizing	Injecting high personal commitment to achievement of your change goals and the delivery of the strategy
Know-how	Using the appropriate change theories, tools and processes to accelerate your progress

Table 1: Leading change in IT – your roles (Higgs and Rowland, 2000)

Skills and behaviours

Throughout this chapter I have endeavoured to take a practical approach to the role of IT leaders and during that process I have identified a range of skills and behaviours that managers need to adopt.

I could draw upon a whole series of academic and consultancy models that seek to describe skills and behaviours needed, but I would like to draw only on two approaches; one which I believe summarizes the issues that we have been exploring throughout this chapter, and the second lists a series of skills that you are likely to draw upon in your role as an IT manager.

The first describes the characteristics required to deliver engaging leadership and which provides a great summary of the challenges that we need to rise to as leaders within the IT function and the business at large.

Engaging Leadership	
Enabling	Managers are important to the extent that they help other people to do the important work of developing ideas and delivering
Interacting	The function and the organization is an interacting network, not a hierarchy. Effective leaders work throughout, they do not sit on top
Evolving	Out of the network emerges solutions, as engaged people solve little problems that grow into big initiatives
Implementing	Action and reflection operate fluidly together to find the best solutions. Collaboration enables people to formulate and implement iteratively
Energizing	Leaders activate the positive energy that exists naturally within their people. Managing thus means inspiring and engaging people and teams
Rewarding	Rewards are given for making the organization a better place to work for everyone.
Leading	Leadership is a sacred trust earned through the respect of others

Table 2: Engaging leadership (Gosling and Mintzberg, 2003)

To me, this model beautifully captures the essence and the fluidity of your role, whilst recognizing the practical reality that much of what you must achieve is done through influencing others and winning their support. It seems grounded in the reality of relationships between people and does not seek to make finite distinctions between roles, activities and objectives.

However, despite the appearance to me of being 'easy on the eye', I believe that delivery of this approach will be demanding. This is appropriate because you will need to raise your game in order to achieve successful delivery of your strategy.

In contrast, the second model is much more specific and some would say much more practical. It is for this reason that I have included it, particularly for an IT community which may find my first approach much too 'soft'.

Working	Relating	Thinking
Planning & organizing	Teamwork & collaboration	Visioning
Delivering results	Influencing & persuading	Innovation
Quality focus	Managing others	In-depth problem solving
Continuous improvement	Team leadership	Decisive judgement
Customer focus	Coaching & developing	Championing change
Customer service	others	Adapting to change
Integrity	Relationship management	Courage of convictions
Business acumen	Negotiation management	Resilience
Functional acumen	Interpersonal skills	
Continuous learning	Communication skills	
	Presentation skills	
	Meeting leadership &	
	contribution	

Figure 8: Working, relating or thinking – what should you be doing?
(*Strategic Success Modeling, Bigby Havis & Associates of Dallas*)

This model breaks down the skills required into three distinct elements; Working, Relating, and Thinking. In each area, there is a list of possible skills that managers could deploy. The aim is not to pretend that managers can exercise all these in their role but to provide a menu from which you can choose the top eight or so that are critical to successful delivery of what you do and how you deliver.

The best way to choose the 'top eight or so' is by way of discussion with your own manager to explore what the skills and behaviours are needed to perform at the levels discussed here.

This model has the potential attraction of providing a more tightly defined approach, specifying skills that could apply to the leadership role in IT and recognizing more fully the need for functional and technical skills.

The development of leaders in an IT environment

Many organizations fail to deliver their strategic goals because they do not have enough leaders to enable them to deliver the success to which they aspire. Hence, there is a need to develop more highly capable IT managers.

TOUCHING

Therefore, in this section, I wish to look at the process of development rather than the specific skills that need to be developed. I will start by thinking about our objectives and then looking at the key issues that you need to bear in mind in the development process.

In a quite brilliant book, *Good to Great* (2001), Jim Collins (2001) explores what companies do to make the leap from good to great and sustain high levels of performance over the long-term. Within that book he describes an approach to leadership which he calls 'Level 5 Leadership'. He uses it to explain how the highest performing companies have leaders that exhibit very specific skills which sustain performance. He describes these leaders as 'Level 5 Executives'. He contrasts these executives with lesser mortals and provides a ladder of capability against which we can assess our performance. More importantly and for the purposes of this section, this simple analysis helps us to target the level that we wish to achieve or wish our colleagues to achieve.

Level 5	**Level 5 Executive**
	Builds enduring greatness through a paradoxical blend of personal humility and professional will
Level 4	**Effective Leader**
	Catalyzes commitment to and vigorous pursuit of a clear and compelling vision, stimulating higher performance standards
Level 3	**Competent Manager**
	Organizes people and resources toward the effective and efficient pursuit of predetermined objectives
Level 2	**Contributing Team Member**
	Contributes individual capabilities to the achievement of group objectives and works effectively with others in a group setting
Level 1	**Highly Capable Individual**
	Makes productive contributions through talent, knowledge, skills, and good work habits

Figure 9: Attaining Level 5 Leadership, (Collins, 2001)

As you can see, the distinctions are clearly made and permit us to identify current and target performance levels in a simple yet effective manner. This approach allows us to set a goal for our leadership performance. As a result, we can also identify the skills that we will need to develop and how we may to attain those skills.

In this sense, the development of specific skills is undertaken as part of a bigger picture in which we are developing our overall leadership capability. Equally, the development of those skills also provides us with the capabilities to deliver the objectives that have been set to the short and medium-term in respect of business performance.

But what is it that we know about the development of managers and leaders that we should bear in mind before we embark on this journey. It appears that there are both positive and negative lessons for us.

Firstly, the positive:

Discovery
Initiate and take every opportunity to discover the sort of leader and person you want to be, and what you want to do

Selection
Select yourself, the people you work for and your assignments. Your career is your responsibility. Don't wait for others to do it for you. Selecting wisely means being brutally honest with yourself

Development
Learning from experience rather than going through the motions will develop the right stuff. Reflect, talk, listen and examine. What have you learned; how will you use it?

Recovery
You will have failures as well as successes. The difference for your career will be your ability to experience failure, learn from it and bounce back

Learning
Business never stops changing and the opportunities to learn are enormous. Learning is continuous, find sanctuaries, but keep learning again and again

Figure 10: Career development – the essentials (McCall and Hollenbeck, 2002)

The message is simple; your development is in your hands. Do not wait until somebody takes the trouble to help you to develop the skills and capabilities that you need because they may never do it. As reflected in the schematic it is much better for you to find opportunities that purposely take you on a journey towards becoming the manager to which you aspire. If that means that you have to force yourself onto projects and programs then you have to get on and do it. On the way you may make mistakes, but you will also enjoy success; learn from both and test your new found skills until you have mastered them.

IT managers should be conscious of two issues:

– Business awareness: Firstly, it must be clear to you from this book that awareness and understanding of how the business operates is a core skill for any manager within IT, and is an absolute must for anyone aspiring to be a CIO in the future. Therefore, you must spend some time managing business units so that you experience the demands and pressures of those roles. For this to be meaningful demands a lengthy spell, not just a short-term secondment.

– Big impact projects: Secondly, you should be seeking out those IT projects that are the most demanding and which have the greatest potential to change the performance of your business. Sometimes these will succeed, and other times they will fail. Your involvement is not about short-term reputation and your focus shouldn't simply be on 'looking good'. The reason for your involvement is so that you test and stretch every skill that you have, develop new ones, and build experience in managing large scale programs that may result in wholesale organizational transformation.

Turning to the negative side of management development, we know that the common errors that managers and leaders make are as follows:

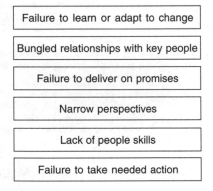

| Failure to learn or adapt to change |
| Bungled relationships with key people |
| Failure to deliver on promises |
| Narrow perspectives |
| Lack of people skills |
| Failure to take needed action |

Figure 11: Career development – the fatal flaws (McCall and Hollenbeck, 2002)

Once again, the messages are simple and obvious. The first is about flexibility of mindset and the need to be mentally agile.

Secondly, you have to be able to work with the key people who have impact both on your career and the performance of the organization. This is not about sycophancy; it is about productive relationships that derive from your increasing ability to perform at ever higher levels.

These relationships are pre-requisites for you to become an effective IT manager in any event. Whilst you may have been able to pursue a solo career whilst cracking code, it would have been clear to you throughout this book that the role of the IT manager and the delivery

TOUCHING

of real value cannot be achieved alone, but only through the creation of powerful relationships with your colleagues in the business.

In closing

Up to now we have been dealing with the impersonal aspects of strategic alignment; competition, strategic planning, performance measures, systems and technology.

By contrast this chapter has focused on the individual and in particular the leader's role in providing the impetus and energy that initiates change and makes the strategy happen through your people, systems and processes.

Thus the manager's role is instrumental and as we have seen it is insufficient to see your role in the narrow sense of the IT function alone. The role of the leader in IT reaches right across the organization to create the context in which your function can perform and the business can enjoy success.

For you to achieve, you need to be skilled at setting the direction for the business and IT. This demands that you play an integral role in both the development of the strategy and telling the story throughout the business.

You need to become a highly effective performance leader using a wide range of capabilities in the areas of motivation, coaching, and supporting and reviewing performance.

And you need to be able to deliver change in a wide variety of settings.

It is unlikely that you have the skills today necessary to be able to do all these things. Hence, you need to stop and candidly reflect upon the skills you will need to be able to perform at the levels I have outlined in this chapter. And later today (yes, today) you need to start the immediate and urgent task of building those skills, otherwise your strategy will remain an aspiration and you will be left doing what you have always done – which is far less than you are capable of.

TOUCHING

Looking

Attention: Please leave this room as you would like to find it

So says the sign in a training room I was working in the other week. However, the sign and its juxtaposition with the day's topic of leadership set me thinking. "What would it mean if we applied the same sign to our leadership styles and roles?" I wondered.

Attention: please leave this *organization* as you would like to find it

In terms of our leadership roles, then surely the big challenge we face must be one of getting the organization into shape so that it can perform at the highest levels, in a sustained way. Indeed, wouldn't it have been great if you had taken custody of an organization in this condition when you took up your duties in the first place. What a foundation on which to build.

Ho hum, and back to reality. So let's assume that it is down to you to build this level of capability. If it is, then the challenge for you is about building a high performing team and this is about your ability to:

- Help people to visualize the success to which you aspire and help individuals and teams to see and believe in their own potential.

- Trigger the desire in people to perform at higher levels.

- Act as performance coach to maintain individual and team belief, managing doubts and anxieties, and increasing individual expectation and conviction.

On the other hand, perhaps my training room sign is pointing us towards creating a culture that makes the business an 'employer of choice', makes people feel welcome, and provides the type of environment that supports and reassures people.

Some of you reading this will dismiss such language as inappropriate in today's fast moving, aggressive, target driven world. But perhaps you should not be so hasty to judge. For years we have known that to successfully implement your strategy you need a culture that fits well with your strategic aspirations (Miles and Snow, 1984). So whilst in some circumstances an aggressive culture is just what is needed, in many others it would only serve to undermine delivery success. For example, the cultural demands of running a mobile phone retail network such as Phones4U, or Carphone Warehouse are very different from a hospitality environment or a social services team.

– What is right for your organization?

– Have you really stopped to think what culture is required for you to deliver?

– Are you working towards building the right culture for your strategy?

In other words, what type of culture will enable your people to perform at the highest levels of their capability in a way that reinforces your strategic goals (especially in front of the customer)?

Or perhaps the sign was simply about the legacy you will leave behind when you move onto pastures new (Jones and J.Gosling, 2005):

– What will be your greatest achievement and what will you be remembered for?

And surely this is the most elevated of all the challenges raised by my sign and the most demanding of them all. But how often does this issue capture your attention as you struggle with the day to day tasks?

However, if you were to stop, reflect and plan for your legacy, what would you need to consider?

– How big a challenge would it be for you?

– What would you do differently if you really intended to deliver your legacy?

– Would your team benefit more if you were to focus more energy on this challenge?

– How would you benefit emotionally and personally from pursuing such a rewarding goal?

I will leave you with these thoughts and remind you that it's up to you; you have responsibility for your organization and its condition when you depart. Grasp that responsibility and that opportunity. And next time you are in a room that implores you to 'leave it as

LOOKING

you would like to find it', ask yourself again whether you are really fulfilling your potential in your leadership role.

Some further thoughts on leadership:

Heroic Leadership – attractive but dangerous?

David Beckham, J-Lo, Hugh Grant. Isn't it funny how celebrity names catch your eye. Indeed, it is possible that the listing of their names drew you to this piece in the first place. I believe that we would all recognize that the culture of celebrity is a dominant feature of life in the 21st Century in Anglo American societies.

And it is a culture that seems to be transferring itself to the business environment, particularly in terms of the managers and leaders that guide and shape our organizations. Today, it is not uncommon for the world at large (and the business community in particular) to be very familiar with the names, faces and characteristics of the chief executives of many of our businesses. This knowledge comes about through books, articles, appearances on television and radio, and of course speaking appearances at conferences. Admittedly, the adoring crowds don't yet hang on their every word and autograph hunters are simply confined to asking for a signature on the fly leaf of the 'great leaders' latest book, but the path towards the cult of leadership is well trodden.

Is this right; is this appropriate; is it important and does this reflect a dangerous trend?

Clearly, the leadership and management of our organizations is important because one of the key roles of managers is to effectively deliver the strategic goals and success of the business. And the interest in leadership by business schools and the business community generally evidences the importance that is attributed to this aspect of organizational life.

Now, I don't believe that the intent of business schools and the business community is to create a culture where the celebrity or 'heroic leader' is dominant, but this is something that has crept up on us. In turn there exists the danger that up-and-coming managers don't aspire to the delivery of long term performance of the business but primarily seek the recognition that being a high profile leader brings.

Alongside, this high profile approach is centred on the individual, not on the organization; it is centred on ego and the 'chosen one' leading us to a point where it becomes increasingly difficult to challenge or question the thoughts and ideas of that heroic leader.

In turn, board and management meetings become increasingly politicized and are led by dominant individuals seeking short term results. Fear becomes a common trait, with managers frightened of criticizing or challenging 'the boss'.

But does this heroic form of leadership deliver the other goals of long term performance and strategic success? I propose that it doesn't; that it doesn't help the long term performance of the organization; nor the development of capable high performing teams where diverse view points are valued and utilized to develop fresh thinking and the creation of new opportunities; where customers and their needs are understood by the organization as a whole and where stakeholders and shareholders can have confidence in the management team.

So is there another option?

I believe that there is, and to make it distinct from 'heroic leadership' let me call it 'quiet leadership'. Here, the common traits are not ego, personality, power and politics, but humility, a quiet resolve to achieve, driven by long term motivation and goals focused on the development of organizational capability. It is leadership that seeks to energize others and engage people in the long term success of the organization.

All well and good, but does this help us to better achieve the goal of delivering long-term high performance by the organization? I believe that it does, but let's test it.

I think we would all agree that we live in a more unpredictable environment where organizations have to be able to better respond to customers' changing and developing needs. To be successful in this environment we know that businesses have to be more flexible; more entrepreneurial; able to think strategically whilst continuously improving their operations; and at the same time getting ever closer to the customers so that they can understand and then predict their evolving requirements. To succeed, these need to be organizational traits developed across the whole organization not just across a group of managers. Which style of leadership achieves this best – quiet or heroic?

In turn, we know that strategic success also demands that the business as a whole understands, and is committed to its plans, goals and aspirations. Again can this degree of clarity and commitment best be served by heroic or quiet leadership?

To build organizations like this, demands that management teams can refresh and renew their thinking, avoid insularity of thought, provoke insight, and encourage critical debate

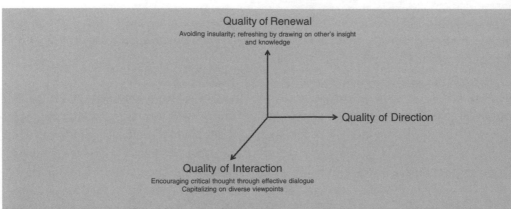

Figure 12: Three dimensions of high performing boards, (Herb *et al.*, 2001)

so that they can bring a quality of direction to the business that focuses people, engages teams and delivers a momentum so that the whole organization is capable of, and willing to do something quite special over the long term.

In reality, of course, managers utilize both heroic and quiet leadership because life is never as simple as the polarized picture I have painted. But in light of the identified pressures, we need our leaders and managers to be conscious of current trends, fight against them and draw upon a broader range of skills and approaches than the apparent short-cut offered by 'heroic leadership'. Yes it is attractive, but it carries dangers.

LOOKING

Doing

I am going to take a slightly different approach to the Doing section in this chapter. Management and leadership are not linear activities where you do one thing and it leads to another. Accordingly, the approaches I have adopted to the Doing section in earlier chapters are not appropriate here.

However, there are a number of things that need to be considered and I need to highlight these for you. Also, I believe that much of your improvement as a leader will come about from self-reflection and practicing and developing new skills. I am therefore providing an approach that will allow you to reflect on your current performance, identify the key things you should be doing, and set yourself some targets for improvement.

Below you will find three blank radial graphs, each one focusing on a different aspect of your leadership role in your organization. In each case, the descriptions at the end of each of the spokes of the radial graphs will provide you with a clear prompt as to the roles you should be undertaking as a reader and manager.

By rating your performance and completing the graphs you will be able to assess how you are currently doing and identify those areas where you either need to become more active or need to develop your performance.

In each case I encourage you to set targets for your performance so that you have something to work towards. You will see that I have used a simple scale, where 1 is the lowest score and 5 is the highest. I fully accept that self-assessment is full of inherent weaknesses and it will be much better if you got others to assess you and provide feedback. Do this if you wish, but this should not stop you from reflecting on your own performance and identifying those areas where you believe improvement will have the greatest impact.

As I say, there are three graphs:

☑ The first asks whether you have put in place the necessary conditions in which strategies can be implemented. (Consider this from either the perspective of the executive team for the whole business or simply the IT function.)

☑ The second graph explores your role and performance in terms of your IT function or team. Have you created an environment in which the IT function can perform over the long-term?

In each case, you need to rate your performance both now and in terms of where you would like to be in order to deliver the necessary results. The following graph provides an example.

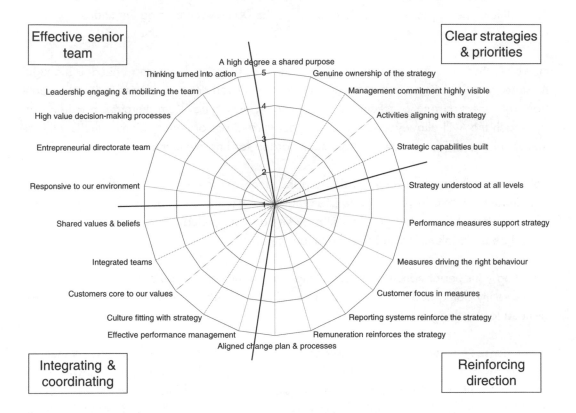

Figure 13: Successfully implementing strategy (Beer and Eisenstat, 2000)

☑ And the third asks how effective are you in the performance management role?

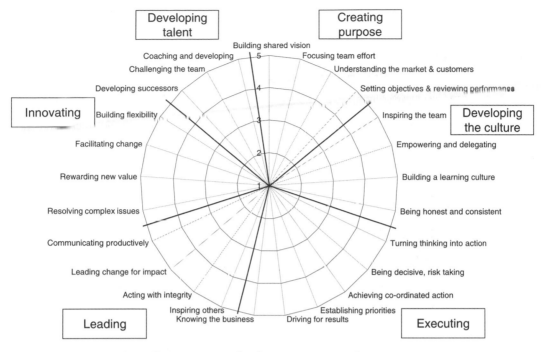

Figure 14: Creating the context the long-term performance

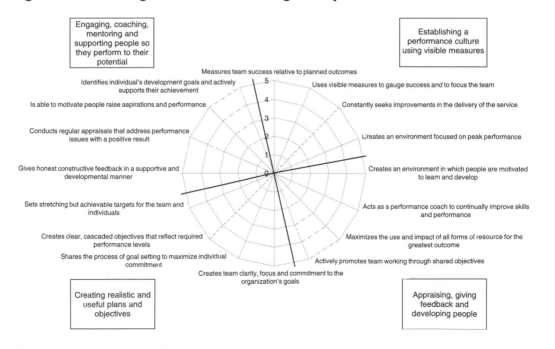

Figure 15: Being an effective performance leader

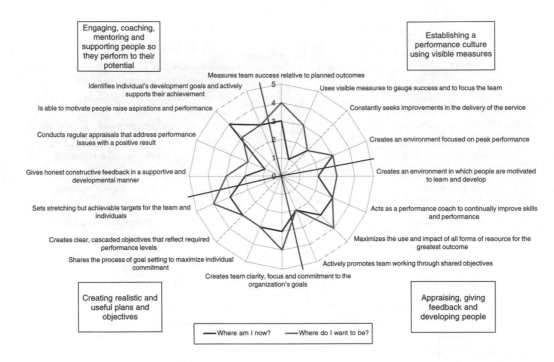

Figure 16: Being an effective performance leader – an example

As a result of undertaking these assessments, you will be able to clearly see the sort of things you should be doing, how you are currently performing and where you need to develop and improve. It would therefore seem sensible as a result to capture your thinking in a simple action plan to keep your development focused and to the front of mind.

	What do I want to achieve?	Why do I want to do this?	How will I know if I am improving?	How will I achieve this? i.e. stop /start / continue doing?	When do I need to do this by?
1					
2					
3					

Table 3: Your personal development plan

It is not possible to address all the development needs that you may have identified above. Most people can only work on one, or perhaps two things at a time. Therefore, you need to identify the priorities for your development.

DOING

11 Building and sustaining your brand

- Where? – Where are you going, what are you trying to achieve and what are your objectives?

- The brand

- Who? – Who is involved in successfully building your brand?

- The relationship management role

- How? – Making it happen on the ground.

Our starting point is one where the perception and reputation of IT is often negative. Thus, IT managers must be able to manage their brand across the business and often across outsourced providers. Unfortunately, they have very little guidance of what to and how to do it. This chapter provides you with the necessary approaches to managing the IT brand.

Touching

I have purposefully and provocatively included the word 'brand' in the title of this chapter, for the simple reason that you need to build a brand in the eyes of the business as a whole and your staff in IT; a brand that they can relate to, understand what it means and what it delivers.

At this juncture some of you will be saying "hype, puff and superficial claptrap". You are wrong. By brand I don't mean just a logo, I mean the depth of consistent delivery and communication which results in people understanding who you are, what you are about, and willingly putting faith in your ability to perform.

By this I also infer that this is a concerted program and series of activities over a period of time with clear purpose and deep-seated impact. In this respect, you need to understand when entering this chapter that you will not communicate effectively with the business and win their hearts and minds by simply relying upon a single or disconnected activities, nor upon the personality and relationships of a single person, nor upon the Chief Information Officer getting a place on the board, nor upon some short-lived promotion regarding IT and its aspirations. No, you have to do all these things, at the same time and over a long period of time. Like courting and marriage, relationships and trust are built over time through multiple contacts, through delivery of promises, through perseverance and put simply, bloody hard work.

Indeed, like a marriage where a lot of wood is thrown onto the fire in the early days to create some roaring flames of passion, the fire and the marriage eventually settle down to a warm and reassuring glow, in which both parties live happily and comfortably, as long as the fire is occasionally stoked and some additional fuel added.

In the same way, you are going to need to put substantial effort into your brand and business relationships in the early days to get into the position where you can operate effectively and comfortably with your partners and where they understand you, what you can and can't do, how you behave, the things you can and can't do, and why you do those peculiar things that make up the quirks and your personality. And whilst this initial heavy workload is important, so is the need to keep stoking the fire and adding fuel. In other words you have to maintain this program over time by way of ongoing activities to reinforce the brand message and the relationships you have built.

However, you will know that as a member of the IT community the concept of positive brand management is not something that you are likely to be familiar with. Indeed, I find that most

IT departments spend their lives undermining the good things they have done, talking about their problems, appearing negative, appearing uncertain, and generally undermining their own confidence, let alone the confidence of the business in their ability to deliver.

IT functions do incredible things every day that people in the business just take for granted. Things that without which the business could not operate, everyone's lives would be much more complex, costs would be greater, jobs would take longer and we would not have information to hand to enable us to make key business decisions. It's just that we don't tell people and we allow discussions to centre on the negative, where the failure of one PC or PDA amongst many thousands dominates conversation and organizational rumour mills.

There is an old saying "the man who stands for nothing, falls for anything". This rings true more in IT than in any other function in the business. So often, we do not stand for anything and therefore our customers and our staff are free to fall for anything. And that 'anything' is often a negative. As a result, people start to believe (indeed, are happy to believe) that IT doesn't deliver, they are always late, nothing ever works, they are always over budget, they are a bunch of wasters, they have no skills, etc.

You know, and I know that this is utter gibberish. It is our job through the approaches in this chapter to change this perception for good and for ever.

In part this is about a coordinated, consistent and continuous brand campaign in the same way that the major brands around the world keep themselves in our faces so that we cannot forget who they are and what they stand for. It is also about your confidence and the confidence of your team. Confidence in this context will be aided not just by the activities set out here, but also is built upon four key components:

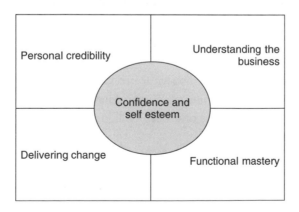

Figure 1: Developing confidence in the CIO

In this respect, confidence in a CIO is built on the personal credibility of the individual, the depth of business understanding that they possess, the skills and knowledge they have regarding IT and their track record in delivering change.

Confidence is more important than you may think and can provide a rich source of power and energy. You only need to think about what you can achieve when you are feeling good about yourself as opposed to when you are feeling negative and you will quickly recognize and realize the benefits confidence can bring. Therefore you need to consider, and find ways, by which you can build, develop and sustain your own confidence and, I would suggest, your resilience.

This chapter is divided into three main parts:

Figure 2: Building the IT brand – the core elements

Where?

– Where are you going, what are you trying to achieve and what are your objectives? I will explore issues regarding your IT brand and its fit with your strategy.

Who?

– Who is involved in successfully building your brand. This section will consider the differing roles of the CIO, your staff, and most importantly the relationship managers, or as they are sometimes called business analysts. I will look in greater depth at their role and the skills that they need.

How?

– How do you go about making it happen on the ground? What you need to do and how can you structure your approach?

Where?

You need to make sure you are clear about what you are trying to achieve in the context of the business, your own strategy, your proposition, and your brand. Therefore, we need to set objectives in each area.

Strategy

In respect of the business strategy and your own strategy I would hope that you are clear about this from the issues we have explored in the earlier chapters and I don't wish to expand much further here.

However I must make the point once again that the key aspect is understanding the business; what it is trying to achieve, how it creates value and how it competes. Without this understanding you cannot focus your efforts and those of your team. It is no good building an IT brand which does not resonate with the needs of the business community that you serve.

Equally you cannot build an IT brand without having clarity regarding your own IT strategy. A brand does not replace a strategy; it personifies it and makes it tangible and accessible on the ground.

Your proposition

As we discussed in Chapters 7, 8 and 9, you need to be clear about the proposition that you are making to the business and what this comprises. Again I don't intend to repeat what has been covered elsewhere, but I do intend to pull out some salient points as they relate to this topic.

There is a good chance that the proposition you have developed is quite detailed and contains a large number of component elements. However, this amount of detail does not provide you with the basis of a good brand message. Somehow, you need to distil this into key words and phrases that are:

– Accessible: your target market can easily understand what you are talking about.

– Memorable: the concepts are sticky and stay with your target market after you have left them.

– Applicable: your target market can see how the issues you have highlighted relate to them and their needs.

Imagine a pot of yoghurt. Inside is a rich mix of bacteria, flavourings and fruit. However, if the marketer tried to sell the product by using the ingredients list she would fail miserably, and the chances of winning market share will be greatly eroded. They don't, they pick out three or four key words that describe the ingredients and which excite you and entice you to open the lid. If you open the lid then you will find out about all the various and multiple contents, and if you are so inclined you may also read the contents list on the side of the pot.

Our challenge is much the same. We need to describe what we are about and the value we bring in a way that excites people and energizes a desire in them to work with us.

Some of you will say that this really is about hype and language only. As I reflected earlier, it is not. This is only one dimension of building the brand and cannot be separated from the hard edged delivery and all the other components that we talk about here and the rest of this book.

However, I am conscious that many IT functions will be starting from a point of being defensive because they are not yet delivering at the levels required by the business and hence may feel unable to shout about their plans and aspirations.

Perhaps though, marketers offer us a way to resolve this concern. In any marketing proposition there is a promise. Sometimes it is tangible and often it is aspirational. For example when you buy a Rolex watch you are not necessarily getting any greater accuracy of time than you would get from a Casio watch. What you are getting is the joy of belonging to the 'Rolex club' and the opportunity to say something about yourself to others.

In IT we are slightly different, but we are still making a promise and should be keen to tell the business about our goals. Indeed there should be a good fit between our plans and their needs, so they should be delighted to hear that we are pointing in the same direction as them. However, we must temper our promises with a sense of reality because we are dealing with hard-headed business people who at this moment may be pretty cynical about IT and our ability to perform.

For example, if we draw on my concept of 'Following, Enabling and Leading', it is possible that your function is currently struggling to 'Follow' but you maybe be putting initiatives in place that will enable you to deliver an efficient, effective, and reliable service, and you may aspire to be taking a 'Leadership' role in the future. If this were the case, you may wish to play down your 'Leadership' aspirations at this stage even though you know that this is where the true value of IT lies in your business.

However, the business does need to know that you recognize the importance of getting to a 'Leadership' state so that you can indeed deliver the value that they are seeking. This does not mean that you are promising to get there tomorrow, nor underestimating the difficulties involved in achieving that success, but it does help them to see where you are pointing.

So to me, it is fine to be saying "Our aspirations are to be able to be 'Leading', but right now, we are going to focus on getting the basics right and being quite brilliant at 'Following'."

Now, of course this may put pressure on you and your team to deliver, because failure will be clear to everyone. Good. I have no problem whatsoever in everyone feeling the pressure of the need to raise the game and deliver what is expected and needed by the business.

In this example I used my concept of 'Following, Enabling and Leading', but in your case the proposition will fall out of your main strategic themes. For example, a firm I worked with in financial services had determined that the role of their IT function was to:

"Enable immediacy

Enabling immediacy with its (business) customers

Enabling immediacy of knowledge, and

Enabling immediacy through technology processes and people."

If IT could deliver on this then the business could deliver the immediacy it needed with its customers on the front line. IT decided that for them to achieve these goals, they need to pursue three key themes:

Being efficient and effective, which involved them in:

– Delivering what is promised on time

– Providing a reliable service

– Responding to business timescales

– Managing out the legacy problems and simplifying systems

– Delivering at a lower cost

TOUCHING

Listening, learning and leading, which involved them in:

– Customer-focused behaviours

– Actively managing relationships

– Leading, challenging, educating and informing

– Delivering a service, not a box

– Jointly solving problems and issues

– Operating at the same pace as the business

Creating value, which involved them in:

– Innovating

– Delivering long term capability

– Being commercial

– Delivering the promised benefits

– Resilient and adaptive to change.

Beneath this existed a series of plans relating to key initiatives, the development of capabilities and various performance measures. The business did not need to know all the detail; what they needed to understand was that IT were going to:

– Deliver a reliable service at a lower cost, which helped them to be more productive.

– Get closer to them and understand the issues they faced and help them find practical solutions.

– Bring them new ideas and possibilities which help them win loyal customers and beat the competition.

On my yoghurt pot it says 'Fruit Corner, peach and apricot – thick and creamy yoghurt. Now with more fruit.'

Only on the ingredients list does it tell me that it contains yoghurt, peach, sugar, apricots, pectins, carob bean, gum, guar, citric acid and milk. And do you know what, I really don't care.

Customer needs

Remember, customers have different levels of need.

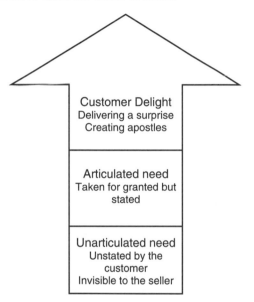

Figure 3: What customers need – creating delight

The base level relates to the unarticulated need. Here the user expects to have a PC that works reliably. They assume it will be there and available to them at all times and won't even bother asking for it.

However, at the next level they <u>will</u> articulate the need for strong project management throughout a large systems implementation program so that it delivers the expected results on time. This is not to say that they will expect anything other than strong project management, it is just that they will be a lot more open about their expectations.

TOUCHING

There is the opportunity for you to enjoy a real win by delighting and surprising users of IT. If you can do this, then you will win credibility and loyalty which will give you the freedom to become a creator of value across the business.

In summary, you are looking for a short, sharp, simple message that tells people where you are focusing your energies and the benefits that they will get as a result.

The brand

At this point, can I ask you to picture in your mind a Porsche 911? What do you see?

Some of you will see a car, others will see a thing of great beauty, others power, others speed, others envy, others testosterone, others aspiration, and others an overpriced form of transport.

For me, I see it as a laptop and information system on wheels. It has a hard drive, display screens, a type of keyboard and a battery. It provides management information, but it does it for the right people at the right time.

- The speedometer runs all the time to tell me how fast I am traveling,

- The oil warning light only comes on when the oil is too low

- The engine management system connects with the computer at the garage to carry out a systems diagnosis. The engine management system does not report to me as the driver because I don't need the depth and range of information that it can provide; but the garage mechanic does.

There are a number of messages from this analogy:

- Porsche cars are packed full of technology in the same way as the systems in your business. However, when people look at the Porsche car, they do not view it as a piece of technology. They view it in the ways I described above – beauty, power, speed, aspiration. In other words, they see it in terms of the benefits it brings.

- Your challenge in this respect is to get people to the point where they view IT in terms of the benefits that you bring not the bits of tin that you put on people's desks.

- You need, therefore, to understand how your customers behave, what value they want and the benefits that they desire. You should be able to do this in a business sense from the work you have already undertaken.

- In other words, you need to become 'benefits'-focused and value-driven.

- The Porsche car provides information by which you can make decisions. It provides this information to the right people at the right time. The question you should ask yourself is whether your IT function is indeed providing the right information to the right people, in the right format, when they need it so that they can make the right decisions. Many IT functions provide too much information to too many people at the wrong time. How do you become like a Porsche car and build a reputation that matches theirs?

This exploration of Porsche leads us nicely into considering the issue of what actually is a brand. Philip Kotler provides us with one of the most effective summaries:

Attributes	What we are known for
Benefits	The benefits we bring
Values	Our values and beliefs
Culture	The way we do things
Personality	Our character
User	Our type of customer

Figure 4: What makes a brand? (Kotler, 1994)

I am going to describe briefly each of the terms that he uses, but in each case you need to consider what it is you are trying to achieve, and how you want to be perceived in each aspect.

Attributes

Whenever you think of a leading brand (Microsoft, Intel, Oracle, Apple, Dell) you can, quickly articulate what they are known for, and what they do. You could easily tell others that they should use Dell kit because it is reliable, made of good components and can be bought for an economical price. And if you asked your colleagues, they would say much the same thing. In other words, the attributes attaching to the brand are clear and recognized broadly.

Benefits

Similarly, Oracle technology 'enables you to better manage all your information, so every employee can make better, more informed decisions.' "Hey" you may say, "that's just what I need." Clearly, those benefits need to relate to the needs of the customers you have chosen to serve. The better the fit, the greater the value and the tighter the bond that exists between the two parties.

Values

What are the principles against which you make your core decisions? How can you tell right from wrong? What are the standards by which you operate? These questions do not illustrate superficial issues of performance or even strategy, but the deeply held rules and guidelines that everybody holds in their head and which tell them how to behave.

Culture

The 'counterculture' at Apple has been a key element in its differentiating itself from IBM and others by encouraging people to 'Think Different'. This has created high levels of demand and the concept of the 'Cult of Mac', where the use of an Apple product is a lifestyle choice.

Personality

This may appear to be a strange one compared to the others but really it tells a story about the organization. Of course, Disney has taken this to the extreme by associating its brand with the personality of Mickey Mouse, but Microsoft is also synonymous with Bill Gates and Richard Branson with Virgin. These are strong examples of personification of the brand. They allow the buying public to shortcut their decision-making. Instead of having to undertake a full assessment of the suppliers credentials they simply say "Oh yes, Mickey Mouse/ Richard Branson/ Bill Gates, they must be okay. I will buy from them."

User

Because of the other five elements in this list and the way in which they come together a company or a brand tends to be attractive to a certain type of user. In other words different people buy Apple to those which by Microsoft. One person buys BMW, another Mercedes and another Audi. This is why when you go into your favourite store there are a lot of people in there just like you.

In the case of your IT function, who are the users who will be attracted to you? Who are the users with whom you will work well? If you know and you are looking to win some credibility in the business then you can do yourself no harm but focus on these people, deliver success to them and then tell the story of your success to others.

Of course, you cannot just work with those who you want to work with, you have to support the whole business. All I am suggesting is that in the first instance it may make sense to practice and develop your skills in a conducive environment.

Consistent delivery

To build a brand, you need consistency of delivery of these factors. Therefore, you need to determine the principles by which your IT function will operate and which underpin your brand. When operating well, as in the examples given above, it will be implicitly and explicitly understood by your customers so that they know who they are dealing with, how business will be carried out and the results that will accrue.

A brand also operates in relation to both your IT staff and your business customers. Internally, the brand provides clarity, standards and direction for your staff. It can also provide a sense of belonging.

Externally brand, on the other hand, gives your customers an understanding of what they are buying and why.

You need to be clear about what you are working towards and trying to be recognized for. Like all the major brands I have cited here, success in a brand sense arises from hard work over a sustained period, supporting a consistent approach and message.

Who?

In the last section we considered strategy, your proposition, and your brand and identified the messages or actions you are going to pursue. As CIO you will not be doing this alone.

In this section we need to look at who it is that is going to be involved in this communication activity, both by way of storyteller and audience. Thus, we will consider the roles of the relationship manager, the CIO, and the IT team.

Firstly, though, I have to point out the obvious. Everyone who will be involved, either storyteller or audience is a human being with a personality and a way of behaving. We have to recognize this and tailor our approaches accordingly. In other words people behave because of who they are, not their job title. Yes, their behaviour will be influenced by the job they do, but at the core is the person who goes home at the end of the day and spends time with his family, who has hobbies at the weekend and has interests out of work. As I say, they are human beings.

TOUCHING

In particular, we need to identify how we are going to communicate with the differing types of people with whom we have to work. To achieve this I am going to introduce a simplified behavioural profiling model which helps us to understand their differing communication styles and guides us to choose appropriate tactics in different circumstances and with different people.

In the grid below I would like you to read the four descriptors and identify which box most closely resembles your way of behaving.

Analyser	Conductor
Concern for quality Attention to detail High quality standards Analysis of facts and data Investigating and planning Logical	Results-oriented Competitive Task focused Sense of urgency Seeks to direct others
Supporter	**Promoter**
Routine work Guidelines to follow Seeks security Relaxed pace Likes being part of a team	Seeks interaction with others Not fearful of change Rather talk than listen Varied activities Intuitive

Figure 5: People behave differently – which one are you?

(Adapted from The Success Insights DISC model from Target Training International of Scottsdale, Arizona.)

Having done that, also identify one of your key business partners and see where they sit on this grid.

You may notice that if you are an:

– Analyser or a Supporter you will enjoy the Touching sections of this book,

– Promoters will focus on Looking, and

– Conductors will tend towards the Doing section.

If you are finding it difficult to identify people using this approach, try the following matrix which describes what it is like when you meet with them or go into their office:

My point is that people are very different in the way that they behave and act. In consequence they are very different in the way in which they wish to communicate. The following grid shows the same four groupings, but this time provides guidance on how you can communicate with each of them:

Analyser	Conductor
Organized desks Work in neat tidy piles Talk in a considered way Will be careful in their choice of words Will talk about the task rather than the people	Will quickly start to talk about objectives and tasks Tend to talk in a direct staccato style Will use performance charts and graphs Clearly ambitious and forceful
Supporter	**Promoter**
Will talk about the team Tend to have photos of the family and team events Will be relaxed and modest Will seek to clarify and check understanding	Will talk about themselves and their achievements Will be friendly and enthusiastic Use the 'I' word a lot Will exude energy and passion Trophies will evidence their success

Figure 6: People behave differently – spotting the different types

Let's say you identified from the first two grids that your chief executive sits neatly in the Conductor box. These are people who like to be in control, they work at a fast pace, and enjoy change, finding solutions and getting the job done. Therefore your language and approach needs to reflect this.

Analyser	Conductor
Do: Prepare your case in advance Stick to business Be accurate and realistic Use words such as: Great accuracy Proven through research because knowing is better than guessing Minimize your risk Tested / Proven reliability	Do: Be clear, be specific and to the point Stick to business Be prepared with an organized package Use words such as: Your opinion counts Making a big contribution Getting the results you want Lead the pack
Supporter	**Promoter**
Do: Begin with niceties to break the ice Present your case softly and non threateningly Ask 'how'questions to draw their opinions Use words such as: Nothing complex about it Staying in the mainstream Free of controversy Easy for people to use	Do: Provide a warm and friendly environment Encourage them to use their energy Ask feeling questions to draw their opinions Keep off detail Use words such as: Exciting, new & unique Getting recognition Gain respect Creating the right image

Figure 7: People behave differently – communicating in their language

You need to be direct, to the point and you need to make them feel that they are in control. As a result, it is best to give them options rather than simply telling them what to do.

By contrast, Supporters just love security, routine and a much slower pace. So being direct, task-focused and assuming that they will love the idea of a new way of doing things will only cause them to retreat from the relationship and discussion.

Therefore, the need is to recognize these differing types and to find ways to communicate with them that recognizes their differing needs. This will demand different styles when talking to them, writing to them, presenting plans and ideas, choosing the media you use and the support that you offer.

Equally, it demands that you practice communicating in these different ways with these different people. It will not come naturally, but the more you can adapt to their style the closer you will get to them and opportunities will present themselves to you to engage in a more positive dialogue. Additionally, you will find it less likely that personality gets in the way of your brand message.

This is not to propose a Machiavellian approach to manipulating people. This is about recognizing that people are different, and it is about being sensitive enough to respond to their needs. It is about empathy not cunning.

The Relationship Manager

Some may refer to this as the business analyst or IT consultant. All the terms are appropriate but in this book I am going to use the term relationship manager because this is the key element of the role in which I am interested. It is the ability to understand and relate to the key players within the business in a way that enables the relationship manager to act as the linchpin and key conduit between the business and the IT function.

It is the customer facing role of the IT department, translating needs, desires and language in both directions, acting as a strategic partner to the business managers, learning about the business, anticipating their needs and translating these into IT projects and solutions.

This is where the IT brand is personified; it is the human face of IT and its brand. I struggle to see how IT functions can really understand the needs of the businesses in which they work without this key role. My experience is that relationship managers open up communication channels, minimize tensions, and provide focus on both sides which results in greater value being delivered. In other words, they provide a vehicle by which strategic alignment can be achieved and delivered and I have rarely seen IT functions achieving the degree of alignment that is necessary without these roles in place.

For me therefore, they are a key component in the structure of any IT function that really wishes to Align IT.

You may ask where you fit in this as the CIO? I believe that in this sense you are the highest level relationship manager in the company. In other words, what the relationship managers do in the business units, you needs to do in the boardroom. Additionally, the you 'personifies' the strategy as well as the brand.

So if your strategy is about Following and hence delivering an incredibly productive, efficient and optimal IT system and processes, then you need to evidence that through your words, actions and knowledge. If your IT strategy is about Leading, then you need to be at the forefront of evolving technologies and identifying strategic and competitive opportunity. Alongside you will be undertaking the same relationship management role that you ask of your relationship managers, but with the executive team.

Centrally the relationship managers represent your brand in the business and you need them to be the brand managers that you deserve and require.

So what does this mean in practice?

– What skills and behaviours are needed?

– What goals are you trying to achieve?

– What type of relationships are you trying to build?

What type of relationship manager?

Firstly, we need to understand what type of relationship we are asking our relationship managers to embark upon. Often people refer to relationship management in a generic term in the same way as they loosely used the word 'quality'. There are many different types of quality, in the same way as there are different types of relationship management.

What type of relationships?	
Supportive – learns about the customer and has empathy	Developing norms and processes for customers to follow
Solving problems for the customer	Bringing new ideas and options
Resilient and adaptive to customers changing needs	Challenging, perceptive, yet sensitive

Figure 8: Building relationships – choosing your approach

Supportive

Are you looking for your relationship manager simply to put an arm around the business, offer them cups of tea and let them know that we understand their problems?

Developing norms

This approach to relationship management has its foundation in the Following strategic theme and is about standardization, efficiency, productivity and reliability. If you want them to do this for you, then your relationship managers need to understand issues around operations management thinking and processes.

Solving problems

These relationship managers are good at getting close to the business, understanding the intractable issues they face and finding solutions both in the IT and business arenas.

Bringing new ideas

This is about the relationship manager acting as a catalyst to change by leading the business units to the possibilities that exist through the evolution of technology and knowledge management.

Resilient and adaptive

These relationship managers are able to cope in fast moving, fluid environments where agility, entrepreneurship and flexibility dominate, both in terms of behaviour and the environment in which the business operates.

Challenging and perceptive

This more demanding and possibly confrontational approach is about getting the business units to rethink their assumptions, and to show the consequences of their existing thinking.

It may be implied from these descriptions that the choice is down to the character and skills of the relationship manager. This is an incorrect assumption. The approach to be adopted is one based upon the needs of the IT strategy and the business in which it is set. It is then up to you to pick the people and build the skills necessary to deliver the type of relationship management approach that you wish and need to adopt.

Having identified the approach, you are then in a position to consider how the role will work on a more practical basis and how it will add to our brand presence.

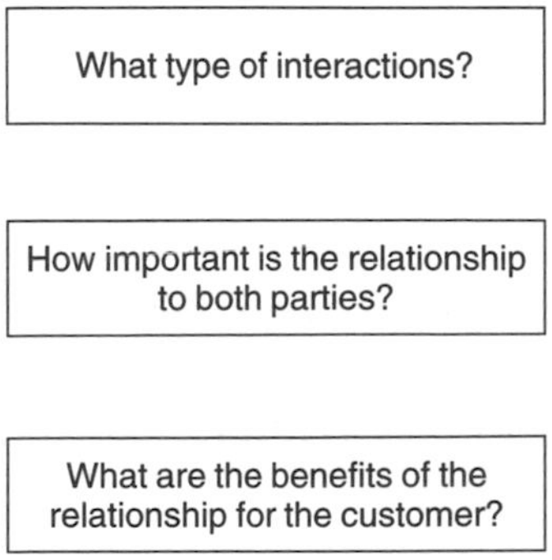

What type of interactions?

How important is the relationship to both parties?

What are the benefits of the relationship for the customer?

Figure 9: Building relationships – focusing on benefits

TOUCHING

This demands clarity over the type of interactions you want between your relationship manager and the business. This can only really be determined by identifying the benefits that will accrue to the customer because of the relationship manager's intervention.

By this I mean that I worry about businesses that have created the role of relationship managers, but the role is often one centred on the business itself rather than its customer. They never stop and consider whether there is a benefit to the customer in taking time out to meet with the relationship manager. In other words, is the 'relationship' solely for the benefit of the supplier but not for the benefit of the customer?

In the same way, your relationship managers must be clear and be able to articulate to their business partners why they should take time out of their busy lives to meet and explore the ways in which IT and the business unit can work more closely together.

The relationship manager's objectives

In line with our discussions in Chapter 6, and to clarify the relationship manager's role, it important to adopt strategically aligned objectives for the job. Thus, their objectives need to be directly linked to those set for the IT function. This link needs to be explicit so that the relationship managers can see clearly what they have to deliver and how this fits into the delivery of the IT strategy.

Indeed, it is likely that a new relationship manager will come with their own views about what they want to deliver and what is the purpose of the role. This may be okay, but you need to ensure from the outset that they are pointed in the right direction in order to deliver the right results and to behave in the right way.

To achieve this, I find that using the structure in Figure 10 is very helpful. This is an approach I use when agreeing objectives with individuals in a wide variety of roles. The concept is built around the idea that you need to have a conversation with the individual involved in order to identify with them three or four key objective areas and to make clear what it is they are expected to deliver and how.

Through the use of the word 'conversation' I am seeking to reinforce that this is about a dialogue between you and the relationship manager where you explore the focus of the role and what the relationship manager needs to be doing in order to be successful.

An in-depth conversation such as this with your new relationship managers is important at the outset of the new role so that you jointly gain an understanding of what the role is about

What the relationship manager needs to deliver...					
	Example	Objective 1	Objective 2	Objective 3	Objective 4
To enable our organization to...	Successfully deliver our new department				
...the RM needs to deliver...	The building to plan (cost, time, quality) The planned customer numbers				
...by doing these things...	Exercising strong project management Delivering the marketing plan				
...who they need to get on board and influence...	Senior and middle management, Construction team, Marketing department				
...using these key skills & behaviours...	Planning Project management Leadership Influencing & negotiating Marketing knowledge				
...with these resources...	Financial budgets Senior management's experience and support				
What success will look like and how we will measure it...	Operational by September, Target customer numbers achieved by December				

Figure 10: Setting objectives – a focused conversation

and what it needs to deliver. If you have not had a role like this in your organization before, it is very likely that there will be a lot of learning to be done and a good deal of flexibility demanded as you find out what does and doesn't work.

The purpose of the form is not to be a prescriptive route map but simply to structure and facilitate a conversation around the key areas that need exploring. I have provided an example to show generally how it works and also to show the limited detail that needs capturing. These are simply notes that record the outcome of your conversations.

It is probably worth making some points about each of the aspects that I have proposed that you should discuss.

To enable our organization to...

In these boxes you are trying to provide a strategic context for the individual objectives. So your goal is to be able to enter a headline statement which establishes a functional or organizational purpose. For example, you may insert, "To enable our team to... respond more quickly, or reduce costs, or increase customer satisfaction, or reduce the number of errors, etc"

...the RM needs to deliver...

This is the essential high level statement of the objectives that you would like the relationship manager to pursue and achieve. The most critical issue here is that you define the objectives in terms of outcomes, i.e. what will the relationship manager have achieved or created as a result of delivering on the objective. It is important that you represent this as a description of a future state, rather than a description of the activity that we wish the individual to pursue.

...By doing these things

At this level we want to identify the key three or four activities that will be required to achieve the outcome defined above.

The description should allow the individual sufficient scope to go about their work with some discretion and personal input, and they must be clear enough to ensure that the relationship manager goes off at a tangent.

...Who do they need to get on board and influence...

It is critical that the right people are involved (or at the very least consulted and informed) at the right stages in any particular phase of a project. Therefore, you need to consider who needs to be involved and managed as an integral part of the delivery of the objectives. Answering this question will enable you to see the levels within the organization at which the relationship manager needs to operate.

...Using these skills and behaviours...

Here you are simply looking to identify the 2 or 3 key skills or behaviours for each objective that will really make the difference. (In this regard, please see the section on relationship management skills below.)

...With these resources...

You need to be absolutely clear about what resources the relationship manager needs in order to deliver their objectives, and equally you need to give consideration as to what is realistically going to be made available to support delivery.

What success will look like and how we will measure it...

Here you are looking for measurable goals for each of the objectives that you have identified. These will be used to judge whether the objectives are being achieved or not. Measures should be stated in SMART terms, and in terms of an outcome rather than an activity. (SMART – Specific, Measurable, Agreed, Realistic, Timebound.) It is key that the individual knows on what basis they will be assessed, and what they must deliver for you to judge them a success.

In conclusion, you will have created a shared view of what is required and how it is to be achieved. Alongside you will have written a pretty good job description for the relationship manager role. This will enable you to go out and find the right candidates for the job and be able to explain to them what it is you are expecting them to do.

Relationship management skills

So, what does all this mean for the relationship manager in terms of the skills that they need?

Firstly, and as noted above the skill needs are determined by the focus that you have decided is right for the role. In other words, if you want your relationship managers to simply be 'supportive' then the skills required will be very different from those needed by a relationship manager whom you expect to bring 'new ideas and options'.

Secondly, and more specifically, the skill needs are determined by the objectives that you set for the role as described in the preceding section. In that section I proposed that you need to identify the skills that are demanded to deliver on each of the objectives, and my aim in this section is to provide you with a broad range of competences from which you can draw. I do not propose to provide you with a specific set of skills or competencies for each of the different type of roles as this would be too prescriptive. However, I will provide you with an à la carte menu from which you can select the competencies required.

Like a good meal, this menu has three courses. They are:

– the relationship elements of the role,

– the change aspects, and

– the analytical skills that are required.

From these menus I suggest that you identify a total of eight to ten competencies that are critical to success. I know that you could pick many more, but in reality there will only be eight or so skills that are really required to enable the relationship manager to be successful. Indeed I would suggest that over time you will find that there are only four or five of them that really drive massive impact and results. However, at this stage, trying to narrow it down to this smaller number will be very difficult.

Having identified the top eight or so competencies, you will be able to see quite clearly the key skill demands of the role. As I said earlier, you will then need to identify people who can fulfil this role for you. Do not pretend that the people you select will already have all the skills in abundance; indeed it is likely that you will have to work with them to develop their skills over a period of time so that they become effective relationship managers. This situation is particularly acute with IT staff as their exposure to the business and commercial mindsets is often limited due to their focus on technology in a narrow sense.

It is however, a superb development opportunity for the right people and prepares them for future roles as CIOs by broadening their perspectives and letting them manage the wide-ranging and often conflicting demands of technology, systems, process, business needs and different types of people.

Do not narrow your search for good relationship managers by simply focusing on members of your IT team. There may well be staff in the business that are suitable and of course they will bring with them an understanding of the business, the way it operates and existing contacts. Whilst this may mean that you forego an opportunity to develop one of your own people, it can accelerate the building of relationships between IT and the business, and also accelerate the ability of IT to understand the business demands. In this respect, is quite useful to use a relationship manager drawn from the business as a change agent within IT.

As said earlier, I see the skills demanded by a good relationship manager as being grouped into three main zones; relationship change and analytical skills. These three groups are shown in Figures 11, 12 and 13:

The first of the three sets of competences relates to core relationship management role (Figure 11) and focuses on the importance of interpersonal skills in a variety of dimensions. It reflects the individual's ability to work with different levels of people within the organization, not just in a passive way responding to their demands, but also establishing the ability to set agendas and lead discussions and negotiations that will result in positive outcomes for the business as well as IT.

Building effective relationships	
Reputation	Having the credibility with key players in the business to be able to influence their agendas and win their support. A reputation that is built out of trust, professionalism and a proven ability to deliver
Networking	Able to build a network across business units at a variety of levels and particularly with senior management and key users
Communicating	Able to frame the key issues for individuals and groups in ways that are received positively by them and which lead to action being taken. Ability to use a variety of media and approaches to influence the debate
Constructive	Challenging, perceptive, yet sensitive. Bringing new ideas and options and helping to solve problems
Personal attributes	Having integrity and being trusted. Empathic, politically astute and sensitive. Self-motivated by a determination to deliver improvement and results
Trader	Able to negotiate and trade to reach positive solutions that carry the commitment of all parties
Team player	Seeks a team oriented to problem solving and decision making. Seeks and sees the value in collaborative working
Encouraging change	Encourages new approaches/solutions to problems; encourages strategic thinking and behaving
Supportive & developmental	Supportive when mistakes are made; encourages critical feedback of him/herself and the service provided

Figure 11: Relationship management competencies – Building effective relationships

A relationship role of this nature demands that the individual has the ability to lead and manage change both within the business, and also within the IT function. This set of competencies (Figure 12) identifies the key skills that may be required. Again, the relationship managers will not require all these competencies to carry out their role and you will need to identify the key ones that will be needed to deliver success.

These more technical competencies are demanded by the need to understand the business and identify likely technology and system solutions. (Figure 13)

Which eight or so competencies you select from the three lists will be determined by the role you wish the relationship manager to adopt, their objectives and the organizational context in which you set them.

It is likely that you will do this in conjunction with your colleagues in HR. The discussions that you will have around these competencies will enable you to explore the role and identify what is required in greater depth than simply choosing on your own. You may also use this activity as an opportunity to build the relationship with HR.

TOUCHING

Leading change	
Igniting & influencing	Ability to create the case for change and secure credible support
Challenging	Ability to test and challenge the thinking of key players in the business so that they can see the long term implications and issues
Enabling	Ability to help others, through effective facilitation, to align their plans and change goals to deliver the strategic objectives
Leading	Ability to influence and enthuse others, through personal advocacy, vision and drive, and to access resources to build a solid platform for change
Leveraging	Ability to identify the levers that can be pulled to deliver results
Controlling	Ability to manage implementation of a credible change plan (including appropriate goals, resources, metrics and review mechanisms) despite being outside the formal hierarchy of the business unit
Energizing	Demonstrates high personal commitment to achievement of change goals through integrity and courage, while maintaining objectivity and individual resilience. Able to stay the course
Know-how	Knowledge, generation and skilful appreciation of change theories, tools and processes
Self awareness	Knows strengths and limitations, both in terms of skills and emotions, and uses failure as a basis for learning

Figure 12: Relationship management competencies – making change happen (Higgs and Rowland, 2000)

Critical thinking	
Technical knowledge	Having the functional knowledge of technology, systems and processes to influence and challenge senior management and directors. Has the capacity to deal with a wide range of complex issues
Technical application	Being able to apply the knowledge to identify practical and creative solutions. To have deep knowledge of chosen specialisms in order to be able to lead discussions and problem solving
Accountable	Accepts responsibility for decisions made and has high personal commitment to deliver
Performance manager	Able to agree strategic direction, targets, development plans and hold others to account for delivery of those plans
Analyst	High capability for scanning and networking for information. Keeps abreast of the environment to shape strategic direction and influence others
Decisive risk taker	Decisive when required; willing to take difficult decisions and risks when appropriate
Intellectual flexibility	Able to asses a situation and draw pragmatic conclusions. Able to switch between the big picture and detail as circumstances dictate

Figure 13: Relationship management competencies – using knowledge for impact

Managing relationship managers

Relationship managers are a peculiar being within an IT function even though they would be very readily recognized in sales or marketing, or even HR. Whilst the normal principles of performance management tend to apply there are some differences that you need to bear in mind. Principally, these arise from the fact that the role is more closely aligned with sales than IT, and this has implications for both the relationship manager and their own line manager; both of whom are likely to be inexperienced in this area.

I covered the core performance management principles in Chapter 10, and I only propose to highlight those issues that relate to be the relationship management role.

Our aim in any environment is to maximize the performance of our people, by challenging them to deliver more, but also offering them the support that they need to enable them to perform at the highest levels.

The relationship management role is challenging. They will be a central thrust in the delivery of your strategy, overcoming existing business prejudices, establishing new ways of working, learning about a business that they don't fully understand and acting as a change agent across the IT team. Do not pretend that this is an easy task. If you are going to challenge someone to this degree, then you need to ensure that you provide commensurate support. This too will come about through implementing the basic principles of performance management:

As stated in Chapter 10, you need to establish a cycle of management that helps the individual to understand what they have to deliver, provides them with the necessary support and utilizes performance reviews to achieve a shared view of how the individual is performing.

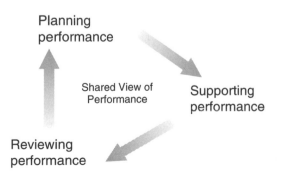

Figure 14: Performance management – the building blocks

This is not just about skills, but also about building the confidence of the relationship manager, especially if they are new to the role. This will be even more important an environment that may be hostile towards them, or at best uncertain of their purpose and remit.

Line managers need to consider the tasks that they need to undertake to support the relationship manager, and I have endeavoured to summarize these below.

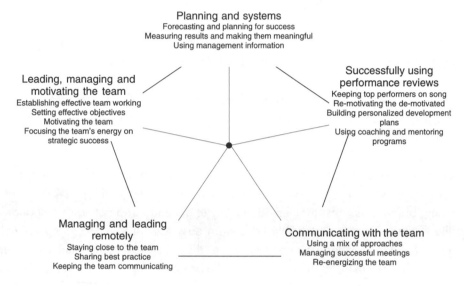

Figure 15: Supporting and managing the relationship manager

The management role is not just focused on setting objectives and supporting and reviewing performance, it also encompasses learning and motivational techniques. It is about managing your relationship managers as a team so that they jointly have greater impact and benefit from being part of that team. It is about recognizing that your relationship managers are more disparate (both in terms of role and possibly also physical location) than many of your IT team and that you need to provide them with a solid foundation and sense of belonging on which they can build and perform.

Touching the business

You will find that new relationship managers are happy when exploring and planning their role. However when you ask them to make their initial contact with the business, they suddenly become very reticent and find that they are busy doing other things. This is an easy excuse if undertaking the relationship manager job on top of another role within IT. This role suddenly becomes very demanding and doesn't permit the time needed to meet business managers.

I suppose this is natural, but I raise it because you need to be aware of this common problem and help them over this initial hurdle. You can do this in a number of ways such as:

- Being very forceful and setting tight deadlines

- Accompanying them on their first visit

- Helping them by undertaking role-plays with them

- Getting them to identify and meet with an easy target relationship first

- Working with them to construct a structure for the meeting so that they have a clear path through their discussion.

In terms of the structure of the meeting, then the obvious place to start is by utilizing the tools I provided in Chapter 2 (see Figure 16 overleaf). The relationship manager needs to understand how the business or function with which he or she is going to work competes and what it needs to deliver.

As I suggested in Chapter 2, simply being asked these types of questions by someone from IT will surprise people in the business, add credibility to the relationship manager and start the relationship on a sound and strategically aligned footing.

In most instances, these questions will provide the relationship managers with sufficient information to understand the business and what it is trying to achieve. Relationship managers should not accept answers from just one director or manager, they may need to meet with a number to gain a broad picture. By doing so they will become more skilled at having these types of conversations and will also broaden their knowledge.

If you are creating a team of relationship managers, then get them back together afterwards to exchange their experiences and the knowledge that they have gained. This can be achieved by getting each of them to do a presentation to the others, and then by combining the lessons from each of the presentations to pull together a business wide understanding.

It is insufficient to see this as a one-off exercise, and the relationship managers need to build ongoing relationship management plans that will guide their activities in the coming months.

TOUCHING

What are your key 3 year goals?

Describe 5–6 headline key issues.
Delineate between the external market-based goals and internal, development-based goals.

What are the growth challenges you face?

If success is going to be achieved in the external market, what are the key issues that will have to be overcome as an organization – internally and externally?

How will you measure strategic success?

How will you know when you have arrived and what measures will you use to quantify that success?

How do you manage risk?

How risk tolerant are you?
What are the key risks you face?
What is your strategy for managing & minimizing the potential effects of key risk areas?

Revenue Growth Strategy

How are we going to grow the business? Is it from new businesses, existing or new products, or from existing or new customers?

Deliver more value to our clients

An additional way of increasing income is to offer more value to the existing served market. What is your strategy here?

Productivity Strategy

What are your plans for continually improving breakeven/overheads, direct costs and asset productivity?

Figure 16: Understanding the business strategy

To achieve this, I suggest using the following tables (Figures 17 and 18). The first identifies the target relationships and asks them to specify what it is they need to be doing and achieving in respect of each of those relationships.

Our primary customers are...	Their top three objectives are...	We can best help them achieve their objectives by...	Our objectives for the relationship are...	By when...	We will really have impact if we...	The skills, resources and support we need to achieve are...
Enter names of business units or support functions with whom the relationship manager is working	What is the business unit trying to achieve?	What can we do to help them succeed?	How will we know if we are successful?		What are the most important things we should be doing?	What do we need to help us to be successful?

Figure 17: Understanding your target relationships

The second is activity-based. Here relationship managers plan the contact they are going to have in the months ahead with their target relationships and then record whether or not those activities have taken place and the benefits that have resulted. This provides a tool that both helps in terms of manpower planning but also in terms of monitoring activity levels and outcomes.

TOUCHING

Customers	Key contacts in each group	Planned Activities (do they support the objectives and issues noted above?)						Key successes	Learning points
		June	Jul	Aug	Sept	Oct	Nov		
Enter names of business units or support functions with whom the RM is working	Who are our key contacts?	What do we plan to do in each month? (e.g. interview, planning, telephone, social meeting)						What have we achieved and have we achieved our objectives?	What have we learnt?
		Completed activities							
		What have we done in each month?							
		Completed activities							
		Completed activities							

Figure 18: Contact planning for your target relationships

Approaches such as these are a very visible approach to managing the role of the relationship manager and provide a vehicle by which you can have outcome focused discussions regarding plans, activities and progress.

The IT team

The focus in the last session was the relationship manager and given that they spearhead the strategic relationships that IT have with the business, it has been right to allocate some time to this important, and possibly vital, resource.

However, they do not work alone and delivery is achieved by the IT team working as a combined unit to deliver the strategy and build the IT brand.

In this respect, the following diagram summarizes the stages a brand goes through in the eyes of the customer, and it reflects our attempts (by using a brand) to move customers from being rational to emotionally driven decision makers.

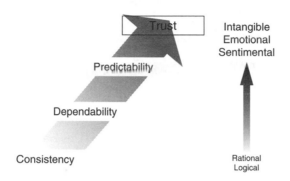

Figure 19: Building trust in your brand (Mitchell, *et al.*, 1998)

Ideally, customers move all the way up the ladder to the point where they place trust in a brand. During their climb up the ladder they become less rational and calculating and increasingly place reliance on the brand and what it stands for. As a result, they are less likely to consider switching or considering other propositions on simply economic terms.

To encourage the customer to go up the ladder demands:

– Consistency: the first thing the IT has to do is to be consistent. Variable or unreliable delivery of products or service undermines the reputation of the IT in the business' eyes.

– Dependability: once consistency of delivery is established, the customer is willing to depend on IT.

  – For example, once we know that our commercial stationers will always deliver the next day, we reduce our stockholding of stationery and rely instead on the stocks held in their warehouse.

– Predictability: eventually the customer is so familiar with the consistency and dependability of the service that they start to predict how IT will act on behave in certain circumstances.

  – For example, if you use a consultant in your business and have built a relationship over a long period of time you may well be in a position of predicting how that consultant will approach a particular problem even before you have spoken to them about it.

TOUCHING

— Trust: Ultimately, the relationship developed to the point where the business is able to place enormous faith or trust in the performance of IT. This does not happen by accident. This happens because you have delivered consistently, dependably and over a period of time.

Why is this important in IT?

Well in terms of brand, the same principles apply to IT as any other brand. In other words, unless we are consistent, dependable, and ultimately predictable the business will not place trust in us and will continue to be rational and logical in their decision-making. In this sense, you should realize that the way they view you and make their decisions about you is a result of how you have performed in the past. In other words, if you have not been consistent and dependable it should be no surprise to you if they take what appears to be an over cynical approach to your promises.

However, if you can be consistent, dependable and predictable then strangely you will find the requests for the service level agreements, outsourcing, benchmarking, etcetera will fade away. Therefore, in respect of your brand, the way they perceive you is in your hands.

And a key player in bringing about that shift in perception is the IT team itself. The relationship manager can make the promises, can understand the business strategy and can build strong personal relationships, but if the IT team doesn't deliver then the perception of IT will remain at the bottom of the brand ladder.

Thus, the relationship manager's role does not only extend outwards into the business. It also extends inwards into the IT function. In this sense they become change agents who communicate the need to change, raise the desire for change, and articulate what has to change. In this way, they also become representatives of the business within the IT function.

This part of their role is often forgotten and does not receive sufficient attention. It is an important element of the role and should form part of their objectives.

Equally, though, line managers within IT must work with their teams to focus on delivering the necessary consistency and dependability so that the business can start to predict how they will perform. But of course, this is just about becoming a very effective 'Follower'.

Making it happen on the ground

The last and shortest section of this chapter provides ideas on how you will make things happen on the ground. It is the shortest because in reality I have covered many of the aspects throughout the chapter already and I do not propose to repeat them here. However, It Is worth identifying some of the things you can be doing that will build your brand and accelerate your progress. So under a few headings I am pleased to suggest some ideas that you can pursue:

A clear and loud message

– Ensure that you have absolute clarity of what it is you offer the business. Turn it into a short and sharp message that people can readily articulate and understand.

– Be clear about where you add value, deliver it and tell people about your success.

– Keep repeating the message to people inside and outside of IT.

– Establish a coherent campaign that reinforces the message through a wide range of media.

– Identify who you are communicating with and use language and media to which they relate.

– Establish a formal system for board sign-off of IT projects that forces the executive to make decisions about priorities and hence ensure that your IT resources are applied to the right things.

Being in their faces

– Identify brand champions who can go out there and tell the story for you. These may be people within IT, but they may also be members of the business for whom you have done a good job and who appreciate the impact you have delivered.

– Advertise (like soap powder) what you can do, what you do and what you have done.

– Identify the important meetings in your business and make sure you are represented.

– Ask yourself whether you are located in the right place. Should some of your staff be relocated to sit alongside business staff?

TOUCHING

TOUCHING

- Daily bulletin boards can be used to keep people informed on current performance levels. This can be achieved through the intranet or you could apply a simple solution similar to that used by the London Underground whereby at the entrance to every platform there is a board which tells you how the services across the network are operating.

- Often the business does not know how much you do because you are almost invisible. So why not give all IT staff a uniform (it need only be a polo shirt) with a distinctive colour and logo so that you are visible within the business?

- Always keep the CEO in the loop and don't let him be exposed to shocks.

- Undertake short and sharp staff training activities at people's desks to small groups (e.g. 20 minutes to a group of five people in marketing on some of the common difficulties with MS Access and how they can be overcome would not cost too much but add lots to your credibility).

- If systems fail, get a message to the business as quickly as possible and put a recorded message on the helpline so that people know what's going on.

Being seen as a centre of excellence

- Attend staff meetings and offer to do presentations on latest developments and issues.

- Offer to do more to staff training so that you become seen as a source of advice, but also expose your staff to the concerns and issues that are troubling business staff.

- Run an IT strategy day with the board.

- Get your relationship managers to meet with relationship managers in other businesses who have had years of experience (e.g. banks and accountancy practices).

- Look outside your industry for changes that are taking place in terms of business models, technologies and systems and come back and tell the story.

In closing

This is a meaty chapter and it covers a lot of ground. This is because it is a topic that gets insufficient attention, is not natural for most IT managers and yet is a central part of successful delivery.

As I said in opening, this is not simply a case of "hype, puff and superficial claptrap". If you are going to get into a position where IT is recognized for the value it can and does bring you are going to need to develop and implement a coordinated approach which tells a consistent story, links the key players (the CIO, the CEO, key stakeholders, the IT team and relationship managers) and sustains the delivery of that message over the long-term.

Central to this is the role of the relationship manager for whom you have to clarify objectives, develop skills and provide support so that they can represent you and your strategy across the business. Accordingly, selection of the right people is important and so is the way in which you manage them in order to build their confidence and their capability.

Overall, you will recognize that not only is this a meaty topic but it is one that will present you with some of the biggest challenges that you will face. Therefore you need to become skilled and become 'marketing savvy' if you are going to enjoy the success to which you aspire.

TOUCHING

Looking

Dancing with the enemy?

Do you remember your first dance with your husband or wife? Indeed, do you remember your early experiences of dancing with the opposite sex? Whilst there are some warm memories I am sure there are also memories of early rejections and rebuttals and some discomfort whilst you learnt to fit with the rhythm of your partner and build and develop the necessary dancing skills.

The challenge facing IT departments is much like this. They seek to engage (dance) with the business and find that initially, and on a number of occasions, their approaches are rebuffed. And when they are actually engaged by the business in delivering high value work they find they are missing some of the core skills or don't understand quite the way the business works. Alternatively, the business doesn't want what we offer or doesn't see the value of what we deliver.

So we need to promote the value that we bring in a way that excites and energizes our business partners so that they actively engage with us and involve us in their decision making and delivery processes. Much in the same way as a Porsche car is packed full of technology, it is not the technology that excites the businessman, it is the overall package and the way in which it is delivered.

So what can we do? Perhaps we can learn from world class marketing companies; in terms of how they understand the needs of their customers and build the ability to deliver the value and skills that are required.

Five key principles seem to stand out: (McDonald, *et al.*, 2001)

– World class marketing companies have a profound understanding of the market place

– They position themselves and their brands as something noticeably different

– They have built organizations that are flexible and innovative

– They have customer focused skills and behaviours

– They are vigorous about implementation.

Profound understanding of the market place

These leading companies clearly understand the peculiar ways and needs of their customers. Likewise, we in IT must understand the peculiar needs and wants of our business partners. This involves us in understanding strategy and how it works today, and it also involves us in developing in three key areas:

- First we must build a culture and set of values that are dominated by flexibility and an externally facing perspective on the world.

- Secondly our strategic thinking must be driven by market knowledge, passion and a desire to continuously improve.

- And thirdly we have to build the capability to sense the evolving needs of our customers, and deliver reliably and consistently the services they need.

And I am afraid that for this to have substantial impact, the change in mindset and capability that is required in the IT function is quite profound. The understanding of strategy and the willingness to engage with the business and its environment cannot be superficial. It demands a continual focus on the customer, the environment they are in, the unpredictability they are subject to, and the vagaries of their own customers. This cannot be done by bold statements; it is done by getting your team out there and interacting with the business (outside of specific projects), it means interacting with their customers, it means experiencing all the other change programs that the business is having to deliver, it means being on the front line and seeing the end customer being served. In essence, it means exposure and regular exposure, until your decision making, your culture, your focus, your meetings, your controls, your stories, your processes are driven by the absolute desire to serve the business and their customer.

Positioning the brand as something noticeably different

I am sure you will recognize and understand the messages that go behind the major brands in the world today, from Mickey Mouse, to Nike to Starbucks and Ferrari. You know what these brands stand for and you know what you will get when you buy from them. Is it the same for your IT department? Do your customers know what you stand for,

LOOKING

the benefits you bring, the way you work? Indeed do your staff? And can they deliver it time and time again?

So, strange as it may sound you need a brand strategy and plan to make it happen. So that one day, the business can articulate (positively and accurately) what they get from you and why they use you. So that one day, they value you for what you offer and deliver.

Organizations that are flexible and innovative

There is no point pretending that the world in which your business partners operate is predictable. It is not, and they have to respond and react to their customers needs. Yes, at times they can lead their customers but very often they are having to deal with events beyond their control. This is how you feel about your relationships with the business. So in reality, you are in the same boat, it is just that you are further down the food chain.

Unfortunately, things are not going to change, so there is no point running away from it. You have to build the skills and ways of behaving in your people so that they are able to respond, be flexible and be innovative in finding solutions to the businesses problems.

And therefore, you need to build a way of working that enables you to offer this flexibility without building uncontrollable levels of stress. Thus you will need to look at your processes, your structure, reporting systems, and your systems. Such a challenge will also beg questions of how you manage the function; what skills do you need, how will you lead, and what behaviours will you exhibit so that your team reaches a point of offering market leading flexibility and responsiveness.

Customer-focused skills and behaviours

To facilitate many of the issues discussed already, IT functions have to be able to build the ability to sense the developing needs of their customers. This is not just about relationship building, although this is an important element. It is also about the ability to deliver what the business values consistently. On a higher plain again, you should be able to get to the point of predicting their needs, and leading them to see the potential that information offers them, so that they can compete in tomorrow's markets.

Vigorous line management and implementation

Unless you can regularly score goals and make things happen, then the businesses will not place sufficient trust in you and will not wholeheartedly engage with the potential value that you can bring. As a result, opportunities will be lost and the business will not benefit from your skills and knowledge. So, you have to be able to build a function that can deliver consistently, reliably and efficiently.

I use the word vigorous and not rigorous on purpose. Rigorous is a given, the vigorous is what makes the difference. This is about bringing your implementation and brand marketing to life and making it happen with the pace and passion which has impact in the business and your IT function.

None of this will happen if you don't ask your business partners for a dance, and you don't practice and develop the skills that are necessary to be a valuable dancing partner. Along the way, your confidence will take some knocks as you are rebutted and rebuffed. Take the knocks, bounce back and keep asking them to dance. Eventually, you will move jointly in a flowing rhythm that will excite all around you.

Doing

If you are going to build a brand for IT which results in IT being properly recognized for the value it can deliver, clearly you must perform consistently at the highest levels.

Equally there are steps you can take so that the business better understands what you are about, what you are trying to achieve and the value that you bring. If the business can understand this and can readily see what it is you are trying to achieve, the brand and the reputation of IT within the business can be enhanced. This will result in an audience that is more receptive to the strategy that you are seeking to deliver.

The following are the key steps that you can take to manage your brand within the business:

☑ Setting the context

☑ Making your proposition

☑ Building your brand

☑ Using relationship managers

☑ Touching the business

Setting the context

The main steps are:

☑ Clarifying the business strategy (Chapter 4)

☑ Setting the IT strategy (Chapter 5)

☑ Understanding how the business currently sees and perceives IT.

So that you achieve:

☑ Clarity over the value the business delivers

☑ Clarity of IT's role in the delivery of the business strategy

☑ Understanding how you are currently viewed.

Unless you know where you are now and where you are going, your journey cannot have meaning nor can it succeed. So whilst this first set of actions repeats topics we have considered already in this book, it is a point that cannot be repeated too many times; everything we do must align behind the business strategy. In turn, the brand must support the IT strategy.

Equally, you need to understand how the business currently views the IT function and its performance. If the perception is positive and they support your strategy, the task is easier and may require less intensive effort. Conversely, a negative mood amongst your customers will demand greater effort, more powerful influencing skills, a more sustained program until the point where you have a critical mass of support.

It is not always necessary to carry out detailed surveys of current moods and perceptions, and in most instances you will have a pretty good idea of the prevailing feeling around the business and should have complemented this by the interviews that you have undertaken with managers, directors and staff whilst developing the strategy.

Making your proposition

The main steps are:

☑ Identify the key components of the service that you provide (Chapters 7 and 8 and 9)

☑ Identify the needs of your target audience

☑ Make the proposition accessible, memorable and applicable.

So that you achieve:

☑ A short sharp, simple message that tells people where you are focusing your energies and the benefits they will get as a result.

It is likely that the proposition that you have created within your IT strategy is quite detailed and possibly inaccessible and hard to describe in a short, sharp and punchy manner.

DOING

The aim of this stage is to be able to create a story that people can easily explain and easily understand. Marketers talk about the 'elevator pitch' – the ability to explain to someone else 'what you do and the benefits you bring' in the 30 seconds available to you when traveling in a lift form the first floor to the 10th floor.

Your message must be:

☑ Accessible: so your target market can easily understand what you are talking about.

☑ Memorable: the concepts are sticky and stay with your target market after you have left them.

☑ Applicable: your target market can see how the issues that you have been talking about relate to them and their needs.

Building your brand

The main steps are:

☑ Identify the key components of your brand

☑ Specify how these will be communicated and made tangible

☑ Assess your current performance in each of these areas

☑ Fill the big gaps.

So that you achieve:

☑ A consistent and coherent message

☑ Agreement on the ways by which you will tell the story

☑ An understanding of where and how you need to improve.

Your brand is not simply a logo, nor is your proposition. To be successful you need to put together a number of elements that complement and support each other so that a consistent and coherent message is delivered and received in a wide variety of the ways.

DOING

This means that you understand what you want to be known for, the benefits that you will bring, what you believe in, and how you will behave.

Alongside, you need to identify how your will make your brand more tangible and visible by approaches such as:

☑ Your presence in the business

☑ The messages that you will leave on the intranet or on the help desk answer phone or in the staffroom

☑ Where your staff are located

☑ What your team do to help people achieve more through the use of IT.

Additionally:

☑ How are you currently performing?

☑ Where are the big gaps and how are you going to fill them?

☑ How are you going to communicate these key components of your brand message?

Using relationship managers

The main steps are:

☑ Identify the types of relationships that you want to establish

☑ Specify objectives

☑ Identify the skills required

☑ Recruit the right people

☑ Provide the necessary support to lift performance levels.

So that you achieve:

☑ A strong brand personality which is brought to life by effective relationship managers who have the skills and the focus to deliver strategically aligned results.

Whilst logos and signs will help to represent your brand, it will only come alive through the interactions that take place between your staff and the staff within the business. The most effective way to achieve this and to accelerate improved relationships between IT and the business is through the use of relationship managers.

This demands that you recruit the right people with the right skills. You can only do this if you know what type of relationships you want your relationship managers to have with the business (a supportive, empathic relationship is very different to one that is challenging or seeks to solve problems).

Equally, it means that you must set strategically aligned objectives and help your relationship managers develop the capabilities that will enable them to perform at the highest levels over the long-term.

Touching the business

The main steps are:

☑ Establishing initial contacts and understanding the business

☑ Planning the ongoing contact program

☑ Managing performance

☑ Supporting change within the IT function.

So that you achieve:

☑ Value creating relationships with the business

☑ High levels of performance by the relationship managers

☑ Accelerated change within IT.

DOING

If your relationship managers are going to have a meaningful impact then they must quickly establish robust, business-focused relationships with their targets in the business community.

This demands introductory meetings complemented by a contact program which enables relationships to be built alongside the visible delivery of benefits. This will In turn further deepen the relationship and build the trust that is required for success to be enjoyed and the IT brand to be recognized for the value it delivers.

This will demand that line managers actively involve themselves in the performance management of their relationship managers to improve their skills, their activity levels and the focus of their work.

Relationship managers must bring back into IT the knowledge that they gain from their contacts in the business to help the IT function see the need for change and accelerate its implementation.

DOING

12 Change plus

- The context for change

- Taking the pulse

- Building the route map

- Telling the change story

- Managing stakeholders

- The CEO's role

- Maintaining momentum

Any strategy will demand change. In this chapter we identify the key components in designing and implementing a change plan, with particular focus on the people and organizational capability issues rather than the technology and procedural elements.

Touching

You may argue that the central issue for change in IT is around technology and systems. In some ways you are right, in that the implementation of the right technology and systems is tangible evidence of your success in delivering change. However, strategic change of the nature demanded by the challenges in this book is achieved by and through the people in your organization focusing their efforts in new directions, changing their behaviours, developing new skills and working in totally different ways with the business. Once your people are suitably directed, motivated and skilled, they can implement the necessary technology and systems for you. But if they are not willing or able, no amount of technology investment will save you.

Centrally, therefore, you will have to energize the individuals in your team and organization to behave in different ways and deliver different results. So for the purposes of this book, I am going to focus on and build from this foundation stone, rather than spend time on the infrastructure which will vary in every organization.

In terms of structure of the chapter, I am first going to layout background principles. Then I explore how you can understand the current state of your organization so that you can identify the approach that you need to adopt for your change program. With the benefit of that knowledge you can design a route map for the change, and we need to consider how you maintain momentum during the life of the program.

The context for change

The first principle relating to change in IT is that for you to enjoy success you have to change both your IT function and the organization in which it is situated. Let me expand. Let's say you manage to change your IT function and as a result it is able to both Enable and Lead the business to the point where you can compete in new ways, drawing on new technologies and benefiting from the evolving behaviour of customers. As a function you are now able to respond more quickly and can introduce new systems and technologies at a pace not previously dreamed possible. However, unless the business is able to absorb and utilize this new-found capability you will not be able to use it to the full.

Indeed, it is possible that the business will still perceive you as you were in the old days; simply expecting you to buy and provide PCs and servers and offering a help desk facility. Alongside, they still see IT as a function to be blamed when they get things wrong.

Therefore, unless you set out both to change your IT function and prepare your business to absorb and fully utilize your potential, your efforts will be wasted and your chances of success will be minimized. As a result, when I talk about building a change plan throughout this chapter, I mean that you need to build a change plan for both the IT function and the business as a whole.

Some underlying principles

When starting out on change it is worthwhile asking yourself three simple questions in order to get your bearings.

Figure 1: Managing change – where, what, how? (De Wit and Meyer (1998) and Pettigrew and Whipp (1991))

These provide you with a simple context and overview of what you want to do.

Why does change fail to deliver?

Before we embark on our journey, it is also useful to know the core reasons why strategic change fails. Often it is the implementation stage that gets the blame; "people didn't follow through on the change plan, we should have prepared a Gant chart, our critical path analysis was inaccurate, etc". However, as you'll see from the following chart, poor implementation is not the primary reason why change programs fail to deliver the results that we expect.

As you can see from Figure 2, the major reason that change fails is that in over 50% of cases, there is insufficient clarity of what we are trying to achieve and why.

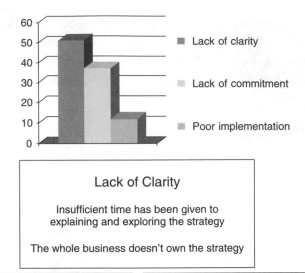

Lack of Clarity

Insufficient time has been given to explaining and exploring the strategy

The whole business doesn't own the strategy

Lack of Commitment

Management believes that it has more important things to do

Performance incentives are driving the wrong behaviour

Poor Implementation

Change plans have not been agreed or understood

People don't have the necessary skills

Figure 2: What stops strategic change programs delivering? (Darragh and Campbell, 2001)

I would like to say that the lack of clarity reflects a hierarchical issue where the information is not passed clearly from one level to the next. However, this is not the fundamental problem. In truth, too many boards and directorate teams spend insufficient time deeply understanding their strategy. Directors walk out of strategy day events, team meetings etc, with differing views of what the organization is trying to achieve and how they are going to go about it. They each go and present to their managers their own interpretation of the strategy. In turn their managers create their own interpretations to suit their personal agendas. By the time the strategy reaches somebody on the shop floor, the core principles have been lost and your aims changed almost beyond recognition.

Even if you do manage to get the clarity that is necessary, it does not necessarily mean that people are willing to implement your plans for you. Something like a third of programs fail for this reason. So often this problem is exacerbated by the fact that individual objectives and incentives encourage people to do other things. Also, people carry on doing what they did before, if only for the reason that it's hard work to change (and if you are not convinced of the need to change, then you won't anyway).

These two aspects serve to underline why it is that I am focusing this discussion on change around the issue of people. It is because you have to get a shared and deep understanding by your team of what you want to achieve and then, somehow, you've got to get them believing in it to the degree where they:

– Will change what they have been doing

– Adopt differing behaviours

– Drop pet projects

– Run the risk that they may not earn as much in the coming year because their bonuses may be reduced.

Whilst the issues covered in the preceding paragraphs represent negatives that we need to overcome, there are also positives to aim for in order to improve our chances of success.

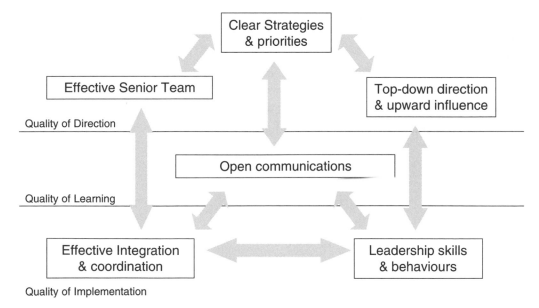

Figure 3: Creating the environment for successful change (Beer and Eisenstat, 2000)

From this, we can see that there are three areas of particular focus that demand our attention:

Quality of direction

– We must provide the organization with clear direction which demands focused strategies and clarity over our priorities. In other words, what projects do we focus on and which ones do we drop? And this clarity comes about from building a senior team that operates effectively by utilizing its diverse skills and experiences, and which is able to learn from the rest of the business.

Quality of learning

– On top of learning from the business, that same top team must be able to communicate its strategy and priorities to the business.

– However, if that downward communication of goals and the upward communication from the shop floor are to work well it is necessary to create an environment where open communications can flourish and the organization is able to learn.

Quality of implementation

– At the point of implementation, success can be enhanced by ensuring that teams and business units coordinate their efforts and compete jointly against the external competition rather than each other. This is aided by possessing the leadership skills and behaviours in middle management that can support and accelerate delivery.

Another point to bear in mind in these initial thoughts about change relates to knock-on effects of making a change in one area of the function.

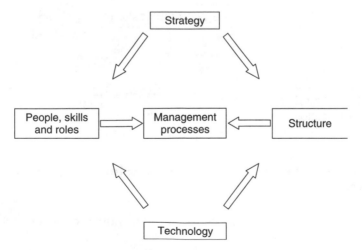

Figure 4: What happens when I touch this? (Scott Morton 1991)

In other words, if you change one thing it will have an impact elsewhere. For example, let's say you introduce new handheld technology for your sales force which enables them to capture and utilize information regarding the customers that they meet in the course of their work. On the face of it, this is a simple technological change. The truth is that this is a pebble thrown in the lake and the ripples will be experienced across the organization. The skills and roles demanded of the salespeople will change immediately. They will need to be able to use the additional information that will be available to them. This information will allow them to approach the sales process in a different way. Over time the type of people you employ will need to change.

The availability of information and the changing role of the sales force will demand a change in the processes that are adopted by management. Chances are that they will have more information which is more readily available to them which will enable them to manage salesforce activity more tightly and also enable them to make different decisions about the deployment of their sales team. In turn, this will pose questions about the structure of the sales team and the support staff that may have been required previously to capture the data that they collected.

The information that is now available to you becomes a critical resource that may alter the strategic choices you take in the medium term; you will the have knowledge that presents the opportunity to compete in new ways or the ability to enter new markets. All this, from a small hand-held terminal.

Drawing all these thoughts together and recognizing the importance of people in delivery of change means that there is a natural focus for our endeavours; we have to energize the individual. How can we do that?

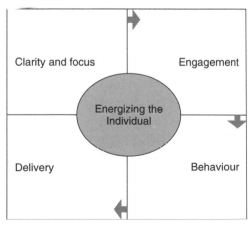

Figure 5: Energizing the individual

- Providing clarity and focus

- You need to have painted a picture of the goals and aspirations in a way that brings them to life for people without overselling or over promising the benefits.

- Engagement

- You need to win the desire to change in individuals. This is not about telling them to change, but achieving a deep commitment arising from personal choice.

- Behaviour

- You will have to change long held patterns of behaviour across the business and nourish and embed new behaviours which support success.

- Delivery

- You must draw on these achievements to deliver performance targets and accelerate the change by learning and embedding the new organizational culture.

Taking the pulse

Okay, the direction and focus of your change effort is clear, but where do you begin?

How fit am I?

The first issue is to understand where you are now. This means that you need to undertake a detailed analysis of the current state of the organization that you are about to change, and in IT this means assessing both the business and the IT function.

Imagine that you have decided to participate in the New York Marathon. The first thing you might do is go to your fitness trainer and get them to assess your health and your readiness to run such a long distance race. They would do a number of tests, including measuring resting and active pulse rates, blood pressure, muscle strength and stamina. As a result, they would make an assessment of your abilities and make recommendations for the training necessary to prepare you to participate and succeed. It is very likely that the training program recommended to one person will be very different from that required for another runner, because of their relative starting points in terms of fitness and general body condition.

It's no different with organizations. Strategic change is very much like a marathon and it is certainly a long race. It will demand an assessment of the current health of the organization, some changes in lifestyle, the development of new skills and the strengthening of latent capabilities, all with the purpose of achieving the goals in the plan (or alternatively crossing the finishing line).

What then can you do to assess your organization's readiness to change? There are a host of approaches available to you and every consulting firm and business school will provide you with their own individual methodology. I am in danger of repeating that here and really do not wish to do so. My aim is to help you understand the key principles that you need to bear in mind and provide you with the sufficient direction to undertake focused exploration and analysis of your own organization. Therefore, I am simply going to highlight the main areas that you need to consider:

- People

- Culture

- Leadership

- Organizational capabilities.

People

Here, I am interested why people put up barriers to change, how they respond to change and whether they have the necessary skills to deliver the change.

When I did my MBA at Warwick Business School, my Organizational Behaviour Professor, Martin Corbett, always used a simple but incredibly effective analysis tool. He called it 'soggy'. Actually it's S. O. G. I., and it asks you to analyse an issue or an organization at four levels. His belief was that we too often blame the individual, whereas it is the 'stage or platform' that we put them on which causes them to underperform. And it is our job as managers to provide the stage or platform on which they can excel.

However, this model can also be used in change programs to consider why people seek to block the progress that you believe is necessary and appropriate. (See Figure 6)

When considering this approach will I find it best to start with the individual and zoom out to look at the other levels, ultimately ending up with a helicopter view of the issues.

	Why do people resist change?	
S Society	– Too much change already – What's the point? – National culture – Short termism	– Comfort zone – What's in it for me? – Too hard to understand – Does not emotionally engage me
O Organization	– Doesn't fit with our culture – What's wrong with how we do it now? – Conflicts with structure – Performance measures	– Restrictions on site – environmental issues – Doesn't embrace change – We are already committed to something else – Wrong technology
G Group	– Resistance to and fear of change – Lack of involvement in process etc – Different evaluation/goals/agendas – No time to learn	– Don't want to learn – Conflicting performance goals – Difficult terms and conditions – Different norms of behaviour – Our leader wouldn't like it
I Individual	– Lack of vision – Loss of power – Fear of failure – Fear of learning something new – Misunderstanding of instructions – Imposed lack of involvement in process	– Unable to see wider picture – Insecurity – loss of safety – Will it take longer? – Lacking time to consolidate – Not motivated to change – Previous experience & lack of training

Figure 6: SOGI – why do people resist change? (Martin Corbett, Warwick Business School)

Individual

People block change for a wide variety of reasons, and the greater the personal impact for them, the more they will resist. If you take power away from people, or make them feel insecure, or do not give them sufficient motivation to change they won't.

Groups

People belong to groups and teams. These may be formal ones (created by the hierarchy of the business) or informal ones (social teams such as football, book reading clubs or coffee shops). Like individuals, these groups find reasons why change shouldn't proceed. They may do this overtly or it may just become a unspoken norm shared between the people in the group. However it arises, you need to understand the thinking of all of these groups, how they will respond and how you will overcome the barriers they raise.

Organization

On a larger scale again, organizations present their own barriers and blockages. It may be the existing culture, or perhaps the current structure doesn't allow you to do what you want to do, or perhaps you have recently invested in a new piece of kit which would go to waste if you pressed ahead.

Society

Finally, there is the society in which organizations and people exist. If the feeling is that life is already going too fast, people are working under too much pressure, working too long hours in economically difficult circumstances they may not be motivated to deliver your change.

This is not to say that the issues identified are going to stop you achieving success. The important thing is that you identify what the barriers are and what you are going to do about them; by way of removing them, going round them, or possibly by going straight through them.

Individual responses to change

Individuals respond in a wide variety of ways to the challenges of change. Some welcome it and look for it, others are frightened by it and look for stability. Some are ready to jump in and do, others need to analyse any change proposals to ensure that they are well considered and thought through.

None of these people are wrong in their response, it is just that they naturally behave in different ways. Often, though, managers do not recognize these different types of people, and think everybody should be like them. Additionally, and unfortunately, the people leading change are very often those who think it should be done tomorrow, if not today. They then incorrectly assess the response of somebody who needs time to consider the implications and identify that individual as a 'blocker' and negative. It may well be that the individual will arrive at the same point as the change leader but may just take them longer to get there. It doesn't make them wrong; it just means that their thought processes are different.

Similarly, different people need different reasons to embark on change.

Some will require more information regarding the 'why' and what the benefits will be. Others will need a more practical explanation which helps them to understand what they will be doing in the new world. Some will not be able move forward until they know that they have got the skills required, whilst others simply need to see the importance of the shift required to enable them to embark on the journey.

TOUCHING

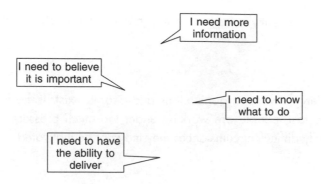

Figure 7: What will help me change?

Once again, none of these responses is wrong; they are just different and they reflect the different needs of different people.

The challenge for you in preparing for the change, is to understand what sort of people you have in your organization and identify the implications of the change for them and try to predict how they may respond. In consequence, you need to identify how you can help them to understand what is required, and how you can get them started on the journey. This may well (almost certainly) mean that you have to adopt different approaches to the different groups that you find in your business.

Individual skills

Similarly, there is a need to compare the current skill levels to those that are required in the future. The assessment should range over the full set of competencies which may be required, including; IT technical and systems skills, operations management, service delivery, relationship management, leadership and management, interpersonal, project management, change management, market place awareness, brand management and strategy.

The skills that you will require to succeed will have been identified during the strategy development process. However, it is necessary to review those conclusions and check for any obvious gaps. Equally, you need to identify the target level of skills required. This compared to the current base case will tell you the degree of shift required.

At this stage, you are doing this on a functional and organizational wide basis in order to assess current levels of competencies and to identify the major development needs. You also want to see where skill gaps may act as blockages to successful implementation. It will also enable you to identify any organizational wide interventions that may be needed.

Separately and later, individual skill gaps and development needs can be addressed through the performance management process.

Culture

Culture has been described in various ways by various authors but for the purposes of this book I am going to describe it as "the way we do things round here". It is important because unless "the way we do things round here" fits tightly with the needs of the strategy, you will be unable to deliver your full potential and your chances of successful implementation of the strategy will be diminished. For example, if you have determined that your IT function needs to be agile and flexible, and yet you have a culture built around hierarchy and bureaucracy, you will really struggle. Visually, the challenge you have looks like this:

Culture is but one element in this schematic, but it highlights the challenge that we face when delivering strategy. Unless there is a good fit between the culture and the strategy you will find it difficult to successfully bring about change. Equally, though, unless the strategy fits with the needs of the environment, and unless you build the skills necessary to match the demands of the strategy and to support culture, you will not be able to maximize your performance.

Therefore, it is necessary to assess the current culture and see how this matches with that which you need.

Culture, is a sizeable and important topic in its own right, so rather than damage the flow of this chapter by exploring the ins and outs of it here, I have allocated a separate chapter for this, so please see Chapter 13.

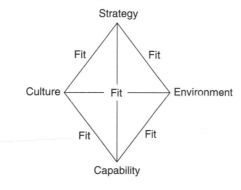

Figure 8: The importance of fit (Miles and Snow, 1984)

TOUCHING

Leadership and management

Similarly, the subject of leadership and management gets its own chapter (Chapter 10), and so I do not need to consider this in depth here. However, I have to reinforce the point that I make in that chapter which is that leaders and managers provide the focus, impetus and reinforcement that is critical to the delivery of change.

Consequently, the capabilities of your leadership and management team to bring about the change required demands detailed assessment and development so that they can perform to the levels required to guide the organization through this demanding journey, and ensure that you arrive at your destination.

When making an assessment of your management team's ability to deliver change, I find it helpful to assess their skill levels against the following set of competencies:

Leading change	
Igniting & influencing	Ability to create the case for change and secure credible support
Challenging	Ability to test and challenge the thinking of key players in the business so that they can see the long term implications and issues
Enabling	Ability to help others, through effective facilitation, to aligntheir plans and change goalsto deliver the strategic objectives
Leading	Ability to influence and enthuse others, through personal advocacy, vision and drive, and to access resources to build a solid platform forchange
Leveraging	Ability to identify the levers that can be pulled todeliver results
Controlling	Ability to manage implementation of a credible change plan (including appropriate goals, resources, metrics and review mechanisms)despite being outside the formal hierarchy of the business unit
Energizing	Demonstrates high personal commitment to achievement of change goals through integrity and courage, while maintaining objectivity andindividual resilience. Able to stay the course
Know-how	Knowledge, generation and skilful appreciation of change theories, tools and processes
Self awareness	Knows strengths and limitations, both in terms of skills and emotions, and uses failure as a basis for learning

Table 1: Change management competencies (Higgs and Rowland 2000)

As you will recall, I avoided producing a wide range of leadership and management competency models in Chapter 10 and I don't wish to start here. But you do need to assess their broader management skills, and put simply:

– Can your managers provide clarity of direction?

– Can your managers engage and energize others?

– Can they establish the right patterns of behaviour and ways of operating?

To do those things, they are going to need to be able to communicate, build trust and in difficult times draw on every ounce of knowledge that they have about the business and the way IT operates.

Please refer to Chapter 10 for much greater detail on the leadership and management role.

Organizational capabilities

The final specific assessment we need to make of the fitness of the organization relates to the broader organizational capabilities that you possess.

Clearly, there are those competencies that relate specifically to the strategy that you are adopting. If for example, you have decided to take on Google, you will need the search engine, marketing capabilities and balance sheet that will enable you to successfully pick a fight with them. I have covered these issues in Sections 1 and 2 of the book.

My focus here, though, is on the capabilities you need in an organization to bring about change.

Once again, there are a host of approaches that you could adopt and all consultancies around the world will provide you with slightly different approaches and competency requirements. Once again, therefore, I am not trying to prescribe a solution for you but seeking to provide you with some points to focus your attention and stimulate you to think about the readiness of your function and its ability to adapt.

With this in mind, I have found that the summary provided by Turner and Crawford (1998) is simple and accessible. (Figure 9)

In essence, they identify three sets of organizational competencies that are important for competitive performance today, and three sets of organizational competencies that enable you to bring about change. The point that I am making is that you need the combination of these two sets in order for your business to perform in the future. In other words:

TOUCHING

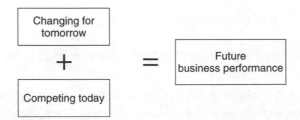

Figure 9: Organizational change capabilities – an overview (Turner and Crawford, 1998)

As I say, in each of these two groups, they identify three sets of organizational competencies that are required. These they describe as follows:

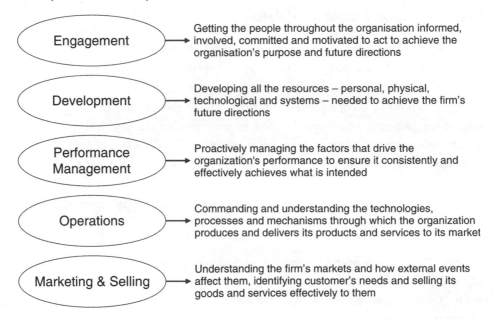

Figure 10: Organizational change capabilities – the competencies

You will have noticed that there are only five competencies listed here. This is because the Performance Management competency is regarded as central to success on both dimensions, with the result that the full model looks like Figure 11 with performance management straddling the two dimensions:

Thus, I have quickly provided you with some key areas on which to focus your assessment of your functional and organizational capability. As with the earlier topics in this chapter,

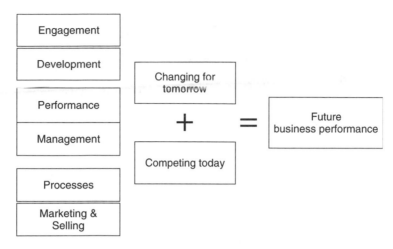

Figure 11: Organizational change capabilities – a reinforcing jigsaw

you need to assess your current levels of capability and what is required to enable you to perform in the future. Turner and Crawford's book goes into much greater detail regarding the issues underpinning these competencies but for the purposes of our discussions in this chapter, this overview is more than sufficient and provides you with the necessary focus.

A final point. You may say that marketing and selling is not a relevant competency in respect of an IT function. If you do, you have missed completely the point underpinning Chapter 11 regarding the IT brand, and the need to understand the business environment as discussed in depth in Chapters 1 and 2.

Pulling it all together

As a result of your analyses, you now have a better understanding of both the organization and the IT function's ability to change.

At this stage I find it incredibly helpful to be able to pull all my thinking together in one simple summary which enables me to see the key issues. From there I can determine the approach that I am going to adopt to the change program (see Building the Route Map).

To pull my thoughts together I summarize my findings using the model in Figure 12:

By viewing it in this way, I can see quite clearly the component elements and I have a visual reminder that I should draw on my knowledge of all of these aspects to identify the possible options I have for implementation.

TOUCHING

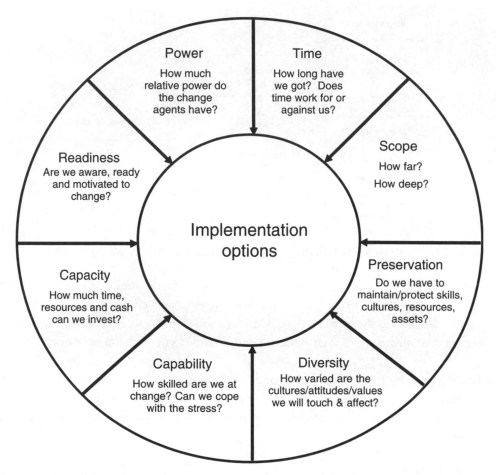

Figure 12: Taking the Pulse – summarizing your findings (Hope and Balogun, 2002)

In this version, I have included an example and added an extra dimension wherein I have made an assessment of whether each of the component elements will help me to deliver the change or will get in the way; i.e. is the factor positive (an enable) which helps me to deliver or is it negative (a constraint) that will slow us down?

We have now completed Taking the Pulse of the organization and have drawn together your findings into a simple summary document which enables you to proceed to the next stage of the change program, namely that of Building the Route Map.

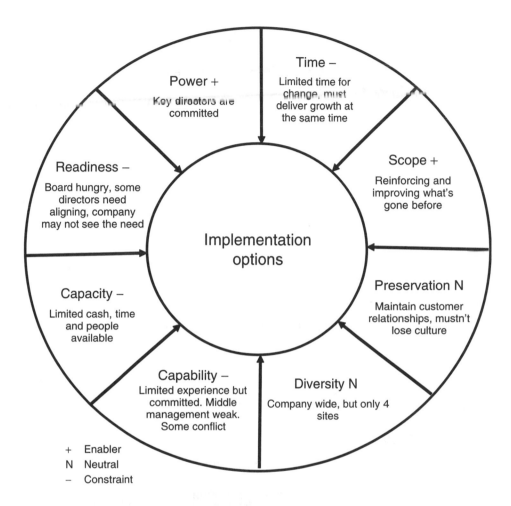

Figure 13: Taking the Pulse – an example summary

Building the Route Map

Taking the pulse is such a key element in any change program but so often it is not done in any depth, if at all. But without it you cannot progress, except by guesswork and this simply is not tenable in a change program where you have promised to deliver so much and your credibility is on the line. So do it, and do it well.

If you do, you will now have a strong understanding of the current state of IT and the organization, as well as a clear picture of where you want to go as a result of developing your strategy. Therefore, you now need to plan the journey that will take you from A to B.

TOUCHING

Figure 14: Building the Route Map – identifying implementation options (Hope and Balogun, 2002)

In determining the shape of that journey, there are a number of options available to you (Figure 14) and I will look at each of these in turn.

Types of change

In essence you need to be clear about how far and how fast you want to go.

		Extent of change	
		Transformational	Re-alignment
Speed of change	Incremental	Evolution	Adaption
	Big Bang	Revolution	Reconstruction

Figure 15: Building the Route Map – How far, how fast? (Dunphy and Stace, 1988)

TOUCHING

Evolution

This is change undertaken through a gradual implementation with multiple stages and lots of interrelated initiatives. Nonetheless it is used when you need to fundamentally change the organization because it is not fit enough to do the job demanded of It.

Its focus is on having a long-term performance impact rather than short-term results and works primarily by shifting the values and behaviours of the organization.

Because of the degree of change required, it is likely that there will also be an emphasis on financial performance which will be driven through a focus on approaches such as operational redesign, organizational structures, overhead reduction, product portfolio changes, entry into new markets and supply chain realignment.

It is often driven by change agents and demands substantial resources.

Adaption

This is less fundamental change, but is implemented in much the same way, through staged initiatives.

It tends to be less focused on values and behaviours and more on operational systems and improving the performance or focus of the business.

In some ways it is about fine tuning and appropriate when time is available.

Steps will be taken to improve the competence and skills across the business.

Again, results are likely to be seen in the medium to long term and more particularly, impact on the value delivered to customers as opposed to fundamentally shifting the returns to shareholders.

It is often driven by line managers.

Revolution

Multiple initiatives are undertaken on many fronts at the same time in a very short period of time to bring about a substantial if not seismic shift in the organization.

Change of this nature is initiated and driven from the top of the organization and seeks rapid improvement in performance and the shareholder proposition.

TOUCHING

Changes will be driven by the leadership and external change agents and will focus on business culture. The top team need to develop clear and tightly focused strategies and related performance measures to create a performance culture at every level in the organization.

These changes will be complemented by reviews of organizational structure, reductions in overheads, substantial changes in the business portfolio and most likely, restructuring of the balance sheet.

Reconstruction

This tends to be reactive change, forced on the organization and often focused on changing the way the organization operates.

This is often led by new leadership or new owners, which accelerates the speed of change.

It does not necessarily demand a substantial adjustment in the proposition made by the business to its customers. More likely it is about doing it better, and at a lower cost.

Systems and processes will be improved and there is likely to be a new team at the top whose aim will be to mobilize the workforce and instil a more demanding work ethic.

As you will see, each of these approaches suits different circumstances and demands a different focus. You need to be clear about the type of change you are embarking upon both in terms of extent, and speed.

Start point

With an understanding of the type of change which you face, you can now start thinking about where you will start to implement the change. Will you start at the top or the bottom? It will now be clear to you that some types of change have to be led from the top, but that is not always the case.

If you have time, you may be able to establish pilot sites, and if the program is to be delivered over the medium term, then the sharing of best practices can be facilitated and used to incrementally improve performance.

Separately, can you initiate change at both the top and the bottom at the same time? Here, you may make the direction clear from the top but then build a desire, hunger and momentum for the change at the bottom so that the change is driven from within. This may be a valuable approach where you have doubts about the tenacity and skills of middle management to initiate and sustain change.

Change style

Fundamentally, will you to seek to collaborate or coerce? But more broadly, will your approach be about education and communication, or participation and intervention, or direction?

Unfortunately, describing the style in this way implies an 'either or' scenario, but in reality this is rarely the case. What you will find is that you will use a mix of approaches depending on your circumstances and the stage that you are at in the program. Yes, there will be a tendency to adopt some dominant styles, but fluidity is the watchword.

For example, you will use a collaborative approach when your key interest groups support the change, and maybe more coercive when key bodies are working against you. However, over time the circumstances will shift and simply thinking in terms of coalition or collaboration will be too narrow and ineffective.

Change targets and interventions

Be clear about what it is that you want to change. Are you principally looking to change the outputs of people, or their behaviours, or their values?

If your sole focus is output then you can achieve this through interventions in the areas of structure and system. However, changing values and behaviours will demand not only focus on structures and systems, but also the ways in which people exercise power and the rituals and routines of the organization. You should note that this will demand that the change approach includes substantial time and investment in communication and personal development.

Change roles

Who is going to do what and where will the responsibility for leading and implementing lie?

In some of the change types that we considered earlier, it is clear that the leadership role resides at the top of the organization, but this is not always the case. You also need to be clear about these responsibilities and the roles of external agents and other support functions.

TOUCHING

Similarly, clarify the roles of senior and middle managers and front-line staff, and ensure that you put in place levers that will encourage or help them to support delivery of the change. For example:

Senior managers

– You want them to put the initiative at the top of the agenda.

– You need them to communicate the story repeatedly and consistently, and not waiver.

Middle managers

– Need to know what they must deliver and be given sufficient autonomy to enable them to make things happen.

– You will want to check their ability to manage and motivate people and ensure that they have the project management skills to keep the program on track.

Front-line staff

– Need motivating and rewarding in making the required changes.

– Need the skills and tools necessary to deliver. Unless we provide them with the appropriate resources we cannot expect them to achieve the changes that we require.

In many ways, this is about focusing on both the hard and soft sides of the organization:

– Engaging and rewarding people on one hand in order to reinforce change, and

– Putting in place the structures, systems and management processes to provide the framework on which the business can operate in the future.

Piecing it all together

With the benefit of the understanding that you have gained from this further analysis, you are now in a position of being able to outline the structure of the change program and build your Route Map. I am going to provide you with a summary of the main stages and component elements, but these are at too high level to be really meaningful for each and every change program. You need to feed in the detail from the analyses that you have undertaken to create a plan of sufficient depth.

In simple terms, any change program will comprise three main elements, and everything else is the detail that makes it work:

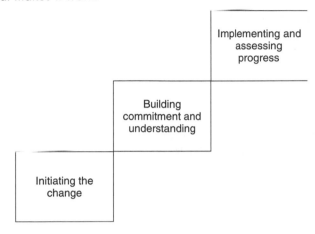

Figure 16: Building the Route Map – the main staging posts

Initiating the change

Anxieties and opportunities

It may seem a strange place to start, and you may expect to start by telling the story of the change to the team, but there is work to be done before this to prepare the ground.

In particular, there is a need to identify how you are going to create an understanding of the need to change, and in turn establish the awareness that we need to move change and at speed.

This can be achieved in one of two ways, and often by way of a combination of the two. Firstly, you can identify such an attractive picture that everybody will be naturally drawn towards it. If you are lucky enough to have such an opportunity available to you, grab it with both hands.

Chances are that your change is not as positive as this and invariably there is an impending problem or crisis that is driving you to make the changes required. If this is the case then you need to find ways to get people throughout the organization to recognize and share your anxiety so that they see the need to move from their current way of doing things.

You can do this by bringing people closer to the potential problems. In an IT team this might be about exposing your staff to the concerns of the business or the strategic challenges that they face. Or you may expose them to the way in which your competitors or outsourced providers are providing the services that you currently deliver to the business.

In this sense you are preparing the ground in anticipation of providing a solution to people's concerns; albeit concerns that you may have created in their minds.

The change team

You also need to determine who is going to make the change happen for you. Is it going to rely on your energy and direction from the top, external change agents or by your middle management team? As a result of the analysis you undertook in respect of the 'change type' you should now be in a position to identify the approach that you should adopt.

Whatever the shape of the team, you need to spend time with them ensuring that they understand the reason to change, the aims of the change and their role within the change program.

Recruitment and selection of this group is important in terms of getting them to work together as a team and I have found that getting them to undertake the analysis described in 'Taking the Pulse' can accelerate this process.

Similarly, the effectiveness and coordination of this team can be improved by undertaking initial work together to develop their change and project management skills so that they have the necessary capabilities and are able to drive the change at the necessary pace.

Clarifying goals

Additionally, the change team should then be tasked to build the detailed change program drawing on the analysis that has been undertaken and the strategy that has been adopted.

Integral to this is the identification of the:

– Main change themes and priorities.

– Performance measures and milestones.

– Creation of the story of change that you will use to communicate to your staff.

TOUCHING

Building commitment and understanding

Engaging and energizing the team

The task now is to tell that story in a way that mobilizes the commitment to and conviction of your staff to do something different. This is not a one-off activity, but the continuous process which removes fear and build aspirations, generates sustainable energy, and helps people to build the mental capacity to absorb the change.

Whilst this stage may include the 'big launch events' it should also include one-to-one interactions, people exhibiting new behaviours, and leaders continually demonstrating their commitment.

In 'Telling the Story' later in this chapter, I will take a deeper look at the communication activities.

Beyond communication, you need to create space for people so that they can make the changes necessary or implement the new projects and programs that are demanded of them. It is no good simply adding to their workload; there is a good chance that they were already feeling overworked and simply adding new tasks will only create barriers and resentment. This is where your work identifying strategic priorities earlier in the program has real impact. As a result, you should know what is and what isn't important. If a piece of work is not important, drop it and give people the room to get on with something that is important.

In this stage, you need to think about how you may use incentives (both the financial and deeper motivational techniques) to accelerate your progress and to reinforce your goals.

Conversely, you need to identify how you will manage the negative impact of any necessary redundancies and job role changes.

Aligning the organization

Working against you will be some extreme cases of negative energy, politics and power, but you should have predicted these as a result of your work during 'Taking the Pulse', and hence you should have strategies to resist these activities.

Some political activity of your own may be demanded to counteract these challenges to the program, but you can also help yourself by increasingly aligning the organization behind the strategy and building a critical mass of support.

TOUCHING

This can be achieved by changing systems and structures in order to make people's lives easier and enabling them to deliver more. Thus, you can reinforce that the strategy is a force for good and one that will bring benefits.

You can also accelerate progress and the pace of change by getting groups within your function and across teams to work together to find solutions to the problems that the change and the new strategy throws up. Your aim is to integrate their efforts and increase coordination.

Implementing and assessing progress

Delivering impact

You need to ensure that you plan for, and get, some early successes that provide evidence to people that you are making progress and there are benefits to be had as a result of the change.

You need also to remove two things; barriers and fear. You should have identified the potential barriers and you need to spend time removing them and negating them.

Equally you need to be conscious that fear will prevent people from doing things. This could be fear of change, fear that they cannot do what is asked of them, and fear that arises out of the existing culture. If people have learnt that managers will jump on them if they make mistakes, or that you will get punished for trying new things, people will not take risks or try to find the novel solutions to the problems that the change throws up.

Fear, can be minimized by:

- Giving people control,

- Giving people information on what is happening, what will happen and why,

- Showing compassion to the understandable concerns that people have during a change program,

- Ensuring people have the skills both to manage the change and to undertake the new roles asked of them. This means that you need to keep assessing whether your change agents are up to the mark as the program develops and what skills are needed by your staff.

Reinforcing the change

Somehow, not only have you got to make the change happen, but you have got to make it stick.

In part, this is about reinforcement and learning; taking every opportunity to capture knowledge gained and reuse it elsewhere. But it is also about utilizing your performance management systems to reinforce objectives and, new behaviours, and to highlight the progress that has been made and the successes being achieved.

Reward, recognition, promotion and opportunity should be given to those that are helping to implement the strategy and who are having the greatest impact on your success.

However, this should not just be about achievement of objectives. This reinforcement approach should be similarly applied to people adopting the right behaviours, because it will be those that will sustain a long-term shift in performance. So if you are looking for people in your function to be more business and relationship centric rather than technology focused, then you need to reward behaviours that seek to understand the customer and put them first, rather than rewarding people who may complete projects but do so without regard to the business needs.

Change will be similarly reinforced by the behaviour of your managers; formal and informal. Not only must they demonstrate ongoing commitment, but they must also be role models who 'walk the talk'. If people see others around them who they admire and respect adopting new ways of working they will tend to follow. This means that you need to identify those who will have impact on others simply by their actions. Having done so, ensure that they are helped to adopt the change quickly and then encouraged to make their actions more visible.

They can do quite simple things. For example:

- Meetings can be structured to reflect the strategy by putting the strategic themes at the top of the agenda.

- They can utilize all their personal interactions with people around the business to reinforce the message.

TOUCHING

– They can show the importance of the strategy by allocating their time and resources to matters that accelerate progress, and dropping things that don't matter any longer.

– They can ensure that they measure and actively manage those projects and activities that align with the plans.

– They can make sure that all the priority projects receive the attention and resources necessary to move you rapidly towards the success to which you aspire.

In this regard the axiom "your actions speak so loudly I can hardly hear what you say" rings very true. It's all right saying one thing, but unless your actions follow through and support your words, people will not believe you, nor do as you ask.

It is also about celebrating success and analysing why you achieve that success. Often we only analyse what has gone wrong, whilst surely we want to learn from what has gone right.

The process of learning can be helped by the change team ensuring that they spend time collecting knowledge from the successes and feeding them back into the team. This will both provide people with new knowledge and skills, and also to highlight the progress that we are making. In the largest programs, it is often done by what is called a Project Office who also have a monitoring role; checking progress against the plan. In change programs, which tend to be slightly smaller and shorter, these are part of the change agents' activities, but important ones.

This simple linear summary gives the impression that you can Take the Pulse, set a plan and simply follow through on it, from one end to the other. You cannot. Once embarked on change, it is a continual process of realigning and adjusting your actions to meet the changing need, mood and progress. Once you change one thing, it will have impact (and most probably unforeseen impact) elsewhere.

Therefore, the change team needs to continually monitor events and make minor adjustments. In large programs, they should reassess their 'Taking the Pulse' analysis and redraw the change plan to account for the current state of your function at say, six monthly intervals.

Telling the story

In every change, there is a story to be told at the outset and on an ongoing basis. What are the issues that you need to consider?

- People need something to believe in; something that make sense to them and with which they can agree.

- People need to understand why the new direction is right and necessary.

- Different people receive and analyse information in different ways, and you therefore need to communicate and help them to understand using a variety of approaches.

- It is not sufficient to simply tell the story; your aim is to get them to:

  - Commit to the change

  - Commit to changing their attitudes

  - Commit to changing their behaviour.

To achieve this, I use the following mix of approaches to structure my thinking:

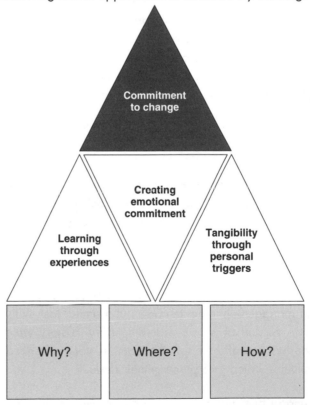

Figure 17: Telling the Story – winning the commitment to change (May and Jung (2000), Ghoshal and Bruch (2003) and Lawson and Price (2003)).

At ground level, is the why, where and how story of the transformation. That which provides your people with the context for the change program. At this initial phase it is also about framing your preliminary plan rather than presenting a final solution. This way people will feel that they have the opportunity to contribute, and be part of the future right from the outset:

Why?

- This is about explaining the internal and external triggers for the change, explaining past crises and forthcoming problems. In IT, it is bound to include an element of the response of the business to your existing performance. Whilst uncomfortable I think is necessary at this stage to have open discussions about the reality of our performance and the current state of the function.

Where?

- This can be a particularly challenging part of the story. You are looking to paint a picture of the company's future and make it real, tangible and very convincing. But at the same time you have to be realistic and not oversell or over promise. In somewhere like IT, I find the best approach is to try and keep away from lofty ideas and visionary statements, and put the strategy in the context of what analysts and help desk staff will be doing in the future.

How?

Here you will be drawing from the knowledge gained from Taking the Pulse and will seek to provide some detail around the journey on which we are about to embark and the route that we will follow. Again, with IT staff that tend more towards an analytical view of life it is helpful for them to see the different tasks, phases, timing and responsibilities and how all the bits fit together in a coherent way.

It is likely that as CIO you will tell this story to all of your staff, but to reinforce the message, you need your management team to carry out a similar task with their teams. They need to create their own version of your overarching story; a story which is more immediate and relates it to the function of their specific team. A story which frames the IT strategy in the day-to-day activities which take place at their desks.

This initial round of briefings alone will be insufficient to win the commitment of everyone. Some will join you immediately and you should be grateful for that. But even those people join you with only a partial understanding of what you are planning, and what is required from them. And then there are those that are not yet convinced. It is necessary to undertake further activities to aid understanding and to seek emotional commitment. This is where the second phase of my approach kicks in.

Here you are seeking to use a mix of approaches that reflect and respect people's different styles of learning in order to make the change real and help them to visualize the end state. You are also trying to bring out into the open doubts and anxieties and encouraging people to make a conscious choice to participate. The result should be that people take personal responsibility to deliver. The approaches you will adopt can include:

Learning through experiences

Here you are trying to expose people to the realities of the pressures and opportunities underpinning the strategy. For example:

- Arranging structured meetings between IT staff and business staff to explore the pressures on the business and the consequent needs for new IT solutions and the important role IT will need to play in this.

- Taking members of staff to companies who have been through similar changes in the past and allowing them to explore the similarity of the issues they had to overcome.

- Creating a series of mock boardroom scenarios whereby team members assume the role of the senior management team. In this scenario, you provide them with the information that you have about the future of the business and let them explore the implications and find potential solutions.

- Exposing staff to the processes and approaches adopted by your partners and suppliers, or even outsourced service providers.

Tangibility through personal triggers

In contrast to 'learning through experiences', which focused on allowing people to explore, analyse and rationalize, this approach is targeted at people who learn more by touching, feeling and seeing. So here, you are seeking to provide physical and tangible examples of the change:

- Create a team that very quickly adopts the new practices and approaches demanded by the change. Then get people to join that team for short spells to see how things will work in the future.

TOUCHING

– Go out and see the practices of other companies who have already adopted strategies similar to your own.

– Create a dummy environment so that people can see and explore the new physical layout of the workplace.

– Get people sat alongside members of staff in the business to experience the issues that they face.

Creating emotional commitment

My target audience here are those who learn by doing and in particular:

– I will look to use role-play, and getting them to teach others about strategy and its implications.

– Getting people to train others, facilitate sessions and also offer coaching support.

– These people are also useful to help you maintain the necessary ongoing communication activities that are necessary in any change program. You can get them to find new ways to explain the strategy to their colleagues and also keep them informed.

– For example, the change will have impact on other people much younger than you, who communicate in their lives outside work in very different ways from you (text messaging, social websites, chat rooms, etc). Get them to tell the story of the strategy and keep their colleagues informed of the progress using their language, not your management speak.

– Get them to create stories, images, story and picture boards, and possibly even games, all of which help others in the organization to understand and explore.

Commitment to change

As noted in the preceding paragraph, there is a need for ongoing communication. This highlights the need to both continue to tell the story and help people understand by using the mix of methods that I have outlined above. Alongside, you will be conscious of the changing mood of people as the program evolves, and you both need to be sensitive to it and shape it.

This is all about protecting and reinforcing the commitment that you will have gained by telling the story in the way I have outlined. It is about providing protection from diversions, reinforcing beliefs and helping people to feel more confident about the change and their role in delivery of the strategy.

Managing stakeholders

One of the biggest challenges you will have in terms of delivering the change is getting your key stakeholders into a position where they can and will support you. For example, a Finance Director with no interest in IT but lots of power on the board can do untold damage to your plans. Conversely, an engaged marketing manager who sees the benefit of using information to better understand the customers can be a powerful ally. However, these states of mind do not come about by accident and your stakeholders need to be lobbied, cajoled, managed, encouraged, informed, and influenced until they support you positively and actively.

To this end, I find that locating key stakeholders on the matrix shown below helps me to see where the key players are currently located and where I want them to be. It also helps me to identify the tactics that I can adopt to get them in the right place.

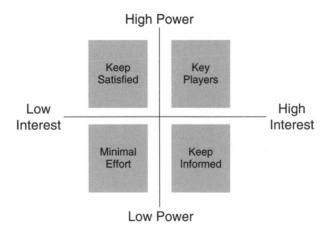

Figure 18: Your stakeholders – how much power and influence? (Scholes et al., 2006)

The general concept behind this approach is that you locate each of the key stakeholders (or players) in the appropriate quadrant on the grid depending on the degree of power and interest that they possess or have. This enables you to see where people are located and what you are trying to do with them. This is not an activity best done alone, but in a group

TOUCHING

where the different perspectives and ideas are allowed to roam so that you can explore all the possible options and solutions.

To help you, may I provide some explanations for some of the terminology:

Stakeholders – those individuals or groups:

– Who depend on the strategy to fulfil their own goals

– On whom we depend to achieve our strategy

– They can be in IT, inside or outside the business

Power – sources of power

– Internal stakeholders

   – Hierarchy

   – Influence

   – Control

   – Possession of knowledge and skills

   – Involvement in decision making

– External stakeholders

   – Control of resources

   – Involvement in implementation

   – Possession of knowledge

   – Informal influence.

Power – indicators of power

– Internal stakeholders

  – Status

  – Claim on resources

  – Representation in powerful positions

  – Symbols of power

– External stakeholders

  – Status

  – Resource dependence

  – Negotiating arrangements

  – Symbols

Key players

– These are the key people whom you need to manage closely and who could have massive influence on your success, or otherwise.

– You cannot have too many people in this box because you will not have the time nor the resource to manage them effectively. Any more than three or four in this box and you should be thinking about how you move some of them out into one of the other zones.

Keep satisfied

– These are people who have the power to influence the shape and success of your strategy, but currently do not have an interest in doing so.

– This may be okay and all you need to do is make sure that they are happy with what you are doing and have no cause to become interested; because if they do they often have negative impact.

– However if these are people who should have a higher interest in the success of your strategy (e.g. CEO) then you need to identify tactics for moving them across into the Key Players box.

Keep informed

– Players who are interested and no doubt keen to see the success of your strategy but are people who have insufficient power to alter your likely course.

– If they are supporters, how can you rally them or transfer power to them so that they can accelerate your progress?

Minimal effort

– The title tells the story and if you have stakeholders in this box, don't spend time on them. Put those resources into managing the Key Players.

If, for example, the managing director of one of your lines of business has a lot of power, but absolutely no interest in IT, then your task is to find ways to increase their level of interest. This can be done by:

– Evidencing the benefits that other companies have gained through the effective use of information.

– Exposure to a peer group of executives in other companies who have had beneficial experiences.

– Education.

– Exposure to emerging technologies and the potential benefits that they can bring.

Alternatively, you may have an HR director who is very interested, and with reasonable amounts of power. But if that director is also very vocal, and causes confusion amongst other senior management, you need to temper excesses and focus energies into specific areas and projects which will deliver substantial impact.

In summary, you should be thinking along the following lines:

– Are the stakeholders in the right place and where do you want them to be?

– How can we move them?

– Who are the key blockers and facilitators of success?

– Do we need to encourage some to maintain/increase their interest in us?

– How are we going to manage the key players?

– What are the key tactics that we can employ?

As a result, you will be able to set objectives and tactics for the management of your stakeholders in a way that facilitates and supports the delivery of your strategy.

And here is an example of a completed one.

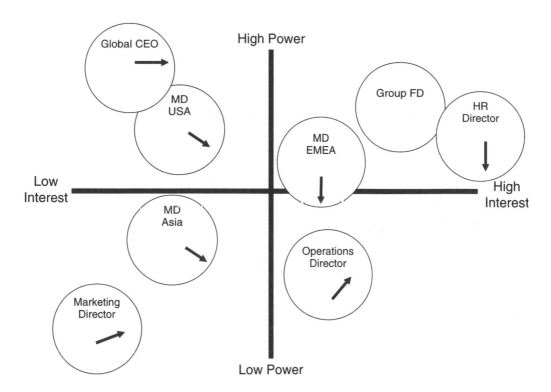

Figure 19: Your stakeholders – how much power and influence?

The CEO

If you are going to successfully deliver the real value of IT for your business, then you are going to need your CEO on board and actively supporting your plans. Regrettably, however, in many companies the CEO is unable, or is apparently unwilling to provide the support necessary to accelerate your progress, and in some cases will undermine your best endeavours.

In the really useful article regarding CEOs, David Feeney and Michael Earl (2000), applied a number of very useful labels to CEOs which help us to understand the different types that exist.

	Characteristics
Hypocrite	Espouses strategic importance of IT Negates this belief through personal actions
Waverer	Reluctantly accepts strategic importance of IT But not ready to get involved in IT matters
Atheist	Convinced IT is of little value Publicly espouses this belief
Zealot	Convinced IT may be strategically important Believes he or she is an authority on IT practice
Agnostic	Concedes IT may be strategically important Requires repeated convincing
Monarch	Accepts IT is strategically important Appoints best CIO possible, then steps back
Believer	Believes IT enables strategic advantage Demonstrates belief in own daily behaviour

Figure 20: Different types of CEO

The most common ones I come across the Hypocrite, the Atheist, the Monarch and thankfully, the Believer. What type of CEO do you have?

Earl and Feeney go on to identify three activities that CEOs should be doing if they are going to have positive impact on the IT strategy:

Believing

– CEOs who are the believers are convinced that IT is the central part of the generation of new business opportunities, strategic decision-making and successful implementation and performance. In essence these CEOs believe in the whole premise of this book.

Living

- Creating context – these CEOs set a context where there is a hunger for change and a desire to venture into the unknown

- Setting priorities – providing a clear set of strategic priorities against which the business has to transact

- Signalling continuously and positively – frequently and consistently making clear their belief in the importance of IT

- Spending quality time – they take time to understand how IT will impact on their business and take time to prepare constructively to discuss IT issues

- Working closely with the CIO – building a good formal and informal relationship.

Practicing

- Scanning and understanding new technologies – these CEOs spend time exploring an understanding involving technologies and how they may impact on their own business

- Forming a vision of the future – spending time developing a picture of the future shape of their sector and their businesses

- Sponsoring internal and external IT architectures – engaging in dialogue with technologists, establishing standards and policies and providing seed corn funding

- Embedding information management processes – ensuring that the right approach is taken to creating IT strategy, evaluating and sanctioning those strategies and ensuring their implementation.

- Challenging the supply side of IT – ensuring that IT has the necessary capabilities and is sourcing supply appropriately either internally or externally.

Unfortunately, not all of you will have a CEO who performs well in all of these areas; indeed it is unlikely. But if you are going to enjoy success with your IT strategy you need to get your CEO closer to being a Believer than now.

Earl and Feeney saw that Believers were IT oriented, not IT literate and IT savvy, or not necessarily IT experienced. They also noted how Believers had confronted the future of the

TOUCHING

industry and their business by identifying key trends and analysing the possible threats and opportunities that existed. Such exposure inevitably brings you face to face with IT and the challenges and opportunities that today's world brings.

Detailed involvement in a large-scale IT project brings exposure, but so can working with a business in which IT is part of its strategic success, or rubbing shoulders with CEOs who believe.

You will need to decide what routes you are going to follow in order to develop the IT passion of your own CEO. But the truth is that your IT function (and no doubt your business) needs a CEO who actively believes in and supports what you are doing.

Maintaining the momentum

From me, this is really a concluding section, but one with a specific purpose. Experience shows that change programs are launched well but have trouble maintaining the initial momentum and succeeding over the long-term. Dips in enthusiasm occur and can be terminal. Much of what has been discussed is about maintaining that momentum and continuing the upward and positive to trajectory. I visualize it like this:

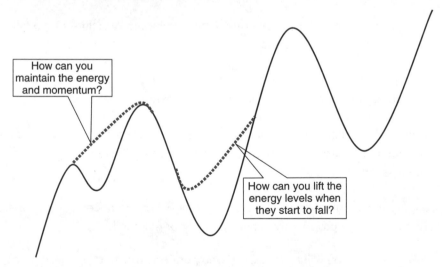

Figure 21: Maintaining momentum through change

The challenge for you is to avoid the small dips and to make sure that the big ones are not quite as deep as they might be.

The tactics and approaches that I have discussed in this chapter will achieve this but if you do nothing else:

– Help people make sense of the change, remove fear and make action a habit

– Give your staff the skills they need, challenge them and support them.

– In your leadership role:

  – Act as a consistent role model

  – Replace vacuums with purpose

  – Up the pace using strong performance management skills

  – Reinforce the right behaviours when you see them.

– Provide people with an organizational context which removes the barriers to their progress and success

– Focus on building a critical mass of people who see the value in what you are doing and who want to change.

Looking

By now you will have a strong idea of the way I approach the strategy and my beliefs in the potential of IT. Equally, you will have a strong understanding of the way in which I look to the outside world for the stimulation. As a result, I believe that in the Looking section in this chapter and the next chapter (Culture), I should provide you with the latitude to spread your wings and look at the world yourself without my views and perspectives getting in the way.

Of course, I wouldn't leave you unsupported just yet, and therefore in both of these Looking sections I will provide you with some initial pointers and direction, and from there you are on your own.

In some ways, therefore, this book is much like a coaching program. I held your hand quite tightly in the early stages and provided a good deal of guidance. But you have now developed, practiced your new skills, reflected on how you are performing, and now you are ready to operate on your own.

So my role here is just to send you off in the right direction and ask you to roam. To maximize the benefits you get from this Looking section, you will need to think freely, talk to a lot people and take time to reflect on what you have learnt. Good luck

The desire to change

It is easy to think, if you listen to what people say and what you read, that people don't want to change and simply want to continue doing what they have always done. Indeed, it often feels like this in the workplace. But all around us, the people we work with, live with, and love are changing all the time. These people strive to achieve some extraordinary things. Some run marathons, others support their communities in amazing ways, others represent local or national teams at their chosen sport, and others overcome serious illness.

All these people and many more have decided to make a substantial change in their lives and achieve something they never thought previously possible. And yet they do it, and they do it with an energy and desire that often they thought they never had. Something, somewhere stimulated them to go out and do something which to them is quite special and quite extraordinary.

I would like you (and would recommend you) to go out and meet these people and find out what they are doing and why. In particular, discover their big catalyst for what they are doing, and what it is that keeps them going, and keeps them energized, and keeps them hungry, and keeps them happy,

Speak to as many people as you can. Take time with them. Listen to their stories.

And when you've done that, reflect on what you have learnt about human beings; their tenacity, their desires, their motivations, their flexibility, their individuality and their sheer reserves of energy.

And when you have clear visibility of the wondrous people around you, think about how you can bring this energy, desire and passion to bear on your change programme. Because if you can, you will achieve more and enjoy life on the way.

LOOKING

Doing

It is not appropriate in a book such as this to identify all the possible approaches that you could adopt to implementing your IT strategy. As a result, I can only highlight the key principles and core tools that you need to consider and apply.

I have also made a conscious choice to principally focus you on the need to energize and win the commitment of your staff to make the changes in their actions and behaviours that will result in different ways of working which can deliver the results to which you aspire. This is because there is no amount of technology investment that will save you if your people are not suitably directed, motivated and skilled.

To succeed the stages you will need to go through are:

☑ Taking the Pulse

☑ Identifying implementation options

☑ Initiating the change

☑ Building commitment and understanding

☑ Implementing and maintaining momentum.

Taking the pulse

The main steps are:

☑ People – identify types, likely barriers & responses to change, & skill levels.

☑ What is your culture like and does it fit with the strategy?

☑ Leadership and organizational capabilities – do we have the skills we need?

☑ Determine our readiness for change and the key areas of focus.

So that you achieve:

☑ Clarity over our readiness to change

☑ Identification of key barriers to change

☑ Knowledge of key levers to accelerate change.

Taking the Pulse provides you with an understanding of the function and its ability and readiness to change.

It is a key component in the change program and is often done in a limited and ineffective way. Without the necessary understanding you cannot build the targeted change program.

☑ Explore and understand the different types of people you have in your function and their natural behavioural responses to change.

☑ Identify the likely barriers to change.

☑ Identify current and required skill levels.

☑ Your culture needs to fit with your strategic aspirations; how would you describe your current culture, what culture do you need, what gaps exist?

You need the management and leadership skills that will carry your function through the change successfully and as quickly as planned.

☑ Do your management have the necessary skills?

  • Which ones are missing

  • How are you going to fill the gaps?

  • Assess the role, beliefs and capability of your CEO.

☑ How good are you as an organization and what do you need to develop?

  • Unless you have an organizational capability that allows you to engage people, develop the resources of the business and apply effective performance management skills, change will be difficult.

DOING

On completion of the analysis you can identify the main levers and barriers to change in readiness for designing the change program.

Identifying implementation options

The main steps are:

☑ Clarify:

- The type of change

- Your starting point

- Your style of change

- Your change target

- Type of interventions

- Change roles

☑ Initiate stakeholder management

☑ Identify the structure and main components of the change program

☑ Determine your readiness for change and key areas of focus.

So that you achieve:

☑ Clarity over the change strategy that you are going to adopt

There are a host of ways in which you can bring about change. Identifying the right strategy and approach to adopt is undertaken by utilizing the information you have gathered from Taking the Pulse and then exploring the possible implementation options that you could use.

☑ Change type – how far and how fast are you going to go, and are you going to do things in sequential stages or one big bang?

DOING

☑ Start point – are you going to start at the top or the bottom or a bit of both. Will you use pilot sites, and how will you share best practice?

☑ Style – will you collaborate or coerce to bring about change? What is the role of education, communication and participation?

☑ Change target – what actually are you seeking to change? Is it outputs, values or behaviours? Each demands different approaches and solutions.

☑ Interventions – what tools will you use to make change happen? You can change systems and structures, or you could use politics and power. Perhaps you will change operational systems or go deeper and seek to change routines and rituals, stories and symbols.

☑ Undertake an assessment of your stakeholders and identify your strategies for managing them.

☑ Change roles – who is going to do what, where will responsibility lie, and who is going to lead the program?

Initiating the change

The main steps are:

☑ Create anxiety and make the opportunities visible

☑ Identify the change team

☑ Review, revise and finalize the change goals.

So that you achieve:

☑ An organization that feels the need to change

☑ The change team who are committed to delivering the strategy

☑ A shared view of success.

Unless people feel the need to change their current patterns of behaviour, they are unlikely to see the reason why they need to embark on change and are less likely to make the changes required:

DOING

☑ Generate anxiety throughout the function which triggers the search for improvement.

☑ Identify and build a team which can make this change happen. Selection and recruitment is important, and so is the need to work with them to turn them into a cohesive unit that can coordinate and integrate their activities.

☑ The change team will need to ensure that they deeply understand the measures of success, and can specify the critical stages and milestones along the journey.

☑ The change team need to monitor and manage progress.

☑ Prepare your stakeholders for change.

Building commitment and understanding

The main steps are:

☑ Create the story that will mobilize commitment

☑ Undertake the initial storytelling

☑ Identify vehicles to continue to tell and reinforce the story

☑ Align the organization.

So that you achieve:

☑ A commitment to change and ownership of the change program and goals

☑ Reinforcement of new behaviours and ways of operating

☑ Everyone pointing in the same direction.

Through the initial announcement and a series of linked and coherent activities we need to win people's commitment to change the way that they do their jobs, the way they behave and the results they deliver.

This cannot be achieved by simply telling people once about the change. We need to help them understand why we are changing, what we are trying to achieve and how we are going to get there:

☑ Give people the chance to explore your aspirations in a variety of ways that meet their differing behavioural needs.

☑ Managers, leaders and change agents need to be reinforcing the new ways of working by their words, their actions and their behaviour.

☑ Maintain contact with key stakeholders to keep them on board and supporting.

☑ Successes need to be shouted about, recognized and learnt from.

☑ Success can be accelerated by building a critical mass of support across the function by changing systems and structures in ways that make people's lives easier and enable them to deliver more.

☑ Cross functional groups can be created to find solutions to difficult change issues and build understanding.

Implementing and maintaining momentum

The main steps are:

☑ Deliver early successes

☑ Target barriers and fear

☑ Reinforce change

☑ Maintain momentum

☑ Determine our readiness for change and key areas of focus.

So that you achieve:

☑ The creation of a feeling of success and an ability to have an impact

☑ Change that sticks

☑ Ongoing progress.

DOING

It is easy for change to stall. The initial launch activities give people a feeling of hope and optimism but this quickly fades unless people see something happening. You need to deliver some quick wins.

Fear prevents people from doing things, so do barriers. They will act as a brake on your progress and you need to overcome them:

☑ Look out for and overcome:

- A fundamental fear of change

- A fear of making mistakes

- The fear of other managers

- The fear of failure

- The fear created by not having the necessary skills.

☑ Give people control and information and show compassion.

☑ Identify barriers to change and remove them, or help people over them, or under them, or round them

☑ Make change stick through reinforcing the right practices and behaviours.

☑ Celebrate, reward and recognize those doing the right things and behaving in the right way.

☑ Ensure managers and leaders across the organization adopt the new approaches and act as role models.

☑ Accelerate the process of learning from success and sharing best practice.

☑ Identify in advance the dips in energy that may slow your progress or which may signal terminal decline. Plan in advance to overcome these by removing barriers, upping the pace and reinforcing the reasons why.

DOING

☑ Keep close to the mood in the function and keep communicating in response.

☑ Create a positive environment to accelerate progress and plan to mitigate the slowing effects of the inevitable doubts and anxieties.

13 Culture

- What is it?

- How to analyse your culture

- How do you change your culture?

Culture is a strange and woolly concept for the IT community, and not only will this chapter provide clear guidance on the issues of cultural change, but it will also make culture tangible and accessible. In doing so it will provide you with an approach and understanding to which you can relate and in turn apply in the workplace.

Touching

Why do you need to know about culture in IT? Quite simply, it is because:

– Your culture has to fit with your strategy otherwise you won't deliver.

– There is a very strong chance that your culture is inappropriate for your needs at the moment.

– Because the culture in your organization determines:

  – The products and services you can offer

  – How responsive and flexible you can be

  – How customer focused your organization can become

  – Your ability to change and respond

  – The speed of your decision-making

  – The management styles that you deploy.

Conversely you could be thinking:

– It is a 'soft' topic that has little relevance in a place like IT

– My culture is okay already.

If you are in either of these camps, you are being complacent. Firstly, because:

– Culture is more pervasive in IT than even technology (and every other bit of your organization), and

– If you don't think you need to improve anything then you haven't challenged yourself sufficiently. Or your strategy is not a strategy, but simply a recipe for the status quo. The business will not accept this flaccid thinking, and nor should it.

So what do you need to know?

– What is culture?

– How can you understand it?

– How do you change your culture?

What is culture?

You will know by now that I believe that strategy, the ability to think about it and the ability to create it is important, but these aspects are not half as important as your ability to implement it. You can have the best strategy in the world but if you can't deliver, it's no good to you at all. It's much like having a Ferrari parked on your drive when you haven't got the keys to unlock it and start the engine. Establishing the right culture is a key component in that success. Why?

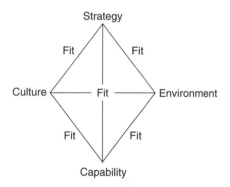

Figure 1: The importance of fit (Miles and Snow, 1984)

In this diagram I have highlighted four main areas for you to think about; your strategy, your marketplace, your culture and your capability. In essence, each of these must fit and be in harmony with the others if you are to succeed in delivering the results that you desire.

So, for example let's consider a company that is looking to compete by being creative and innovative – what has 'fit' got to do with all this?

The fit with the environment and market place

Well, unless your market place actually wants or desires the innovative products and services that you have on offer you won't be able to sell them. Not unless you adopt a 'hard sell' policy so that you can push your products into the market, but commits you to ever-rising marketing and sales cost. These additional costs reduce your profitability and your returns and in due course, your ability to re-invest in the business. And do they create loyalty and repeat business?

If, on the other hand, the market is hungry for your product it will suck it from you in much the same way as enjoyed by Dyson or Direct Line in the early days of their unique product launches.

The capability fit

In this regard, successful achievement of your results hinges upon your ability to deliver. This is about having the skills, the resources, and the know-how to be able to deliver your plans, time and time again.

The culture fit

So that brings us around to culture.

Let's return to our company which is competing through creativity and innovation. If the culture in the company is one bounded in bureaucracy, controls, and stifled thinking then it will not be able to deliver on that more fluid and dynamic approach that the strategy aspires to. Indeed, the cultural constraints will also limit the company's ability to build the capabilities that are required to deliver.

Often the culture also prevents the board from recognizing the reality of its current position. Boards often perceive that they are doing well even when customers are leaving and the competitors are overtaking them. This happens because the internal cultures serve to reinforce existing patterns of behaviour and beliefs. There is a long list of major companies that have been undone by their culture and its ability to blind them to the realities of the world; Marks & Spencer and IBM are just two. Similarly, are you deluding yourself because your culture provides you and your management team with a skewed perception of the reality of your current performance?

Unless an organization is able to see accurately the reality of its performance and capabilities (their starting point), they will never be able to get where they need to go. Just imagine trying to get to Boston if you don't know whether you are currently in Miami or Seattle.

Therefore, if you want to deliver your strategy you have to build, change and develop your culture so that you are able to see the world for what it is, can understand your current position in it, and can you build the capability and skills that are necessary to compete.

We also know that where common values, behaviours and cultures are shared there is a correlation with higher performance which implies that we have a management interest in fostering a common and consistent approach. So it seems, that we do need a common way of thinking and acting and that this needs to fit with our strategy. However, the culture mustn't become so dominant that it creates delusions of grandeur.

Exploring culture

Culture has been described in many ways by many people:

- A set of guiding beliefs and philosophies

- The way we do things round here

- A way of thinking and acting

- Just the way things are

- The glue that holds the organization together

- Shared beliefs, customs and practices which are often accepted without question.

In light of this, it is a strange, yet sad, fact of organizational life that when you join a new organization you are inducted into its systems and processes and introduced to the key people, but it is left to you to learn about the culture. Whereas, if an introduction to the culture was an overt part of the induction process, your ability to fit in and perform in the expected manner would be much accelerated.

Part of the reason it is ignored in the induction process, is that culture is quite complex; the behaviours in marketing differ from those in IT, which differ from those in operations, and everywhere is different from finance! Even within these individual functions there are further sub-cultures that exist in the teams that work together and the groups that socialize together.

Despite these variances, common behaviours and values will form across an organization. The degree of consistency varies in each organization and the depth and strength of the culture is evident by its pervasiveness and the degree to which norms of behaviour are accepted and lived by.

However, and as noted earlier, where the culture does not fit with the market you may find that the performance is held back. This is particularly so in multinational companies, where a culture which is applauded and supported in head office doesn't fit the needs of local market conditions. Coca Cola experienced this when it endeavoured to apply a common approach to its global activities but found itself unable to respond to local needs. As a result it has stepped back from this homogeneous approach and now encourages local managers to take advantage of greater discretion in terms of decision-making, ways of managing and the development of local cultures – in other words 'thinking globally, acting locally'.

The challenges that result for us in IT include:

– Having a culture that permits us to deliver our strategy.

– Benefiting from a culture that fits with the needs of our market place, i.e. the business.

– Having a culture which facilitates the building of the necessary capabilities, the deployment of appropriate management styles and which accelerates our ability to change and respond at speed.

Another way of looking at culture is to view it in different layers.

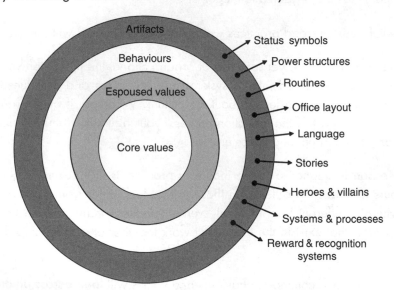

Figure 2: The cultural layers – just like an onion (Thornbury, 1999)

The artifacts

These aspects of culture are very easy to see and can often be very deceptive; organizations often look similar on the surface but may have very differing values.

Attitudes and behaviours

Whilst not as visible as artifacts, they are very important as they often dictate the behavioural norms that indicate whether an individual is going to be accepted and get on in the organization.

Espoused values

These are the values which an organization claims to hold and are often shouted about by management. They can be evidenced by posters, press releases, claims in change programs and the words of managers. However, unless those words are translated into actions, behaviours and practices on the ground they have no meaning and are more likely to cause cynicism than positive impact.

Core values

These can be deeply buried into the organizational psyche that they will determine the nature and shape of your business, what you do and how you do it. Our difficulty is that they are so unconsciously adhered to that they can be often very difficult to identify.

Not only are these elements increasingly hard to identify, but the closer you get to the core values, the greater their impact increases and the harder they are to change;

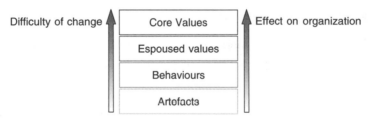

Figure 3: The difficulty and impact of changing your culture

It is much easier to change artifacts and behaviours than it is core values, but the impact of the latter is the greatest.

Culture, though, isn't just reflected in these layers, it is a reflection of your organization:

How old are you and how big are you?

– If you are at the start-up stage, you will find that your organization tends to be more market-driven and informal. Spoken communication is the norm and feedback to the owners or top management is immediate.

TOUCHING

In more mature organizations that have a more decentralized structure, more formal and structured communications and ways of working are more common.

Where are you?

– Your culture will reflect the country in which you are located. Yes you may be influenced by the country of your parent organization, but you will also be subject to the influence of your host nation.

– The German's considered approach, set in an environment demanding extensive sign-off is in stark contrast to the risk-taking, informal and direct approach of the Americans, where hunches and a feel for the right opportunity is often a dominant feature of decision-making.

Who is your dad?

– Culture also reflects the passions of the founding fathers of the business. Whilst this may appear obvious in terms of the smaller company it rings true in much larger organizations; the impact of Sam Walton and Walt Disney is still evident in Wal-Mart and The Walt Disney Company to this day.

What are the consequences?

The existing culture is likely to be representative of a mix of factors; the company we work for, the country we work in, the history of the company, the depth and strength of culture in the business as a whole.

The culture in IT will:

– Reflect the history of the function.

– The role it has been used to undertaking in the business.

– Its experiences in relation to the business and its experience of past heads of the department.

In other words, an IT function which has spent its life just about reacting to business demands and being subject to a blame culture will be very different from one which has established strong relationships with the business, has evolved a strategic way of operating and enjoys a voice in the boardroom.

The existing culture will evidence the technical focus of the function.

− If technical skills are dominant in the hierarchy and the exercise of power in your function it is likely that you can produce solutions of superb technical quality.

− It is also likely that these are solutions that are delivered too late and do not address the needs of the business.

− A technically dominated culture will be of limited value to you if you are seeking to 'Lead' your business and will be similarly inappropriate if agility and responsiveness are core themes in your strategy.

The existing culture will reflect the focus and preferences of your current leaders and managers.

− Where are they taking the function today, what behaviours are they rewarding and what values are they reinforcing?

− If their preferences are for technology rather than customer centricity, or if a defensive and controlling mindset is being established, your attempts to seek and exploit new opportunities are unlikely to be realized.

Unfortunately, it is my experience that the culture in many IT departments remains technically focused with a rigidity that is unsuitable for the challenges presented in this book. Even those IT functions who have identified the need for the approaches we have discussed are finding that their progress is being slowed as a result of a cultural intransigence built out of an inappropriate functional culture.

As a result, leaders and managers in IT have to recognize the need to deliver a change to the culture in their function, and establish ways of behaving that will support and accelerate the delivery of the strategy.

How can you analyse your culture?

The first stage in making that change, is about understanding where you are currently − in other words, are you presently in Miami or Seattle?

This demands that you find a way of exploring and describing the 'soft and woolly' thing called culture. Some say this is not possible to do, but there are a number of tools and approaches that can help us to both describe the current state of the organization and iden-tify where you want it to be in the future. There are a number of ways of doing this, but I am only going to propose those which you can do for yourself, either as an individual activity or with your team.

Separately, there are a number of survey and internet based approaches promoted by vari-ous firms and consulting groups. Whether these provide significantly greater precision or the insight that will accelerate your progress is not for me to debate here. My aim is to give you the ability to describe your culture and to encourage you to engage in debate over your differing views and perspectives and from those discussions, deepen your understanding of your culture.

And let me be clear, there will be many views expressed by different people. And many of those views will be very deeply held. The challenge is to understand why they exist and to be able to draw lessons and deepen your understanding as a result of the debates that ensue.

A new job

As a warm-up exercise, let's start with a very simple but active approach.

– Get a dozen of your IT people together (a mix of positions, teams and departments is fine) and give them each nine post-it notes, and let them know that they must put one idea only on each post-it note.

– Explain to them that a close friend of theirs is about to start work in the IT function the following week, and that their friend has asked them for some guidance on how they can get on in the IT function and enjoy a successful career.

– In particular, they have asked three questions:

  – What three things must they do to get on?

  – What three things can they get away with not doing and yet still enjoy career suc-cess?

  – What three things must they absolutely never do if they want a career in the function?

- Ask your colleagues these three questions in turn, and after you have asked each question give them two minutes (no more) to write down one idea on each post-it note (they will complete three post-it notes for each question).

- Once the two minutes have elapsed, asked them the second question, and after a further two minutes ask the third question. At the end of this they should have nine post-it notes, each with one idea or issue.

- Whilst they are doing this, you should put three post-it notes on a blank wall:

  - Must do

  - Get away with

  - Mustn't do

- Then ask your colleagues to put all their post-it notes up on the wall under the three headings that you have marked up:

  - Having done this, get your colleagues to group the responses in each of the three areas and identify the common themes that arise.

  - Ask group members to tell the others what they have seen, found and discovered.

Very quickly, you will see the key behavioural themes coming out of this grouping activity and the related discussion. Equally, you will start to build a picture of the main elements of your culture, and see which aspects have the biggest impact on people's behaviour and attitudes. In turn, you should be questioning whether these fit with the demands of your strategy.

This is a very quick exercise which provides a great deal of insight on many an organizational culture, and I often use it to get my bearings in a company. The key is to make the group work at pace, and certainly not give them any more than two minutes in each of the sections. This results in people revealing their honest views because they don't have time to hide them behind the normal political correctness.

The emotional essence of culture

One of the elements that you are trying to identify through your analysis of the culture is the shared values and beliefs that exist. Often these are not readily visible and therefore it is

TOUCHING

necessary to identify those tangible elements of the workplace which act as evidence of the underlying shared values and beliefs.

The essence in this approach is the principle that culture is something that is shared by your staff. Therefore, if you can identify those tangible elements of the workplace that your staff share, you can use this as evidence of the underlying beliefs and values.

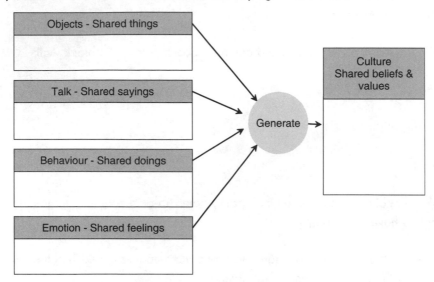

Figure 4: Analysing culture – the things we share

Shared things

What are the physical elements of your business that your staff share? This may be a car park, or a staffroom, a water cooler, or secretaries. It may be PCs or floor layout, status symbols, large and small rooms, cars and pool tables.

Shared sayings

What do people talk about; customers, task or management? What are the jokes about? Is there an office slang? What acronyms do you use and why?

Shared doings

What are the common routines that exist and which everybody abides by without the need for instruction? Where do people go at lunchtimes and who with? What clubs and societies and social activities do people participate in? How do people let off steam?

Shared feelings

What shared views existed either about the organization or the world at large, or the competition, or customers? What do people think about management and what do management think about staff? How do people respond to the bonus systems and the reward structure?

Having done this, ask yourself:

– Why these things occur, and why people seek peace in these common areas of interest?

– What are the common themes in each of the boxes and why?

– What are shared values and beliefs?

The culture web

Whilst you can gain a good understanding of the main themes through the approaches just described, very often it is necessary to have a more detailed description and this is where the cultural web (Scholes *et al.*, 2006) is a very useful tool, particularly as it allows you to describe the culture along a number of dimensions.

The concept behind the cultural web is to provide you with a way of describing the various elements that go to make up your culture, as shown below.

As you will see, the culture web is represented by a series of interlocking rings that come together to represent the culture of your organization. At the centre is a 'summary' circle which serves to capture the overall essence of the culture.

By asking a series of questions you can build an understanding of the various elements that go to make up your culture (Scholes *et al.*, 2006):

Stories

– If you were sat in the staff room, what stories would you hear?

– What core beliefs do stories reflect?

– Do the stories relate to successes or our failures?

– Is conformity or individuality recognized?

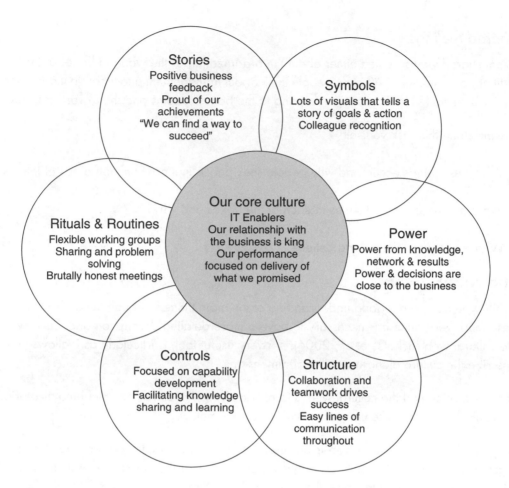

Figure 5: Analysing culture – the cultural web

- Who are the heroes and villains?

- Why do staff say they like working here?

Routines and rituals

- Which organizational routines and rituals are emphasized?

- What behaviours do our routines encourage?

- What do training programs emphasize?

– In what way do people respond to change?

– What is distinctive about the way in which our Managers manage the business and our people.

Controls

– What is most closely monitored/controlled?

– Is emphasis on reward or punishment?

– How do controls reinforce our strategic goals and shared values?

– What does the reward structure reinforce and how?

Organizational structure

– How flat/hierarchical are the structures?

– Do structures encourage collaboration or competition and in what way?

– How do teams operate?

– In what way does the structure enable people to deliver our goals?

Symbols

– Are there particular symbols which denote the organization?

– What type of language and jargon is used?

– What aspects of our strategy are visible across the business?

– How are our customers represented in the business?

– What status symbols are there?

Power

– Where is the power distributed in the business? Why does power reside there?

– What are the core beliefs and principles of the leadership?

– How widely are those beliefs shared across the business?

– Where are the main blockages to change?

– Where does the energy and desire for change come from?

Our Core Culture

– What are the dominant values of the organization?

– If you came into contact with the business what would be your abiding memory?

– How would you describe our people and their attitudes?

As a result of undertaking these activities we are in a position to be able to describe the culture of your function and assess its suitability (fit) with the demands of your strategy. And this is your final task in the analysis process;

– Really explore all the different issues you have uncovered.

– Debate as a team the key lessons that arise.

– Identify the key themes and issues.

– Explore how the culture needs to change in order that you can deliver your plans.

How do you change your culture?

Obviously, I will not repeat here all the change issues covered in Chapter 12 and will focus instead on those aspects particular to culture change.

A sense of direction

One of the real strengths of using the culture web approach is that it provides you with a vehicle by which you can set objectives for your culture change program. So, whilst I accept that you may be dealing with the 'nebulous and soft', a culture web provides you with a way to be much more specific:

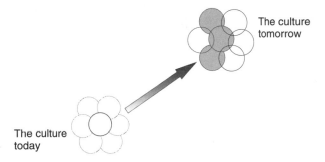

Figure 6: Changing culture – where are you headed?

This is because you can describe the culture as it is today using the culture web and equally you can create a picture of the culture which you wish to build, again using the cultural web.

As a result, you can see clearly what it is you are trying to build and equally you can see the specific changes that you may need to make in any of the circles, e.g. the stories that are told, or creating new symbols, or establishing new controls. Thus, you can identify what changes you need to make and where. You also know where Boston is, and whether you are currently in Seattle or Miami.

Building the Route Map

With the foundation of this sense of direction, it is now possible to build an incremental program of change which focuses on the key changes that you need to make in your culture.

Without repeating the main themes identified in Chapter 12, the issues you need to bear in mind with regard to change in the culture are as follows.

Long-term

Culture change is a marathon not a sprint and therefore you need to prepare yourself to be able to sustain and maintain a program of activities over a number of years, so that new ways of working can not only be adopted but also deeply ingrained. The example of British Airways is often cited; Lord Marshall spent many years changing the culture only to see much of his endeavours undone in months by his replacement Bob Ayling.

Care, support and trust

This will be a demanding change for many people. You need to be conscious of this and evidence it in the ways you handle your staff, provide them with the support that they will need and maximize the trust they place in you. Be particularly careful not to lose their trust.

Changing artifacts

Whilst this is one of the easier elements of culture change it is often an aspect left to change of its own accord rather than being actively managed. So I suggest consciously identifying the physical changes you would like to make that will evidence a new environment, and go out and make them.

If that means moving some of the team to sit within business units, using new performance measures, putting up performance charts, changing the floor layout to integrate analysts and programmers, creating space for informal meetings, changing dress codes, getting members of the business into IT more often or simply changing the structure, format and content of meetings, then get on and do it, and keep doing it.

Changing behaviours

Focus on changing the behaviours of all managers. Give them coaching and guidance on what you expect them to be doing and how you expect them to behave, and get them doing it straight away and continually. If that means managing by walking about and just talking to people, good. Better if they can use those conversations to reinforce the new culture and help people make sense of what is going on and how it impacts on their job.

It is even better if their actions reinforce their fine words. This will show the team that the world is changing. This includes their actions in terms of:

– Giving feedback

– Encouraging people

– Their own interactions with the business

- Their approaches to problem solving and decision making

- The allocation of priorities

- The management of projects

- Their social interactions and language.

Also, look out for mismatches between 'espoused' behaviours and what is really happening on the ground. If your staff see a gap, they will become cynical and your progress will be delayed or even may be halted. Deal with these gaps quickly.

Reward system

Make sure that the rewards that you offer reinforce the new behaviours, values and culture that you wish to create.

- If you want people to be focused on the business, then reward them for trying to do so.

- If you want people to be innovative, then recognize their efforts in trying to identify problems and find possible solutions. In the early days they may not be successful; this does not matter as it is the desire and habit that you are trying to establish. Results will flow in time with practice and the addition of new skills.

And by rewards I don't just mean salary, but also recognition (both public and private), bonuses, project opportunities and promotion.

Whenever you reward someone by whatever means, make explicit the link between how they have behaved, the culture we are working to achieve and the benefits realized by their actions.

Explain, and explain again

Behaviours and attitudes are difficult to change, and initially it is very difficult for people to understand what it is you mean. So you need to plan to include an excessive amount of communication which helps people to understand where you are going and why, and what it means they need to be doing.

This can be a real challenge for IT managers and it is very likely that you will need to help them to build a story and practice telling it:

TOUCHING

- IT people can be quite analytical and detail focused. Therefore you need to satisfy their needs and expectations in these regards.

- Give them the detail, show how the pieces fit together, and let them explore and debate and challenge the consequences.

- They will need to rationalize the change you are proposing and you are not going to win by coercion.

Create a desire

Having helped people to understand, you need to help people to want to get there. In part, that is about rewards and incentives, but it is also about helping people to see how the new world will benefit them personally, and will help them to achieve their own goals and aspirations.

Build the capability to cope

Even if your people understand and want to join you on the journey they will not succeed unless you ensure that they are capable of doing so. This is likely to mean:

- For some this will be about giving them new skills

- For others it will be about getting them to practice new behaviours

- For others (if not all) it is about giving them the context in which they can perform in new ways

- It will be about empowering them

- Making sure that the teams they work in support the change

- It may mean changing decision-making processes and controls

- Making sure that their managers are behaving in the right way and supporting them

- Sharing the experiences and successes of others in a way that reinforces momentum.

TOUCHING

In closing

In simple terms, culture is important and you cannot bring about the delivery of your strategy without changing it in some way.

How deep that change needs to be only you will know. The chances are your current culture is too the pointed towards technology, is insufficiently business focused and too rigid to help you become the fluid and responsive function you need to be to perform in the current business climate.

Culture change can be delivered but it will take a long time and will demand that you know clearly where you are now and where you need to get to. You must help your staff to make the change by both giving them the support that they need and behaving in a way which reinforces the attitudes and values central to the culture you wish to create.

TOUCHING

LOOKING

Looking

Once again and in the same way that I did in the last chapter, my role in this Looking section is to send you off in the right direction and ask you to roam. To maximize the benefits that you will get from this, you will need to think freely, talk to a lot people and take time to reflect on what you have learnt.

This time though, I invite you to go and visit different businesses, places of work, leisure clubs etc and see for yourself the different cultures that exist. In this regard, I want you to feel and expose yourself to those different cultures and then consider how they impact and limit the different strategies that those businesses could pursue.

For example:

– Why is it that receptionists in doctors' surgeries always behave the way they do and how does that constrain the strategic options for those surgeries?

– What is the culture like in your children's school and how is this evidenced?

– If you have two children (or more), how do the cultures differ between the schools they attend?

– How do these cultures vary from that which you see in your local discount store or your favourite furniture store?

– And more provocatively, how does the culture in your own home differ from that of your neighbours and friends?

You could use any of the tools that I described in the Touching section to analyse your culture, but my favourite is the culture web. However, I will leave that to you.

As I say, when you have finished looking, reflect on the differing cultures in the places you have seen, and consider how this impacts on what they can and cannot do.

Then look again with fresh eyes at the culture in your own organization and identify both the limitations and the possibilities that result.

Doing

Culture is a key component in the successful delivery of your strategy. Chances are that your current culture is inappropriate, and if left alone it will slow and possibly halt your implementation plans.

You therefore need to know what culture is, how to analyse it, what you are trying to achieve and how to make the change happen. In this sense, our interest in culture is an extension of our discussions in Chapter 12 regarding change. Therefore, the actions described here are complementary to the issues discussed in that chapter. Thus, I do not repeat those elements again and simply highlight the additional actions that you need to be taking:

☑ Where are you now?

☑ Where do you want to be?

☑ On the journey.

Where are you now?

The main steps are:

☑ Analyse your existing culture.

☑ Identify the key elements of your existing culture.

☑ Test the fit of your culture with your strategy – will it support or undermine?

☑ Identify the main changes that you will need to make in your culture.

So that you achieve:

☑ A clear understanding of the starting point for your culture change journey.

☑ Understanding of what it is you are going to need to change and why.

Changing your culture is a key element in the successful implementation of your strategy. But first of all, you need to understand what it is you're trying to change and why.

☑ This demands that you analyse and understand your existing culture and can describe and see where it does and doesn't support your strategic aspirations. The issues you will explore will include:

- The stories that are told

- Routines and rituals

- Controls that exercised

- Where power resides

- The things people do

- The things people feel

- The way managers manage

- The things that you see and touch.

☑ There are a number of tools available to you to do this and whichever model you decide to use you must ensure that it helps you to go much deeper than simply recognizing the physical symbols and artifacts of organizational life. You are seeking to identify:

- How people behave and why

- The shared belief and behaviours of the function

- The glue pot holds the function together.

☑ You will not be able to do this alone and will need to involve other members of the management team, the function and the business units so that you have a wide range of perspectives and use that will shine a light on these core issues.

☑ Once you have a strong understanding, you will be able to see whether or not your existing culture supports your strategy and if not, where not and why not.

☑ In turn, this will allow you to identify what it is you have to change to deliver your plans.

Where do you want to be?

The main steps are:

☑ Identify the core themes of your desired culture.

☑ Describe the main components of the culture that you are trying to build.

☑ Identify milestones for the journey so that you can monitor progress.

So that you achieve:

☑ Clarity over the final destination of your culture change journey.

☑ An ability to explain to people where you are going and what needs to change.

To be successful in delivering culture change, you need to know where you are heading.

☑ The tools you have used to analyse your culture should be used to help you describe the end state.

☑ In describing the end state that you are seeking to achieve, you need to be able to describe the main components and the main thrust of your culture and the various attributes that will evidence this on the ground;

☑ Not only should you describe the end state, but if possible you should also seek to specify what the world will look like at different stages of your journey. This will mean that you can check intermittently on your progress.

☑ You need to find language and vehicles by which you can explain your aspirations to your team in a way which they can understand, rationalize and engage with.

On the journey

The main steps are:

☑ Identify the levers that you are going to pull to accelerate your progress

DOING

☑ Pull those levers

☑ Monitor progress

☑ Take remedial action and maintain momentum.

So that you achieve:

☑ Accelerated delivery of the culture change

☑ Fast change in the physical environment

☑ A supportive working environment that helps people make the necessary changes in behaviour.

You need to be clear about the actions you are going to take to help people make the behavioural changes that will in turn drive the change in your culture.

Central to this is your management team:

☑ They are accountable for making the shift

☑ They have to identify the changes that you need to make

☑ They have to evidence commitment

☑ They have to be the first people to change their behaviours and actions in order to both evidence their commitment and to provide the environment in which people can successfully change.

☑ You therefore need to ensure that your management team are on board, committed, skilled and supported so that they can fulfil these critical roles.

There are other things you can do:

☑ Change the look of the office so that it fits with what you are trying to achieve

☑ Explain, and explain again what it is you're trying to achieve. Use different methods and different approaches appropriate to the way your individuals think

☑ Create a desire to change

☑ Give people the skills and context to perform

☑ Reward new and right behaviours

☑ And build trust. Build trust across teams and in particular ensure that your staff can trust your managers. A loss of trust will delay or even stop your progress.

DOING

14 In closing

A strategy only has any value when it is implemented and delivers the results that were planned. In that regard, IT has a massive role across the business in aiding and accelerating implementation.

For this reason, this book has focused on providing you with the ability to implement strategy rather than develop it. However, it has done so by building on my passionate belief that IT has the potential to deliver much greater value to the business than you achieve at the moment.

If you are going to deliver to your full potential it demands that you and your teams understand a number of aspects in the strategy arena:

– First, you need to understand what strategy is today in the competitive and fluid environment in which businesses operate. This is not necessarily about analysis and planning, but how strategy operates both as a way of thinking and as a way of acting so that your company can deliver value to its customers.

– With that foundation, and hence a focus for your energies, it is possible for the IT function to develop its own strategy which can be tightly aligned to effectively support the business strategy. This degree of alignment is critical to both the success of the business, the effective utilization resources and the perceived value of the IT function.

– We have seen that different IT functions are at different stages of development; those that simply react to or Follow the needs of the business, those who have progressed to Enabling the business to succeed, and others (a rarer bunch) who are in a position of Leading the business so that new strategic opportunities are facilitated by the IT function. For many of you, this will be an aspiration, and a challenging one.

– Once you are clear about where you are heading, it is possible to be much more specific about what and how you deliver to the business and the service that wraps around your core proposition. Once this is clear to you and your team, this message can be reinforced in words and deeds so that your peers in the business understand what they are buying and adjust their expectations accordingly.

– However this demands that you have the ability to deliver consistently and reliably so that the business starts to place trust in you.

– It will result in you being able to respond more quickly and introduce new systems and technologies at a pace not previously dreamed possible.

– For this to be achieved, you have to develop the necessary skills and capabilities in your staff and managers and set these in a culture that will support and facilitate your success.

– This will be a demanding journey and one that will have its highs and lows and you will need to carry your staff through the stresses and challenges that it will present; but you will see that the benefits to your business, your function and yourself are great.

– However, unless the business is able to absorb and utilize this new-found capability you will not be able to use it to the full; so you have to prepare the business to enable it to work with an IT function with this level of capability.

In closing, this all demands that you and your team build the ability to think and act in a strategically aligned way. This is not about strategy as plans, systems and processes; it is about fluidity of thought, awareness, desire, belief, knowledge sharing and a passion to see IT as the key strategic resource in your business; one delivering value and success continuously.

Good luck and I wish you every success in becoming not just an IT function, but the Department of Value Creation.

References

Andersen, H. V., Lawrie, G. and Shulver, M. (2000) The Balanced Business Scorecard vs. The Business Excellence Model – which is the better strategic management tool? 2GC Working Paper, June

Beer, M. and Eisenstat, R. A. (2000) The silent killers of strategy implementation and learning. *Sloan Management Review*, Summer

Bennis, W. and Nanus, B. (1985) Leaders: *The strategies for taking charge*. Harper and Row

Boston Consulting Group (1977) *Using PIMS and Portfolio Analysis in Strategic Market Planning: A comparative Analysis*. Harvard Business School CIO Connect / SAS Census, 2005

Collins, J. (2001) *Good to Great*. Random House, London

Darragh, J. and Campbell, A. (2001) Why corporate initiatives get stuck? *Long Range Planning*, 34(1)

De Wit, R. and Meyer, R. (1998) *Strategy Process, Content and Context*. Thomson Business Press

Dunphy, D. C. and Stace, D. A. (1988) Transformational & coercive strategies for planned organizational change. *Organizational Studies*, 9(3)

Feeney, D. and Earl, M. (2000) How to be a CEO for the information age. *Sloan Management Review*, Winter

Ghoshal, S. and Bruch, H. (2003) Going beyond motivation to the power of volition. *Sloan Management Review*, Spring

Gosling, J. and Mintzberg, H. (2003) The five minds of a manager. *Harvard Business Review*, November

Hagel, J. and Brown, S. (2005) The Only Sustainable Edge: *Why business strategy depends on productive friction and dynamic specialization.* Harvard Business School Press

Herb, E., Leslie, K. and Price, C. (2001) Teamwork at the top. *McKinsey Quarterly*, No. 2

Herzberg, F. (1968) One more time: how do you motivate employees? *Harvard Business Review*, 46(1), 53–62

Heskett, J. L., Sasser, W. E. and Schlesinger, L. A. (1997) *The Service Profit Chain.* Free Press

Higgs, M. J. and Rowland, D. (2000) Building change leadership capability. *Journal of Change Management*, 2(1)

Hope, V. H. and Balogun, J. (2002) Devising context sensitive approaches to change. The example of Glaxo Wellcome. *Long Range Planner*, 35

Introducing Excellence: *The EFQM Model.* EFQM, Avenue des Pléiades 11, 1200 Brussels, Belgium

Ittner, C. D. and Larcker, D. F. (2003) Coming up short on non-financial performance measurement. *Harvard Business Review*, Online version, November

Jones, S. and Gosling, J. (2005) Nelson's Way: *Leadership lessons for the Great Commander.* Nicholas Brealey Publishing

Jones, A. and Williams, L. (n.d.) *Public Services and IT. Why ICT? The Role of ICT in Public Services.* The Work Foundation

Kaplan, R. S. and Norton, D. P. (1996) Using the Balanced Scorecard as Strategic Management System. *Harvard Business Review*, January–February

Kaplan, R. S. and Norton, D. P. (2000) *The Strategy-focused Organization.* Harvard Business School Press

Kotler, P. (1994) *Marketing Management: Analysis, planning, implementation, and control.* Prentice Hall International

Lawson, E. and Price, C. (2003) The psychology of change management. *The McKinsey Quarterly*, Special edition: The Value in Organization

Leavitt, H. J. (1965) Applied organizational change in industry: structural, technological and humanistic approaches. In: March, J. G., editor, *Handbook of Organizations*, Rand McNally, Chicago, IL

Marchand, D. A., Kettinger, W. J. and Rollins, J. D. (2000) Information orientation: people, technology and the bottom line. *Sloan Management Review*, Summer

Markides, C. (1999) Six principles of breakthrough strategy. *Business Strategy Review*, 10(2)

May, D. J. and Jung, M. (2000) Corporate transformation without crisis. *The McKinsey Quarterly*, (4)

McCall Jr., M. W. and Hollenbeck, G. P. (2002) *Developing Global Executives*. Harvard Business School Press

McDonald, M., Christopher, M., Knox, S. and Payne, A. (2001) Creating a company for customers. *Financial Times,* Prentice Hall.

McFarlan, F. W. (1984) Information technology changes the way you compete. *Harvard Business Review*, May–June, 98–105

McKinsey Quarterly Global Survey of Business Executives, March 2006

Miles, R. E. and Snow, C. C. (1984) Fit, failure and the Hall of Fame. *California Management Review*, XXVI(3), Spring

Mitchell, P., Reast, J. and Lynch, J. (1998) Exploring the foundations of trust. *The Journal of Marketing Management*, 14

Orlov, L. (2005) *Make IT Matter for Business Innovation*. Forrester Research, November

Palmisano, S. (2006) Multinationals have been Superseded. *Financial Times*, 12 June

Petttigrew, A. and Whipp, R. (1991) *Making Change for Competitive Success*. Blackwell Publishers

Porter, M. and Millar, V. (1985) How information gives you competitive advantage. *Harvard Business Review*, 63, 149–160

Scholes, K., Johnson, G. and Whittington, R. (2006) *Exploring Corporate Strategy: Text and Cases*. FT Prentice Hall

Scott Morton, M. (1991) *The Corporation in the 1990s: Information Technology and Organizational Transformation*. Oxford University Press

Slack, N., Chambers, S., Betts, A. and Johnston, R. (2005) *Operations & Process Management: Principles and practice for strategic impact*. FT Prentice Hall

Strategic Success Modeling. Bigby Havis & Associates of Dallas, TX

Thornbury, J. (1999) KPMG: Revitalizing culture through values. *Business Strategy Review*, Winter

Turner, D. and Crawford, M. (1998) *Change Power: Capabilities that Drive Corporate Renewal*, Business & Professional Publishing

Index